Allison's Brain

BY ROBERT MCMECHAN
WITH ALLISON WOYIWADA

ADVANCE REVIEWS FOR
Allison's Brain

A heart-warming story of pain and recovery, but most of all, of hope and belief. Allison's powerful personality and wry wit shine through the pages of this journey, and Allison's Brain *is a tour de force, testimony to how determination and optimism can overcome what at times appears to be the insurmountable.*

LINDA HOLEMAN, AUTHOR

Allison's Brain *is a valuable, inspiring gift for anyone touched by brain injury. Allison and Robert have done an incredible job of sharing their journey, including rich perspectives, insights and experiences of their entire community. They have demonstrated the power and contributions of the patient, family, friends, healthcare workers and the greater community to deal with and recover from the challenges of brain injury. Everyone has a crucial role in advocating, educating, supporting, motivating and offering hope to the client and family. We all need to realize how scary, embarrassing and frustrating it is when recovery takes such a long time. Remaining optimistic was difficult for Allison unless people 'made me believe I could recover'.*

As a professional I have been reminded of the assets, strengths and resiliency of my clients and the importance of communicating and providing strategies for families even while they wait for services. As a speech-language pathologist I recognize the importance of the ability to communicate – and how hard families need to advocate for services across the globe, including Canada. It is important for everyone, including all healthcare workers to know how to communicate effectively with people who struggle to understand and express themselves.

JUDY MEINTZER, MSLP, R.SLP, S-LP (C)
CHAIR, SPEECH-LANGUAGE AND AUDIOLOGY CANADA

"Allison's Brain" tells the compelling true story of a young woman diagnosed with a brain aneurysm on her journey from illness to recovery from the viewpoint of Allison and her husband Robert. The meaning behind the title of the book is poignant, referring to the name of an email group that provided Allison and Robert's family and friends with updates, sheltering them from worry.

The book weaves Allison's illness narrative with compelling personal texts such as letters written to family and friends, Allison's diary entries and results of various medical tests; allowing the reader a true inside view to this very personal journey of the authors. The authors convey their challenging experience in a manner that opens the readers' hearts and minds into emotional, complex and difficult truths about our healthcare system.

While the story is one of courage, resilience, strength and recovery, there is a warm consoling undercurrent of Robert's love for Allison which is evident from the beginning of the book in his pursuit of the highest quality care for Allison. His unconditional love is evidenced in his voice as an advocate, Internet searches on medical treatments and research on finding the most qualified medical professionals to treat Allison. Allison's spirit and positive attitude are also threads that are present throughout this "hard to put down" story.

The writing throughout the book is genuine, moving and compelling. I think my favourite part was the Epilogue written by Allison in May 2014. Humour is also present in the stories providing a light hearted side to a very tough journey that Allison and Robert faced with bravery and potency.

As a music therapist and University educator, I was particularly inspired to read about how music played a significant role in Allison's life from childhood through recovery. Appendix 1-The Power of Music Therapy written by Cheryl Jones, a neurologic music therapist, provides scholarly detail on the role of music therapy in rehabilitation and describes the treatment plan initiated with Allison, focusing on using music for remediation to encourage a neuroplastic response for speech. Music therapy also focused on word retrieval, and the use of vocal music and also sight reading piano music in order to reach Allison's goals.

On a personal note the book also speaks deeply to me as my father died of a brain aneurysm at the age of 37.

I highly recommend this book to allied health care professionals, doctors, nurses, students and all those who have endured loss and grief. It is a masterfully written narrative that gives readers both personal and professional accounts of surviving a challenging diagnosis. It will leave you inspired, motivated and moved.

AMY CLEMENTS-CORTES, PHD, MTA. MT-BC, FAMI
MANAGING EDITOR, MUSIC AND MEDICINE
WWW.NOTESBYAMY.COM

Allison's Brain is a tale and tribute to the human spirit, power of relationships and the use of music and music therapy to foster recovery. While our advances in medicine provide hope and possibility for so many patients, the process of recovery continues to rely on our humanistic practices. Music therapy played a pivotal role in Allison's recovery and her story illustrates the power of music to heal. Allison's music therapy sessions facilitated by a certified music therapist, allowed for the expertly guided use of music to foster her brain's neuroplasticity and skill re-acquisition. Leveraging the innate power of music to heal through structure music therapy sessions was a transformative process for Allison. Allison's Brain demonstrates how music and the brain were made for each other.

ANNIE HEIDERSCHEIT, PH.D., MT-BC, LMFT, FAMI
PRESIDENT, WORLD FEDERATION OF MUSIC THERAPY

In the military it is essential to plan, execute and review every event in order to execute the next similar event with hindsight, wisdom and lessons learned. Allison's neurosurgeon termed the 12 hour process and operation to remove the aneurysm the size of a small plum from her brain "a military operation." The planning, the medical experts, the right team to be gathered, the training to handle any situation which may arise, the right equipment and locale and the post operation treatment and therapy all indeed resembled a military operation.

There is a huge thread throughout the book on how music therapy played an enormous role in the successful rehabilitation of Allison's brain. One of her music therapists has penned a section in Appendix 1 on how and where music and rhythm affects the brain. This is a fascinating section for all those who find the power of music incredible in being able to rejuvenate a brain or treat behavioural issues.

Allison's daughter Marya has also written a must read section on the lessons she learned and the advice she would give to anyone who finds themselves trying to bring back a loved one from an incredible medical journey.

If you want to read a real life incredible journey with a miracle ending this book is for you. A story of perseverance, dogged determination, love, music, friendship, humour, dedication, and stubbornness has messages for us all. You will love this account and all those in it. Give Allison a hug next time you see her!

VICE ADMIRAL DUNCAN MILLER (RET'D) MSC CMM CD

Allison's Brain *is a personal diary written by two people whose obvious love and commitment to each other shines through each page. Their perseverance and Allison's unfailing positive attitude and sense of humour make this very long journey compelling reading.* Allison's Brain *is also about the healing value of the arts: in Allison's case music. This is a must read for anyone going through major surgery; it is a how to as well — how to connect with family and friends, how to share the experiences and create a support system of those who wish Allison well and grow in their own understanding of how valuable life is and the struggle to enjoy its every minute.*

VICTORIA HENRY, DIRECTOR
CANADA COUNCIL ART BANK

In the 1500+ reviews that I have written since 2001—notably the live performances but occasionally films as well—I frequently know something of the artists involved or the background/previous works of the creators. In the case of this review, I found myself in the unique position of knowing Allison Woyiwada as a performer (through many, many conductor-soprano collaborations from the Gilbert and Sullivan canon), composer-publisher (the wonderfully inventive school musicals) and friend.

As time went on, I also made the acquaintance of husbands Rick, Bob and children Marya and Tyler. In recent years—after a long absence from Ottawa—Allison and I had been planning to work together and raise some much-needed funds for Ottawa's Savoy Society. Sadly, institutional inertia (likely the cause of the money woes in the first place) and then Allison's diagnosis, permanently shelved those musical possibilities. Going ahead without her was never in the cards.

Thanks to Bob's legal background, sense of narrative flow and unwavering support for his life partner—fuelled in turn by the army of friends and supporters that rallied around Allison as she courageously battled her life-threatening brain aneurysm—the world now has a most detailed, very personal chronicle of this truly incredible journey from early warning signs to life after rehab.

As a valuable record of the myriad events and situations that are unfolded with humour (tax lawyer and music jokes abound—comic relief most welcome during the rollercoaster ride of extra-dangerous surgery and just what Allison would become on the other side of the operation), hope and a chorus of voices, anyone finding themselves (or their loved ones) in a similar predicament ought to make Allison's Brain *required reading.*

Not surprisingly—given Allison's considerable talents—the value of music as both healing element and brain stimulant is readily apparent from the overture ("A Brief History of Allison") to the extended coda ("From Where I Sit—May 2014" and the three appendices).

The effects of acquired brain injury manifest themselves in many ways. In virtually every case, survivors report the feeling of rebirth. And as those precious lives begin again, it is for the rest of us to celebrate, reacquaint and marvel at the power of art and love.

S. JAMES WEGG
MANAGING EDITOR AT JWR (JAMES WEGG REVIEW)
WWW.JAMESWEGGREVIEW.ORG

This is a story of tenacity and optimism. It explores the power of music in the rehabilitation process and highlights the critical role played by Allison's family and friends in her recovery. The epilogue is essential reading as it sets in context what Allison was feeling as she struggled with the ebb and flow of the recovery process.

GERALD OAKHAM, PH.D.
CHAIR, DEPARTMENT OF PHYSICS, CARLETON UNIVERSITY

Suite 300 – 852 Fort Street
Victoria, BC, Canada V8W 1H8
www.friesenpress.com

Copyright © 2014 by Robert McMechan with Allison Woyiwada
First Edition — 2014

Cover art, "Allison" by Jennifer Ettinger www.ettinger.ca

All rights reserved.

No part of this publication may be reproduced in any form, or by any means, electronic or mechanical, including photocopying, recording, or any information browsing, storage, or retrieval system, without permission in writing from the publisher.

ISBN
978-1-4602-5177-5 (Hardcover)
978-1-4602-5178-2 (Paperback)
978-1-4602-5179-9 (eBook)

1. Biography & Autobiography, General

Distributed to the trade by The Ingram Book Company

Table of Contents

1	Preface
4	Prologue — A Brief History of Allison
12	1. The Giant Aneurysm Diagnosis
35	2. Waiting for Brain Surgery
73	3. It's Not Rocket Science
80	4. Show Me Two Fingers
97	5. The Last Fifty Cases Don't Matter
170	6. Beethoven's *Sonata Pathétique*
190	7. ABI Rehab and the Benefit Concert
260	8. After the Rehab Centre
293	Epilogue — From Where I Sit — May 2014
316	Appendix 1 – The Power of Music Therapy
340	Appendix 2 – Say No More and It's a Fact Jack
352	Appendix 3 – Lotsa Helping Hands
414	List of Images and Photographs
420	About the Authors

Preface

What would you do if you were enjoying a healthy and vigorous life and were suddenly faced with a choice between complicated brain surgery with an uncertain outcome and a forty percent chance of having what would likely be a catastrophic brain hemorrhage sometime during the next five years?

This is the story of Allison Woyiwada, my wife, who made the courageous choice of surgery.

We are telling her story for a few reasons. The first is as a tribute to a talented team of medical personnel, who do unbelievable work together in the neurosurgery area. As laypersons, it is absolutely mind-blowing to learn that doctors can open up your brain, monkey around in there (more about this later), repair a major brain defect, and make you whole again.

But that's not the whole story. Following this medical wizardry came the indispensable work of scores of health-care workers, without whom Allison's story would have come to a very different end. Here we are talking about a devoted group of front line medical personnel, who do a ton of heavy lifting after the neurosurgery team has done its deeds. It would be hugely remiss not to mention the nurses in Intensive Care, who run the intense, spaceship-like environment of post-surgery; the nurses in the Acute Care and InPatient Units, who tend around-the-clock to patients during their hoped-for recoveries; the therapists who try, often successfully, to get patients walking and talking again; and the social workers who help patients and families adjust to new realities. In *Allison's*

Brain we have tried to patch together the whole story with the benefit of after-the-fact interviews with Ottawa Hospital staff, who generously shared their time with us. For that we owe enormous thanks, and we hasten to add that, to the extent we have failed to properly communicate to you what we've been told, the fault is ours and ours alone.

Another reason for writing *Allison's Brain* is that we feel it is a genuinely inspirational story that speaks not only to the power of the human spirit but also to the profound importance of community. Allison, her daughter Marya, and I have all benefited tremendously from the support of a terrific community of friends and family members throughout a very difficult and trying time. Some of these friends and family members have made splendid written contributions to this account of her journey, which you will find in the *Lotsa Helping Hands* appendix. We also owe enormous thanks to these contributors and to other supporters too numerous to mention.

In Allison's case her story also explores the role that music and music therapy can play in the cognitive rehabilitation needed after a traumatic injury or event. We were very lucky, in this regard, to benefit from the expertise of Cheryl Jones, a researcher and music therapist who specializes in brain trauma and neurodegenerative disorders. Cheryl has generously contributed an appendix (*The Power of Music Therapy*) to the book detailing her experience with Allison.

The speech language pathologists who have worked with Allison are a remarkable group of people to whom we also owe enormous thanks. We were fortunate to interview all of them while writing the manuscript and to receive a written account from Evelyn Tan detailing her experience working with Allison, which you will find in the *Say No More and It's a Fact Jack* appendix.

While we acknowledge that no two people with brain injuries have exactly the same circumstances and prospects, we think that there were lessons learned along the way that are worth sharing. These include the need for strong lucid advocacy when navigating complex medical issues, the value of an engaged support network, the role of determined positive attitude, and how to manage expectations when short-term prospects seem bleak. In this latter regard Marya has written a thoughtful guide for caregivers that you will find at the end of the book.

Finally, we began writing the manuscript for *Allison's Brain* in Antigua during what we've been told was a "polar vortex" (or something like that) afflicting our home in Canada. We are very grateful to our Caribbean friends for their warm encouragement and support!

Prologue —
A Brief History of Allison

Allison was born the second daughter of Doug and Helen (Cobbe) Cameron at Roblin, Manitoba, in the early 1950s. She lived with her parents, her sister Linda, and her brothers Bruce and Richard on a farm at Tummel near her grandparents. Farming wasn't her father's chosen vocation, but his mother had purchased farmland for him with money that was due to him after the end of his service in World War II. The family pulled up stakes when Allison was six and moved on to MacGregor, Manitoba, and soon thereafter to Portage la Prairie, Manitoba.

Allison fondly recalls that, as a young girl, she loved visits with her grandparents near Roblin and with her nearby aunts and uncles, for she could go and walk in their fields, "on my very own." This "on my very own" thinking, at a young age, was a sign of things to come. Allison began taking piano lessons when she was in Grade 4, and by her own account she eventually got to be "pretty good." She became the pianist for the McKenzie United Junior Choir and also for the Indian Residential School Glee Club. She travelled with the Glee Club to San Antonio, Texas, and to Anaheim, California, during Grades 11 and 12, in a bus with a banner on the side proclaiming "Canada's Singing Indians." The following year she had the opportunity to serve as the Glee Club's pianist again on a trip to the World's Fair in Osaka, Japan, but she was anxious about not delaying her post-secondary education, and so she declined.

As music has a great deal to do with the *Allison's Brain* story, it is worthwhile pausing here to relate some of her musical memories. Allison says her Aunt Margaret owned a music store in Portage la Prairie, and she was able to pick up any sheet music she wanted from the store, whenever she wanted to do so. She also recalls that, during high school, she was frequently grounded on Saturday night for staying out past her Friday evening curfew, so she stayed home and played the piano, with her parents happily listening. Another telling musical story from her high school days is that she played "O Canada" every morning over the school's PA system. On a dare from her classmates, she prefaced the national anthem one morning with a rendition of "Tiptoe Through the Tulips." Her home room teacher was not pleased with this turn of events, but Allison had wisely gotten the school principal onside beforehand. Plus, she made money from her classmates on the wager although she has never divulged how much.

Allison recalls that when she heard from her high school guidance counsellor that Brandon University offered a Bachelor of Music degree, she thought it must be a mistake, as it didn't seem possible that a person could obtain a university degree just by doing what they loved. Allison, therefore, decided that she should get a Bachelor of Music before the "mistake" was discovered. She auditioned for Dr. Lorne Watson, playing Chopin's Polonaise in A-flat major, Op. 53, and she recalls being asked by Dr. Watson whether she knew she was playing an abridged version. Her reply to this was "no" as, at the time, she didn't know what an abridged version was, and from her point-of-view it didn't matter, as she just played everything in front of her. Dr. Watson, nevertheless, recognized something about Allison's potential, and she was enrolled in and completed a four-year music degree program, the final year of which also gave her teaching qualifications. The caption next to Allison's photo in the Brandon University Yearbook for her graduation year still fits — "If there is no struggle, there is no progress."

During this early formative period, at age nineteen, Allison married her best high school friend Rick Woyiwada, another talented musician. They moved to Winnipeg in the early 1970s, and Allison began her career as a music teacher. She left music teaching for a while to pursue an opera-singing career, and she recalls making a lot of money one summer as an opera-singing waitress at a Winnipeg restaurant. However, being an opera-singing waitress was very hard work, and the cash flow dried up as summer turned to fall. Allison, therefore, resumed music teaching, but left again in the late 1970s to study opera singing at the University of Toronto.

Allison had earlier won a provincial opera-singing title in Manitoba in the mid-1970s, taking home the Rose Bowl in a Kinsmen-sponsored competition. She next proceeded to compete in Toronto, but she recalls that she wasn't quite ready to sing at the national level. A couple of years later, she also won the Rose Bowl in Toronto at an Ontario Kinsmen opera-singing competition, but the judges knew she was a Manitoban, and they sent an Ontario fellow on to compete at the national competition.

Although Allison had a passion for opera singing, she decided at the end of her year of study at the University of Toronto that she was not going to pursue a career as an opera singer. After her return to Winnipeg and the resumption of her music teaching career, her son Tyler was born in early 1979, "super cute and happy." At around this time, Allison served as the music director for Trinity United Church in Portage la Prairie and then as a music director for the United Church in Winnipeg. Rick moved to Ottawa in the fall of 1981 to take a position as a Department of Justice lawyer, and Allison followed in December after completing the first semester at a Winnipeg school as its music teacher. She began her position as the music teacher at Hopewell School in Ottawa in February of 1982, and her daughter Marya was born in December. Allison recalls Marya as being "cute as a button and well behaved."[1]

---

1   This behaviour business took some funny twists and turns, but it eventually ended up not too badly. In fact, after completing a degree in music at the University of Ottawa, and pursuing her own opera singing interest for a time, Marya is, at least for the present, succeeding her mother as the music teacher at the Hopewell School in Ottawa.

Thus began Allison's unparalleled twenty-eight-year career as the music teacher at Hopewell School. It would be fair to say that, during this period, Allison established herself as a bit of an all-star. Over the twenty-eight years, she spent tens of thousands of hours directing extra-curricular school bands, leading school band trips, and staging student musicals that she had written. She also enjoyed twenty years performing in and directing Gilbert and Sullivan operettas with the Savoy Society of Ottawa. Allison has been recognized for her work in the Ottawa arts community on many occasions, including as recipient of the Whitton Award (1993), Arts Advisory Award for Innovative Programming in the Arts (1997), Community Builder Award (2000), Hopewell School Music and Drama Award (2006), Capital Critics Circle Award as Best Director (community) (2006–2007) and Lifetime Achievement Award from Hopewell School students (2008). Upon her retirement from teaching, a wing of the Hopewell School was dedicated to Allison, and the "Allison Woyiwada Music Award" is now presented annually to students at Hopewell School.

Allison didn't accomplish all that she did just by being nice. In the late 1990s, when the Hopewell School music program was running short of funds, author JC Sulzenko penned the story of *Annabella and the Tycoon*,[2] to assist with fundraising. A music teacher is featured in the story, and it isn't just a coincidence that the teacher is described as "funny but fierce." All of this is to say that Allison expected and demanded a very high level of performance from students and performers. This led them to very high levels of achievement. As it happens, Allison also applies these high standards to herself. That turns out to be a crucial part of the *Allison's Brain* story.

Allison and Rick split up in the early 1990s, and they raised Tyler and Marya jointly, with a week-on and week-off custody arrangement. Allison became financially strapped during this period, having bought a second house without speaking to her bank manger first, to his dismay, and then finding she was unable to sell the house she was living in. Not one to be deterred by mere obstacles, she took on boarders and taught private music lessons almost daily in order to make ends meet. Her financial problem was solved when Rick agreed to purchase the house Allison was living in.

That brings me to *me*. For better or for worse, a good deal of what you read in *Allison's Brain* has been written by yours truly. This is all the happy result of an invitation extended to me by Allison, in the spring of 1996, to take part in a murder mystery evening she was hosting. At the time, I was living with my friends, Gordon and Pamela, who were rescuing me from a bad depression brought on by, what seemed to me then, difficult life circumstances. I can still recall what a breath of fresh air Allison brought to my life. We were living together in Allison's house within a few months.

I've since joked with Allison about this, telling her that men in some countries put great emphasis on the importance of finding a woman with a house. The truth though is that finding myself in a romantic relationship with Allison was like winning the life lottery, only much better. Ironically, Allison and Rick had performed

---

2   J.C. Sulzenko, *Annabella and the tycoon*, Blue Poodle Books, Ottawa, 1999.

at my wedding, when they were together in the early 1990s, and I've since said that Allison must have sung real good. I had known Allison and Rick, as a couple, since Rick and I worked together at the Department of Justice back in my Winnipeg days. I'd always admired Allison, but never in a million years did I imagine us as partners.

In the mid-2000s we bought a house together and renovated it. In keeping with her usual high form, Allison pretty much gave the general contractor his daily marching orders, and I was largely free to concentrate on building my new solo tax practice. Just before then, Allison had seen me through another serious depression — for which I was again hospitalized — this time brought on by doing a ridiculous amount of legal work for the Government of Canada in a major tax court case.

When Allison officially retired from teaching in 2008, she kept up her usual vigorous pace, as well as taking on an office manager role in my tax law practice, which had grown considerably. As we approached our sixties, it seemed to me that the level of Allison's volunteer work was at least bordering on unreasonable, and we began to enjoy taking time off for travel together.

It was during a trip in Western Canada, in the summer of 2011, that the *Allison's Brain* story had its beginning. The trip was memorable in many respects, beginning with my family's relay team running in the (I later came to think badly named) *Death Race* near Grand Cache, Alberta, and ending with quite a strenuous climb through grizzly country in the Valkyr Mountains, near Revelstoke, British Columbia, in order to attend my son Phil's wedding to his fiancé, Kristie, at a beautiful high mountain lake.

    This next point isn't really part of the *Allison's Brain* story, but we had to sign waivers in order to go to Phil and Kristie's wedding. You never really think about this sort of thing when your children are small, but the things they eventually involve you in can be pretty surprising. In any event, in order to try to be fit enough to endure the climb to the wedding, we undertook a few mini-mountain climbs earlier during our vacation. It was during this time that Allison gave Phil an affectionate nickname, that isn't fit for print, to wit: $#@+&%$ Phil, or something like that.

    In between the *Death Race* and the grizzly-infested mountain climb, we had quite a nice normal visit with Allison's sister Linda and brother-in-law Jim in the beautiful environs of Clear Lake in Riding Mountain National Park, Manitoba. It was here, while walking by a candy store, that Allison first experienced smelling something horrible that no one else could smell. These bad smell episodes happened again, from time to time, throughout our holiday. Allison didn't make a big deal out of her bad smell experiences at the time, but she had the good sense to tell her doctor about them when she had an appointment with him back in Ottawa in the fall of 2011. Later we came to understand that the bad smells were *olfactory hallucinations.*

A final point that I can usefully add at this stage is that Jane Mahoney, a social worker working in the neurology area at the Ottawa Hospital reminded me, in January 2014 when I was doing interviews for this book, of a description I had given to her of Allison for the Social Work Assessment she was doing in June 2012. This was just an off-the-top of head, unrehearsed description of Allison. I described her as "an active, dynamic, uplifting and cheerful person." I also told Jane that Allison was "extraordinarily determined, and a force to be reckoned with." These traits are prominent in the *Allison's Brain* story.

The level of detail in this prologue might strike some of you as excessive, but I thought it important that you have a good understanding of Allison before taking you to the rest of her story. This is because, as far as I can see, possessing the attributes of determination (some call this stubbornness), fortitude, good humour and positivity all have a great deal to do with where Allison is today. That and having her brain steeped in music.

1.

The Giant Aneurysm Diagnosis

When we returned to Ottawa from Western Canada, Allison did research on the Internet trying to find out what was causing the horrible smells she was having. She unfortunately found that brain damage is one of the most common causes of phantom smells. I also found information about *phantosmia*, a term that is used to describe the condition of people who believe they smell scents when no such smell is actually present. We were relieved to see that sometimes this occurs in people who have no illness.

Allison also kept a diary of the occasions when the bad smells occurred:

> *July 25th — walking by a candy shop and noticed a stink even though there was a strong sweet smell from the shop — several more over the next few weeks of our vacation*
>
> *Sept 27 3:30, my office, 1 sip of wine — start keeping track*
>
> *Oct 7 just before falling asleep — one ounce of wine*
>
> *Oct 12th*
>
> *Oct 18 4:00 at Staples — started Bilbury yesterday*
>
> *10:00 twice in one day*
>
> *Oct 19 made an appt for the 24th*

When Allison went to see Dr. Blake on October 24th and told him about the smells, he was concerned and referred her to the Ottawa Hospital for a CT scan. The scan was then scheduled for December 15th.

In the meantime, Allison continued to keep a record of all of the bad smells she was experiencing.

Oct 24th after Yoga — different smell — not rotten, gassy

Oct 31 evening — less severe

Nov 13th — two minor incidents since Oct 31 and not severe

Nov 17 twice today — one stinky, the other milder

Nov 26 one — less smelly but longer lasting, made me shiver

Nov 30 - evening

Dec 2 - morning, over coffee

Dec 4 - Staples

Dec 5 - evening, home

Dec 7

After having the CT scan on December 15th, Allison received a call from her doctor's office on December 19th, and she went to see him that day to find out the results. Dr. Blake gave her a hard-to-read copy of a fax from Diagnostic Imaging at the Ottawa Hospital, which was a copy of the Report of a CT HEAD SCAN WITHOUT CONTRAST. The report included the following passages.

FINDINGS: There is a calcified hyperdense mass centered over the left Sylvian fissure which measures 2.5 x 2.9 cm. The lesion appears to be bilateral.

Allison's Brain • 13

IMPRESSION: Findings are suggestive of a giant aneurysm arising from the MCA bifurcation. The differential diagnosis would include a calcified oligodendroglioma. A CT angiogram is suggested for further evaluation.

Needless to say, this caused the family a lot of concern, but Allison remained quite calm. Her composure in the face of this unsettling news is clear from her email to my daughter Laurie.

From: Allison Woyiwada
Sent: December 20, 2011 12:50 PM
To: Robert McMechan; Laurie Souchotte
Subject: Re: Hello!

Hi Laurie

Yes, it's not a pleasant situation, but there is a possibility that the problem is calcified mass not an aneurysm — my medical friends and family read the report and came to this conclusion — my doctor did not. The technicians weren't sure. When I read it, I thought I had both.

However, other than the blip that showed up, there is mild swelling in the left temporal lobe (which is where the blip is). Otherwise they said my brain looks good. I'm guessing the swelling could be from the pressure of the extra bit up there and could also have resulted in the smells. Anyway, I'm glad I got it checked. Waiting to hear from a Neurologist today. Might prescribe a CT angiogram to be sure.

Merry Christmas

Allison

ps funny thing about elevating my blood pressure — the doc took it after he told me of the possible aneurysm, and it was normal. He was relieved until I told him that it's usually low :)

Never one to wait for things to happen, Allison called the hospital on December 20th and had someone agree to look for a fax from Dr. Blake requesting a CT angiogram and call her back to schedule an appointment for it. However, there wasn't any immediate news of a CT angiogram being scheduled.

The next day, I found some information about aneurysms on the Internet.

From: Robert McMechan
Sent: December 21, 2011 6:59 AM
To: 'Allison Woyiwada'
Subject: medical stuff

Researchers estimate that about 10 to 15 million people in the United States will develop an intracranial aneurysm during their lifetimes.

Frequent aneurysm locations

Allison's Brain • 15

- *Middle cerebral artery 33%*

Who is affected?

- *Approximately 5% of the population may have or develop an aneurysm; of those, 20% have multiple aneurysms.*

- *Unruptured aneurysms are more common (2.7 million per year) than ruptured (20,000 per year) (1). However, 85% of aneurysms are not diagnosed until after they rupture. Aneurysms are usually diagnosed between ages 35 to 60 and are more common in women.*

Computed Tomography Angiography (CTA) scan is a non-invasive X-ray to review the anatomical structures within the brain to detect blood in or around the brain. A newer technology called CT angiography involves the injection of contrast into the blood stream to view the arteries of the brain. This type of test provides the best pictures of blood vessels through angiography and soft tissues through CT (Fig. 3).

Recovery & prevention

- *Unruptured aneurysm patients recover from surgery or endovascular treatment much faster than those who suffer a SAH (subarachnoid hemorrhage)*

Allison also found information on the Internet about calcified aneurysms.

From: Allison Woyiwada
Sent: December 22, 2011 1:00 PM
To: Robert McMechan
Subject: more info

Aneurysm: Aneurysm is another factor that may contribute to calcium deposits in the brain. It is a condition wherein an artery particularly in the brain develops a weak spot that causes a widening or enlarging of the blood vessel which may eventually start showing calcifications. Though very rare to occur, these calcifications are usually arches or circle shaped and do not contribute to the severity of brain aneurysm.

Not having heard anything about a CT angiogram, Allison called Dr. Blake's office on December 22nd, and she learned then that he had requested that a neurosurgeon be assigned to her and hadn't, therefore, requested that a CT angiogram be scheduled. So Allison asked Dr. Blake's assistant to have him make a request that a CT angiogram be scheduled. By this time, Allison's anxiety had risen to a higher level, and after watching a CTV news clip about the work on aneurysms by Dr. Timo Krings, at Toronto Western Hospital, I emailed him directly on December 23rd at 7:11 a.m. to ask about the possibility of scheduling an appointment.

Remarkably, Dr. Krings emailed me back four minutes later to advise that an appointment could be set up, and by 10:00 a.m. his assistant had offered one on January 23rd. Later the same day, having now determined from Dr. Blake's office that Dr. Howard Lesiuk of the Ottawa Hospital was her neurosurgeon, Allison called his office and was advised that it was closed until January 3rd and that there was a ten month wait for appointments. Allison again spoke with Dr. Blake, and he told her that he had spoken with Dr. Lesiuk the day before, who was going to put in a request for a CT angiogram.

Allison then told Dr. Blake that she was feeling pressure in her head, and he suggested that she go to Emergency at the Civic Campus of the Ottawa Hospital, which she did immediately. Soon thereafter, Dr. Lesiuk's office called to say that a CTA test had been ordered and that it would likely occur within the next few weeks. However, because Allison had gone to Emergency, another CT HEAD scan was done on December 23rd in the afternoon. Allison

Allison's Brain • 17

then waited in Emergency with her daughter Marya for several hours to learn the results, and I joined them later in the day. At about 8:30 p.m., we met a doctor who told us that Allison was being admitted for an angiogram and MRI the following morning.

The doctor we met that evening predicted that surgery would be required. Allison and I remained at the hospital, to complete paperwork related to her hospital admission the next morning, and later we returned home to celebrate "Christmas Eve", with the knowledge Allison had to be back at the hospital before 7:00 a.m. on December 24th. We were having Christmas Eve early because of a tradition that allows Tyler and Marya to have a Christmas Eve and Day with both of their parents from December 23rd to 25th. Marya had returned to our house with her boyfriend, and Tyler with his girlfriend, and they had gotten the fondue ready that Allison loves so much as part of our Christmas Eve tradition. Considering what had happened, we managed to keep our time together jolly, but there was a dark cloud on the horizon.

After the fact, we have learned that the Diagnostic Imaging Report from December 23rd headed CT SCAN THE BRAIN CTA OF THE CIRCLE OF WILLIS included the following.

FINDINGS: The CTA of the circle of Willis demonstrated partial curvilinear enhancement of the left Sylvian fissure lesion, may represent a partially thrombosed partially calcified giant aneurysm. It arises from a left M2 temporal branch, with a possible branch arising off at the superior aspect of the aneurysm; the enhancing part of the aneurysm measures approximately 2.3 x 1.6 by ongoing 1.4 cm in anteroposterior craniocaudal and transverse diameters respectively. No neck noted.

—

IMPRESSION: Findings above-described may represent partially thrombosed and partially calcified giant aneurysm on the MCA territory, with features that may represent dissecting aneurysm. Neurological consult recommended.

Early on December 24th Allison sent an email to family and friends who knew about her aneurysm.

From: Allison Woyiwada
Sent: December 24, 2011 6:32 AM
To: Multiple Recipients
Subject: some action

Went to the Civic emerg yesterday. It was the fastest way my doctor could arrange a CT angiogram. Had one. Was there for 11 hours. Got a neurosurgeon assigned to my case — Lesiuk — looks good. Going back today for a straight angiogram and MRI.

The feeling is that this baby has to come out, if it's possible, because of its size. The angiogram today shows blood flow and gives them a better idea if they can clip the vessel at either end of the aneurysm and sew the vessel back together.

Due back at the hospital by 7:00 so gotta go. Don't worry. I think I'm finally in good hands.

aw

From the moment that Allison disclosed the existence of her aneurysm, we received an outpouring of support from family and friends. This email from our friends Joan and Warren is a great example.

From: Joan Duguid
Sent: December 24, 2011 12:58 PM
To: Allison Woyiwada; Robert McMechan
Cc: Warren Creates
Subject: Re: some action

I am so relieved for you. What the hell happens to people who cannot advocate for themselves? Hope you get more answers to questions and hope you do not have to wait long to have this thing clipped. Aneurysm a better diagnosis

Allison's Brain • **19**

than tumor. Me thinks! Take care, enjoy the holidays as much as you can. Thinking of you both.

Love Joan and Warren

There were many messages of this kind. I have chosen this one partly because it makes the point about the importance of self-advocacy. Not having had much experience previously with the medical system, it was quite an eye-opener to see how much self-advocacy matters. I often wondered, during Allison's medical journey, about how people get along who either can't or just won't be proactive. I think there is a natural expectation, once your medical problem has been diagnosed, that "the system" will take over and that whatever is best for you will be done on a timely basis. The reality is different. "The system" is inundated with demands on it, and there is a chance that you won't receive timely attention unless you also are seen and heard. Allison has never been a shrinking violet, and she kept her medical problem front and centre, to the extent she could. This in turn had an influence on what eventually happened.

Allison had her next diagnostic imaging test on December 24th. The Report of this test is titled MRI OF THE BRAIN WITH CONTRAST.

FINDINGS: There is a giant aneurysm in the left Sylvian fissure pointing inferiorly and arising from an inferior M2 branch of the left middle cerebral artery. The entire aneurysm measures 2.6 x 2.8 cm. The anterior aspect of the aneurysm is filling with contrast and measures 2.4 x 1.1 mm. The posterior aspect of the aneurysm is thrombosed. The aneurysm is pointing anteriorly and inferiorly. There is no other aneurysm seen. There is some hypertense T2 signal present in left temporal lobe. There is no acute infarction seen.

IMPRESSION: Left MCA giant aneurysm arising from an inferior M2 branch. The aneurysm is partially thrombosed.

Allison was released from the hospital late in the afternoon on December 24th on the basis that she would return early on the 26th to have an angiogram. After Allison was released from the hospital, we celebrated the "Christmas Day" with Tyler and Marya that ordinarily would have started much earlier. On the morning of the 25th, Allison and I were together on our own, as we are every second year. Allison is always very excited about Christmas, and with her usual high energy and form she has always made us a special Christmas breakfast. But this year, on the 25th, she came downstairs and lay down on the couch, which I had never seen before. So I set about making a very modest non-Christmasy breakfast, which Allison was barely able to eat. Part way through breakfast, Allison rushed towards our downstairs bathroom but didn't quite make it and vomited all over the place. The day before she had begun taking the anti-seizure medication Tegretol, and my Internet research suggests that it might have been the culprit — rather than my breakfast. That's my story, and I'm sticking to it.

After I cleaned up, we had a quiet time watching the Met Opera DVDs that I had given Allison for Christmas, but I recall feeling this was a Christmas like no other and having a great deal of trepidation about what lay ahead. Fortunately, our great neighbours Don and Pauline had invited us to have Christmas dinner at their house with their family, and that turned our day into a much more jovial one. Besides the benefit of them being terrific cooks, having dinner at Don and Pauline's table is always a high-spirited affair.

Allison was back at the hospital early on the 26th, and she waited all day for an angiogram that didn't happen. Early on the 27th, Allison was again back at the hospital for the angiogram. However, it turned out that one of the doctors who wanted to be present for the angiogram was away until the New Year. So, on the 27th, Allison was sent home part way through the morning. The Discharge Summary by Dr. Amin Kassam says, "Since the patient was neurologically stable, it was decided to send the patient back home with an outpatient angiogram." By this time, we had come to appreciate that Dr. Kassam was also a neurosurgeon involved in

Allison's Brain • 21

Allison's future. Internet research made us feel very good about this, as we found descriptions of him as a "technical wizard" –and– "the Wayne Gretzky of his field — the best."

The next day, Allison sent an email to a large group of family and friends to tell them what had been happening. The group she set up in her email account for this purpose was called "Allison's Brain," which inspired the title of this book. Allison's motivation for setting up this email group had to do with giving people accurate information in order to prevent rumour-mongering and encourage people not to worry about her. Creating the "Allison's Brain" email group turned out to be a stroke of genius although Allison's sister Linda, who has a medical background, suggested before Allison's surgery that "stroke" might not be a good word to use. In any event, "Allison's Brain" group emails became a crucial communications vehicle in the months ahead, and it allowed me to give regular updates on Allison's condition to a large number of supporters, without drowning in email. Many people have told us that they really appreciated receiving these updates. The cutest story I've heard about them came from a friend who told me that she read them to her children, who began to eagerly look forward to more updates.

The first of the *Allison's Brain* emails is classic Allison, and I think it tells a good deal about her.

> **From:** Allison Woyiwada
> **Sent:** December 28, 2011 5:13 PM
> **To:** Allison's Brain
> **Subject:** my newsletter

> *Hello my friends and family. This is a message to tell you all (many of you already know) of a health condition I have, and I want you to hear it from me. I have a giant aneurysm (2.5 cm) in my brain and am being tested and will likely be treated with surgery at the Civic Hospital although I will be sending my test results to a Neurologist in Toronto as well. This will not likely rupture as the blood has clotted in the swollen part and will not likely get free to*

22 • *Robert McMechan with Allison Woyiwada*

wander about. This is all the bad news. I feel fine — almost normal and not terribly worried, and I don't want you to worry either.

This all started with olfactory hallucinations in July — smelling what's not there (usually garbage). Glad to have that diagnosed as this aneurysm might not have been discovered if there hadn't been a side effect. Millions of people have them and never know.

I'm in good hands. The Doctors I'm dealing with have great reputations, and two of the three have been in daily communication with me — the third one is off this week. One has been compared to Wayne Gretzky re his talent — say no more! Got a couple more tests to do and then the surgeons come up with an action plan. They might do this at the Heart Institute as their operating rooms are state-of-the-art apparently.

So this is not a taboo subject. I am happy to email with you. Feel free to let our other friends and family know. Please don't feel doomy and gloomy. I don't feel that way.

I will not be filling your inbox on a daily basis, but I will let you know when there is a development of some kind. I am telling you all this way so you get the message directly and know that I am relatively confident this can be dealt with successfully. I always hate getting news like this second hand about friends. I thank Google for allowing me to do such extensive research (although the doctors don't approve but Google is available 24-7 :). See a sample below.

Cheers and Happy New Year to you all

Allison

http://www.brain-surgery.com/bsictoda.html

This *Allison's Brain* email produced a wave of supportive responses, of which I will share a couple.

From: Paul Kane
Sent: December 28, 2011 6:06 PM
To: Allison Woyiwada
Subject: Re: my newsletter

Hi Allison,

Thanks for the news. I have been wondering since receiving Bob's quick email that you have been undergoing multiple scans. Almost knocked on your door yesterday wondering about the results and what is happening. Discretion and my mother's advice to mind my business kept me moving.

So like you to take the subject by the horns, lift the blanket and get rid of the smoke. Love your attitude which augers well for your recovery. So much easier for others to just know the straight goods.

Will say a little prayer for you in any event. Always good to have the Big Guy working for ya.

Big hug!

Sudbury Sam

I'm also including the next email, for the sake of a great story that I will tell you in a minute. By way of introduction, Lorraine is a friend I met at winter indoor cycling, who basically almost never sits down.

From: Lorraine England
Sent: December 29, 2011 7:35 AM
To: Allison Woyiwada
Cc: Robert McMechan
Subject: Re: my newsletter

Hi Allison,

Thank you so much for your newsletter. You truly do sound very positive, and I will send those vibes back to you as well.

I have to chuckle when I read about your smell sensation of garbage… because it is garbage day in my neighbourhood today. If I don't think of you daily… I will certainly think of you every Thursday when I smell my garbage as I take my bags/bins to the curb… is that at all comforting?

I look forward to your next update and all the good news you can send my way.

If there is any support I can provide for my end, please let me know. I expect you will have a bit of a stay in the hospital, so I can certainly send over a casserole or two to feed the troops as you recover.

A big hug to you Allison.

I am sure your "Wayne Gretzky" will score a goal in your game.

Love Lorraine

P.S. Bob… quite seriously, please let me know when the family may particularly appreciate a casserole or a hearty soup.

I naturally took Lorraine's P.S. very seriously and quickly responded.

From: Robert McMechan
Sent: December 29, 2011 9:56 AM
To: Lorraine England
Cc: Allison Woyiwada
Subject: Thanks Lorraine!!

Tuesdays and Thursdays will be good days I think. :) P.S.
Happy New Year!
P.P.S. I am out of the office these days.

No one has ever accused Lorraine of being a slouch, but this next story takes the cake. Beginning at the end of May, when Allison had her surgery, Lorraine delivered dinners to me for Tuesdays and Thursdays *for seventeen successive weeks.* Many was the night when I arrived home late from the hospital, not having eaten dinner, and when I opened the fridge thought "God bless Lorraine." But all good things must come to an end, and when my sister Joan and brother-in-law Ben came to Ottawa in September to help out, I told Lorraine I was feeling guilty about the work I was causing her and suggested she stop. Lorraine reacted by telling people that she had been fired, and claims not to have made a meal since.

Allison's diary entries will give you the picture of what happened over the next while.

> *Week between Christmas and New Year: Called the Civic many times — booking, Dr. Lesiuk's office etc. left messages, received an appt for a CT scan in the mail for Jan 19th — called radiology to tell them I had already had one and Jan 19th is later than I had hoped*

> *Jan 3 faxed a letter to Dr. Blake telling him of what had happened and what hadn't. He called me back. Will try to get ahold of Lesiuk and set up an appt for me.*

> *Jan 4 called Dr Lesiuk's secretary — she was unaware of the tests that I had already had and would look into making sure that Jan 19 was for an arterial angiogram*

> *No response from her all week so I called many times — left a message asking for confirmation*

> *Jan 6 Dr. Blake called to find out what had happened. Suggested I call Lesiuk's office next week again*

Then came Allison's next *Allison's Brain* group email update.

From: Allison Woyiwada
Sent: January 8, 2012 12:43 PM
To: Allison's Brain
Subject: update #1

Something you should all keep in mind: don't get a diagnosis just before Christmas. Just like you and I, health care workers take some time off. Nice bunch though. I did get great service, except for the two days I waited in the hospital for tests that didn't happen. Many apologies expressed and promises that things would return to normal in the New Year.

I have been in touch with Dr. Lesiuk's office (he heads the team of surgeons — he's originally from Manitoba, like me) and I have an appt for an arterial angiogram on Jan 19th, and an appt with Dr. Lesiuk on Jan 23rd, once he has the available pics of my brain in front of him. My GP, Dr. Patrick Blake, calls me periodically to see how I'm doing and what progress has been made. He makes calls on my behalf to the hospital. Good guy. The hospital may be getting sick of hearing from me — too bad.

I was told by one of the neurologists that exercise was allowed — just not to try to lift 500lbs. However, I have read that I should keep my blood pressure from rising (it's normally low) so I have ordered a mini BP machine to wear on my wrist. Anyone had experience with one of these gizmos?

Still feeling great. Walking on the treadmill at the Y — too icey outside, playing piano, working for Bob, going to parties/dinner/movies and reading. It's a full day.

Cheers
Allison xo

*ps Thanks for all your responses to my first email. Nice to
chat with you. I've gotten smarter and bcc'd you this time.*

One of Allison's many telephone calls to the hospital struck
pay dirt on January 10th. She contacted someone in the Medical
Imaging Department who booked her for a cerebral angiogram on the 16th because he found the authority to do so in
her file. The Diagnostic Imaging Report for this test is headed
CEREBRAL ANGIOGRAM.

> *TECHNIQUE: Details of this procedure were explained
> to the patient. The potential risks include, but are not
> limited to, groin hematoma, infection, contrast reaction,
> vessel injury or stroke. Questions were answered and
> consent was obtained.*

> —

> *FINDINGS: There was no significant stenosis at left
> carotid bifurcation. On the left internal carotid arterio-
> gram, there is a giant aneurysm arising from the inferior
> M2 branch of the left middle cerebral artery. The aneurysm
> is wide-necked with the distal segment of the inferior
> middle cerebral artery branch arising from the medial
> superior aspect of the aneurysm. On the AP view the
> aneurysm lumen measures approximately 1.9 x 1.4 cm in
> orthogonal diameters. On the lateral view, the aneurysm
> lumen measures approximately 1.4 x 2.1 cm. On the left
> external carotid arteriogram, there is a patent left superfi-
> cial temporal artery of good caliber.*

> *CONCLUSIONS: Giant aneurysm arising from the left
> inferior branch of the middle cerebral artery, as described
> above.*

We had a lengthy meeting with Dr. Lesiuk next, which Allison
has described in an email update below. When we first met Dr.
Lesiuk we realized we were dealing with a very smart man, and we

found that he had a splendid patience that enabled him to respond to all of our questions without any dismissiveness. A host of these questions came from Marya, who is not unlike her Mother in many respects. One of these had to do with what the neurosurgeons would do when they were "monkeying around" in Allison's brain, and (I've forgotten what) happened. Dr. Lesiuk even had an answer for that question.

Apart from having a high level of confidence in the medical team, a decisive point in Allison's thinking about whether to go ahead with brain surgery was a finding in a study of unruptured aneurysms that Dr. Lesiuk referred us to at our meeting. According to the *International Study of Intracranial Aneurysms,*[3] there is a forty percent chance that a giant aneurysm will rupture within a five year period. Since the rupture of a giant aneurysm would very likely be catastrophic, not having surgery would be like having a ticking time bomb in your head that could go off at any time.

Dr. Lesiuk had written a letter to Dr. Blake on December 19th, confirming the existence of a "giant aneurysm of the left middle cerebral artery which is partially thrombosed." He also wrote:

> *This aneurysm represents a significant medium- to long-term risk to the patient. The International Study of Unruptured Intracranial Aneurysms [Unruptured intracranial aneurysms: natural history, clinical outcome, and risks of surgical and endovascular treatment, Steering Committee, Mayo Clinic, Rochester, Minnesota, The Lancet, vol. 362, July 12, 2003] suggests that an aneurysm of this size in this location carries with it a 40% risk of rupture over 5 years. Therefore treatment, if feasible, should be undertaken. Because of its size, the thrombus within the aneurysm, and its configuration, its treatment represents a considerable technical challenge. There does not appear to*

---

3   Steering Committee, Mayo Clinic, v. 362, *The Lancet*, Rochester, Minnesota, July 12, 2003.

be any feasible endovascular solution, and open surgery is therefore required. This would involve either:

A direct approach to the aneurysm with temporary clipping of the proximal and distal vessels and likely an opening of the aneurysm with removal of the intra-aneurysmal thrombus to permit a complete deflation of the aneurysm sac followed by a form of aneurysmorrhaphy with multiple aneurysm clips to reconstruct the parent vessels. If this approach was undertaken, some consideration might have to be given to deep hypothermic systemic circulatory arrest to provide brain protection during a potentially sustained period of intracranial circulatory arrest.

Trapping of the aneurysm proximally and distal with maintenance of distal circulation with a high flow extra-cranial to intracranial circulatory bypass procedure which would have some significant technical challenges due to the configuration of the aneurysm and the vessels which would have to receive the vascular graft anastomosis.

I have discussed the general principles of what we are facing with the patient and, with the understanding of the very substantial risks of doing nothing, she is prepared to proceed. I am going to be reviewing this complex case with the rest of the Cerebral Vascular team to formulate a final management strategy. I will report further following this.

Here is Allison's following email update #2 to the *Allison's Brain* group.

From: Allison Woyiwada
Sent: January 20, 2012 1:56 PM
To: Allison's Brain
Subject: update #2

Hello all,

Couple of events happened this week that I'd like to share. Cerebral angiogram on Monday — nice little light show goes on under your eyelids when they inject the dye. Yowsa!

Met with my surgeon Dr. Lesiuk Thursday afternoon. He has 1500 pictures of my brain, and this is the only fault he found — amazing!

After giving the various possibilities that were open to me, he thinks surgery is the way to go, and so do I. He wants to do this before the end of February, and I'm happy with that decision. He will put together a team which will include Kassam (the Wayne Gretzky of brain surgery) and possibly John Sinclair (I've had good 1st hand reports on him as well).

For those of you who want technical details, they will be putting a clip on the aneurysm to cut it off from arterial circulation. This will keep the clotted part away from the blood stream.

The second option is an arterial bypass — takes an artery from my arm and attaches it to the one in my brain bypassing the aneurysm. Hope step one works but glad to know there's an option.

A risk associated with leaving the aneurysm status quo is rupturing. However, this aneurysm has been around for some time (likely since I was a kid although it's still growing) and is somewhat calcified, so there is less risk of rupturing.

Still, there is a 40% chance of this happening within the next 5 years — especially with giant aneurysms.

Too big a risk for me. So if it can stay put for the next few weeks, I'll let the surgeons work their magic.

Allison's Brain • **31**

Recovery is likely to take a while although he said I would likely be able to drive after 4–6 weeks — won't be driving anywhere if I'm likely to scare small children... or big ones.

The suture line will be behind my hairline — however, I won't have all my hair for a while :). All in good time.

So, once more, stay calm. I feel well looked after and will keep you updated.

More later.

Cheers
Allison xo

A crucial point that Allison *didn't* mention in her *Allison's Brain* update is that Dr. Lesiuk estimated a 10–20% risk from the surgery, and my recollection is that when I asked what the *risk* was his answer was stroke or death. I can only say this is my recollection, for although at the time I was trying my best to digest everything being said, it was hard to keep everything straight while feeling pretty shaken by the nature of the news. The relatively high level of risk was associated with the hard-to-reach location and the odd shape of the aneurysm. Dr. Lesiuk drew us a rough sketch of the aneurysm at our meeting, which looked like the sketch below. The number one surgery game plan was to clip the aneurysm — as indicated in the sketch. We were told that clipping the aneurysm involved installing titanium clips while not impeding blood flow.

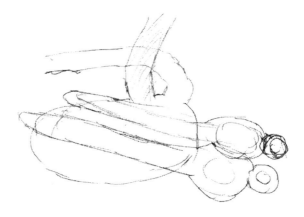

Allison's update did mention the 1,500 pictures of her brain that Dr. Lesiuk had on his computer. The pictures were so vivid that Allison obtained and installed them on her own computer, and showed them, when she could, to family and friends. A couple of the pictures are reproduced below.

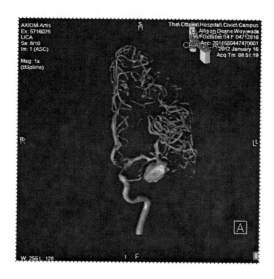

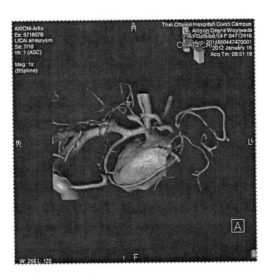

At this point, Allison was geared up for brain surgery in February, which turned out to be badly off-the-mark. The next three months of waiting for her surgery were excruciatingly hard on Allison, and even her relentless cheerfulness took something of a beating. We've come to think, after the fact, and with the benefit of interviews with hospital personnel in preparation for writing the *Allison's Brain* story, that Allison would have fared better if she'd understood how much advance preparation was taking place.

2.

Waiting for Brain Surgery

With a February surgery date in mind, Allison set out to discover and carry out *anything* that would stand her in good stead for the event. She checked into what foods to avoid — any food that thinned the blood might disturb the blood clot in her aneurysm. She adopted a daily routine of doing brain exercises on her computer; physical exercise; piano playing; and reading, all with a view to trying to make herself as fit as possible for surgery. Our understanding was that this would assist in recovery.

I researched the background of Dr. Amin Kassam and found a great deal about his stellar qualifications and international reputation in the neurosurgery area. Among other things, I found that he had done more than 3,000 neurosurgical procedures, written 128 peer-reviewed publications and 32 book chapters, and delivered 119 national and international lectures. He also served for a number of years as chair of the Department of Neurological Surgery at the University of Pittsburgh School of Medicine, which was consistently highly ranked as one of America's best neuroscience centres by *U.S. News & World Report*. We also learned from a medical friend that Dr. Kassam had the training and experience to do the type of deep hypothermic circulatory arrest brain surgery that was being contemplated for Allison. It had only been done in Ottawa on one previous occasion, but Dr. Kassam had experience with the procedure in the U.S.

35

On February 6th, Allison sent out another *Allison's Brain* email update.

> **From:** Allison Woyiwada
> **Sent:** February 6, 2012 7:51 PM
> **To:** Allison's Brain
> **Subject:** update #3
>
> *http://www.youtube.com/watch?v=THNPmhBl-8I*
>
> *Hello all*
>
> *I believe my lead surgeon underestimated how long it might take to assemble the team that will need to be present for my surgery. He told me it would be scheduled by the end of January but, alas... we will have to allow more time. I'm still feeling great so will just have to wait a bit longer. I will let you know.*
>
> *Thanks to my friend, Dr. Fraser Reubens, for doing some ground work for me, for bringing me up to speed on how the medical system works and for giving rave reviews of my surgical team — ones you can truly trust when they come from another surgeon (and a tenor!), not just a rocket scientist — oops, sorry to you rocket scientists and basses out there — and reviews that didn't come from Google :) (wow, that was a run-on.... sorry)*
>
> *Spring arrived here today. Will likely be winter again tomorrow, but it was a nice treat.*
>
> *Cheers*
>
> *Allison xo*
>
> *ps Next time you're in the neighbourhood, drop in and have a look at some (or just one) of the 1,500 pics of my brain — I got a DVD of all 4 tests I had.*

You will notice that Allison included a YouTube link at the beginning of her email update; she left it to her family and friends to find out what the clip was about. I recommend that you watch the clip as it is very funny; however, in the interest of advancing the *Allison's Brain* story, here is a brief synopsis. A brain surgeon tells everyone he meets at a party that he is not just a doctor, but a brain surgeon. Then a rocket scientist comes to the party, and on hearing the brain surgeon bragging the rocket scientist says, "Well it's not exactly rocket science is it?" This brain surgeon at a party story came up a few times post-surgery, and one day it got seriously trumped in Intensive Care — but I digress.

On February 14th, we met with Dr. Lesiuk and Dr. Kassam for a long discussion about what was to come. They explained that they would both be performing the surgery at the Heart Institute and that using a deep hypothermic circulatory arrest procedure would optimize conditions for the surgery. The meeting lasted quite a while, and all of our questions were answered, but once again, given the gravity of the news, I don't recall very much. Allison followed up with another *Allison's Brain* email the next day.

From: Allison Woyiwada
Sent: February 15, 2012 12:15 PM
To: Allison's Brain
Subject: update #4

http://www.5min.com/Video/Saint-Johns-Neuroscience-Institute-Pioneer-Technology-517132304

This is not as funny as the last thing I sent you, but I'm introducing you to the man known as the Wayne Gretzky of brain surgery. Unlike Dr. Wayne, who signed on in one city and stayed there til his contract was up, Dr. Kassam can travel the world to do his wonderful work. I met him yesterday along with one of my other neurosurgeons, Dr. Lesiuk, but today he's in Texas performing brain surgery or lecturing there, and following that, he's off to Vienna. (Marya suggested we follow him and have the surgery

Allison's Brain • 37

elsewhere — he just smiled :) Meeting was fantastic. When you can get them all in one room, they'll stay with you until all your questions are answered.

The downside of having a world-class surgeon is finding a time when he's free and when the rest of the team is as well. And so, the suggested date of surgery is now late March or April. I will have to learn to become better at waiting. I also need a new hobby!

They will do this at the Heart Institute as they may need to drop my body temperature to 27[sic]* to slow my heart (not stop it, as was earlier suggested). They won't know if that's necessary until they get a peek inside, but I told them they had my permission to do whatever.

So, I feel I'm in great hands. They say the surgery is tricky but not impossible — a little crowded in the area they need to work on. All the tests show my good state of health (other than having a giant "frigging" aneurysm in my head :) and my youth (ok, he's a sweet-talker) will make this less of an ordeal.

More later, but maybe not for a while given the necessary delays. I still have no symptoms and feel great, so don't worry about me... until it's necessary :)

Cheers all
Allison xo

[*In point of fact Allison's core temperature was brought down to 16.5 C for the surgery.]

Allison also found out at the meeting that she could address questions about her upcoming surgery to a nurse practitioner by the name of Monika. So Allison began emailing questions to Monika on a variety of subjects, including the effects of the anti-seizure medication *Dilantin* on short-term memory and weight gain; whether to set up a bed for recovery on the first or second floor of our three-storey house; how the heart perfusion machine accomplishes body cooling; whether to avoid being in public spaces where other people might be spreading germs; whether there was any harm in taking products like echinacea or ColdFX; whether a certain probiotic boosts the immune system; what was happening in terms of setting a date for surgery; whose responsibility it was to answer questions about scheduling the surgery; and contacting the hospital administration about obtaining a surgery date. Allison had the highest regard for Monika's responses, calling her a "lifeline," but Monika had a lot of other duties.

Ordinarily, Allison would have had a number of projects underway simultaneously, as a director of children's musicals and other musical productions; however, because of her pending surgery she put all of this on hold. While for most of us this likely wouldn't be such a big deal, in Allison's case, given her constant drive to do more and more, this was incredibly frustrating. A story from her teaching days helps to illustrate the point. Allison says that when things were going smoothly during the school year, she would ask herself what else she could do. Many of the rest of us are happy with smoothly. I also think that being a music teacher with a couple of hundred or more students over a school year, many of whom are playing instruments for the first time, acclimatizes you to a high level of hubbub. On the occasions when I accompanied Allison to her music room at Hopewell School after one of her band concerts or musicals, I was amazed at her ability to interact constantly with so many students.

All of this is to say that the suddenly imposed "downtime" of waiting for surgery, coupled with the anxiety and stress that such an event would naturally bring on, caused Allison to go off the rails a bit. On a day-to-day basis Allison did her best to immunize the rest of us from the anxiety and stress that she was having, and in fact I think her chief aim was to make things as easy as possible for the rest of us. However, it was evident from Allison's demeanour that she was hugely preoccupied with what was ahead, and this led to quite a lot of what manifested itself as forgetfulness, and also to what Allison herself identified as "grumpiness." In the middle

Allison's Brain · **39**

of May, after Allison had initiated contact with the CEO of the Ottawa Hospital about her difficulties in obtaining a surgery date, I wrote to the CEO's Executive Assistant, saying that having to wait for months for communications from anyone at the hospital about when the surgery would take place was having a serious impact on Allison's psychological well-being. I was moved to do this by one of Allison's very few unguarded moments, when she admitted that she was catastrophizing about being found in a heap with a ruptured aneurysm. Lots of people die from having ruptured aneurysms, and the scenario Allison was catastrophizing about didn't seem at all unrealistic.

In early March, Allison emailed Dr. Kassam directly inquiring about the date for her surgery, and he replied that he was out of the country, but was cc'ing Dr. Lesiuk and would try to follow up with him upon his return. Next Allison contacted the booking department at the Heart Institute and found they had never heard of her and that nothing had been done to book cardiac surgeons, anaesthetists, or an operating theatre for the surgery. Then, on a social occasion, when we happened to have dinner with a medical doctor, he told us that the neurosurgery area has a bad reputation in the medical community for not attending to scheduling and that the best course is to keep oneself visible and top-of-mind.

So Allison wrote a letter to Dr. Lesiuk, which is reproduced below.

March 10th, 2012
Dear Dr. Lesiuk:

Regarding upcoming surgery, I was quite composed and confident to face this event initially, but as time passes, more time than was initially indicated, my composure is flagging, and I fear my anxiety is increasing. I understand anxiety is not the best recipe for undergoing surgery such as this, but there are a number of reasons for my concern.

The initial date you suggested as a possibility for this surgery was February 2012. On Feb 14th, you indicated that the date for the surgery could be set within a week to ten days. For this reason, I did not raise the fact that my husband and I may be moving to western Canada this coming summer as he is hoping to be invited to be a Law Professor at a university in British Columbia. As a result, we would be preparing our house for sale, selling it and purchasing a new house in BC. Initially, I thought that if the surgery were to happen in February, all of these plans could go ahead as planned, allowing for some recovery time and follow-up treatment here in Ottawa. Now, this may not be possible and this is causing me some anxiety.

According to details that were given to me yesterday when I called Dr. Kassam's assistant, you felt the surgery date would be set in two weeks; but when speaking to Carmel, she said you had said a few weeks, not two weeks. My anxiety level went up another notch when I got this news.

Another cause for my concern was the fact that you initially told me this was a somewhat dangerous situation for me to be in and that surgery should proceed as soon as possible. As surgery has not occurred and it is uncertain exactly when it will occur, I cannot help but feel that I am at greater risk the longer the delay.

I am following all your instructions by cutting down (and eventually cutting out) nicotine and wine. I am monitoring my heart rate during exercise, I am monitoring my diet and trying to avoid crowded places where I might catch a cold or flu. I have started taking probiotics to boost my immune system. I have been in contact with Monika and doing a lot of online research. I am filling my days with activities like yoga, reading, playing piano and playing word and number games to keep my mind active and exercised. These activities help relieve my anxiety to some extent, but as the days pass and I receive no news, the anxiety creeps in yet again.

Allison's Brain • **41**

I have also been faithful to taking 300 mg of Dilantin on a daily basis, but the impact is becoming more and more noticeable as time goes on. There are times throughout the day when I can barely stay awake. I am suffering some short-term memory loss, and my mood is not as stable as it once was. Before taking Dilantin, I suffered no symptoms of having a brain aneurysm and so I could remain positive; but now these symptoms are with me a great deal of the time as a constant reminder that I am not well.

Being left out of the loop is extremely hard as well. I have received no response to my questions regarding health issues I have asked to be passed on to you. I do not know if you received the message (sharp pains in my right temple) and felt I should not be concerned, or if you did not receive the message at all, and would have felt I required medical treatment. I have asked Carmel to call me from time to time, even with small pieces of info on the progress, and she has agreed to do this from this point forward.

My husband and daughter have both commented that although my normal state is composed and confident, the cumulative stress associated with waiting for more than two months to be informed about a surgery date, after having being advised by medical staff at the hospital about the risk of rupture and that my situation would be given "high priority," is causing me to be agitated and anxious — a condition they have never witnessed in me before.

Thank you for taking time to read this letter. I would appreciate a response and/or a follow-up appointment to discuss how plans are going and how soon I can expect the surgery to take place. Perhaps you could also let me know for how long a period you customarily invite patients in for monitoring following surgery so that I can assess the logistics of moving west.

Yours truly
Allison Woyiwada

The next day Allison sent an email to her sister Linda and brother-in-law Jim, who were spending the winter in Nicaragua. I'm including the email as it also helps to explain Allison's state at the time.

From: Allison Woyiwada
Sent: March 11, 2012 10:21 AM
To: Jim Rennie
Cc: Robert McMechan; Marya Woyiwada
Subject: tired of waiting

As you read this letter, don't be seriously alarmed. All of it is true, but my anxiety is not out of control — it's just that they are really starting to piss me off, and I need to get their attention.

I spoke to a GP at a dinner party on Thursday who told me Neurology [sic] has the worst reputation in the city for letting things fall through the cracks. One reason might be that it's up to the neurosurgeons to put the team together and find a date when all are available. I have a feeling this is not something they studied in school and they have no skills for it — and why should they. I feel like offering to come in and do it for them. After all, I scheduled my own cerebral angiogram, why not take it further and schedule my own brain surgery :)

As stated, I have cut back on wine and Nicorette — may be the cause of some anxiety, but they told me to do it, so it's their fault. I've started to drink fake wine from the grocery store (not bad really) and have only one glass of the real stuff just before bed — may even stop doing that as well. They have allowed me a glass a day. Nicorette is a bigger challenge — I believe wine has always been just a habit because I have quit before for periods and not felt

Allison's Brain • 43

any withdrawal; but nicotine is definitely an addiction. However, replacing it with sugarless mints and gum has been quite successful, and if I feel some anxiety coming on, I pop a Nicorette in my mouth — only consume about 3–4 mg a day.

I'm going to ask for another blood test for the Dilantin levels in my blood — I hope they're too high and I can cut back. I'm a zombie at times — it feels a little like being stoned so not unpleasant, except I can't choose when I feel like this — the drug decides. I sometimes nod off when reading and make up the story from where I left off in my semi-conscious state. Weird!

Sorry — this is long, but I need you to know all this stuff. Can't send a general letter to the masses yet because I'm pissed off, and it would cause worry among the faint of heart — of which you are not... I hope. Marya and Bob are very attentive and supportive (Tyler's working in northern Quebec again) so I'm in good hands.

Keep getting too brown and too hot, and enjoy the balance of your winter getaway.

Love Allison

By mid-March my email messages to inquiring friends were that it was a "Bad week so far for Allison"; Allison was "getting pretty beaten down"; and "Allison had a pretty downer-day yesterday (this never happens)." Then Allison sent out an *Allison's Brain* email update to describe her "no news" situation.

From: Allison Woyiwada
Sent: March 15, 2012 3:52 PM
To: Allison's Brain
Subject: no news yet...

...odd to send a newsletter saying there is no news, but it's been a while so thought I would let you know. If you think this is taking a long time to happen, I agree. They promise I am still on the radar, but it doesn't always feel that way.

Still feeling well except I get sleepy at odd times of the day due to the anti-seizure meds I'm on. I'm not used to ever feeling tired — never happens to me under normal circumstances. Looking forward to "normal" again.

Can't fly anywhere — jury is still out on the impact of cabin pressure, and I won't risk it. Can't visit any rural areas unless they have a hospital with an emergency neuro-surgery department — duh! This leaves driving to Toronto and/or Montreal (I know, tough life) and avoiding crowds of people who may have a bug to pass on to me.

Cheers

Allison xo

ps I'm trying desperately to stay in good health for the big day, whenever it arrives. If I'm ill, they'll postpone, so please don't come around if you have a bug. Thanks.

The next day Allison received a telephone call from Dr. Lesiuk. I should say here that it looks to us as if Dr. Lesiuk's services are constantly in huge demand, with untold numbers of urgent brain surgeries to attend to, and essential follow-up care as part of the package. Over time we came to realize that our own high level of comfort with and respect for Dr. Lesiuk is shared with many others. During Allison's hospital stay, several people who worked in the hospital told us that if they had to have brain surgery, they would want Dr. Lesiuk to be doing it. When I've mentioned this to Dr. Lesiuk a couple of times he is nothing but modest, and he just says that "what they are saying is much better than the opposite."

Following Allison's conversation with Dr. Lesiuk, she sent out another *Allison's Brain* update.

From: Allison Woyiwada
Sent: March 17, 2012 11:22 AM
To: Allison's Brain
Subject: my latest update was too soon

Got a call Friday from my lead surgeon, Dr. Lesiuk, in response to a letter I had sent him asking for more details. He's coming to understand I have a "need to know details" gene and he provided some. (Those jokes I sent out yesterday did not apply to MY neurosurgeons by the way.)

In my letter, I asked why the delay if I was at a high risk. He said I'm not high risk in the short term — the surgery is. That made me feel better, oddly enough. This surgery is not scary for me — I believe these guys can do just about anything.

I asked about my surgery taking a few weeks to schedule. He said it will take a few weeks to happen — scheduling will happen sooner and then pre op for tests, instructions, advice etc. Seems like a small point, but I think I can see a light at the end of the tunnel. He's already speaking to cardiology and anaesthesiology, so the team is assembling as we speak. I'll try to get a group photo.

Recovery is a big question mark. Completely successful surgery means 1 week in hospital and maybe 6 weeks for full recovery — energy level takes a while to return and my brain may need to relearn some things — like my name :) Too much swelling would mean they couldn't replace skull section right away so they'd stitch me up and do it a few weeks later. Fashionable helmet to be worn in the interim. http://www.tmz.com/2010/09/07/ikki-twins-mtv-double-shot-at-love-car-accident-coma-brain-surgery-photos/#.T2SnTsmF9tI

So thanks for reading. Sorry to bombard you with so much info in a short period, but this feels like real "news."

Cheers and Happy St Patrick's Day

Allison xo

This update again produced a flurry of supportive responses, of which I will again include a couple.

From: Geoff & Eileen Wilson
Sent: March 17, 2012 1:06 PM
To: Allison Woyiwada
Subject: RE: my latest update was too soon

Hello Allison,

I cannot imagine not having a "need to know" gene. You have been a successful independent woman for decades and, of course, that independence extends into your interaction with the health care system. Good for you for asking precise questions.

Doctors sometimes think that they are gods and patients are puppets. And in a certain way they are gods and we want them to be gods but we are never puppets. In my mind, that's the difference. I appreciate your clear explanations included below; it makes your situation clearer to me. Uncertainty is the worst part of an illness. You are managing this uncertain waiting stage magnificently.

Love to you and Bob,

Eileen

From: Howard Kaplan
Sent: March 17, 2012 9:29 PM
To: Allison Woyiwada
Subject: Re: my latest update was too soon

This is progress… no apologies necessary, bombard away my friend. You're right when you say surgery is not scary for you. That's because you're fearless. You have more guts than anyone I know. It's inspiring.

Howard

One of the ways I thought of to try and give Allison a bit of a boost was attending the Cirque du Soleil Michael Jackson show in Montreal. We were both big fans of Michael's musicianship and were mesmerized by his obsession with perfection as depicted in the movie *This Is It.* We couldn't believe that the night we went to see the movie at our local Mayfair Theatre that we were two of only a handful present. In any event, I purchased tickets, and Allison found a Groupon hotel deal at the Delta Inn in Montreal. She bought the certificate, but when she called to make a reservation she was told there were no Groupon rooms available for that evening. She made the reservation anyway, and when we arrived at the registration desk Allison presented the Groupon certificate. The clerk informed Allison that there were no Groupon rooms available, but Allison persisted, whereupon I beat a retreat. Although I have spent a good deal of my life as a litigation lawyer, I have never especially enjoyed conflict. From a distance I could see that Allison continued to press her case, eventually involving a hotel manager. After some time had passed, Allison came to fetch me, advising that the hotel was honouring the Groupon deal. Then, as we walked towards the elevator, Allison read the fine print and saw that the Groupon hotel deal wasn't available on Tuesdays. As it was a Tuesday we were in quite a predicament, which we never quite figured out how to solve. We went to the show, which was so-so, but we had a splendid dinner with our friend Pierre Barsalou, who also happens to be tax lawyer.

By the end of March, and perhaps earlier, we had come across the "Ted Talk" by Jill Bolte Taylor, who wrote *My Stroke of Insight.*[4] Jill was working in the neuroscience area when she suffered a stroke

---

4   Jill Bolte Taylor, *My Stroke of Insight: A Brain Scientist's Personal Journey,* First Viking Edition, Penguin Group, New York, 2008.

at a relatively young age. She gives a fascinating account, with the benefit of expert insights, into her entire experience, beginning with a description of how her brain behaved during the stroke itself, and tracing through her entire recovery. This was hugely inspirational stuff for us which we consumed eagerly.

At around this time I was scheduled to do the oral defence of my Ph.D. dissertation at Osgoode Hall Law School in Toronto. My topic was a taxation law one (much more about this later) concerning the role of economic substance in tax avoidance cases,[5] which almost no one but me has ever found interesting. As luck would have it, Allison's surgery had been delayed, and she was able to accompany me to Toronto. I had worked pretty hard to get ready for this and was feeling fairly comfortable, so I tried my hand at an April Fools' joke as Allison took over driving on a Sunday morning part way from Ottawa to Toronto.

From: Robert McMechan
Sent: April 1, 2012 9:41 AM
To: Robert McMechan
Subject: Big Snow Storm

Trapped in Napanee. Hope it blows over soon as I need to be at Osgoode in the a.m. for my oral defence. Wish us well.

As there is a bit of history here, my adult children both ignored my plight, and some knowing friends countered with incredible stories involving one-upmanship. But I shall remain forever proud that my mother and sisters were apparently concerned about the possible impact of the big snow storm. Not the least of it was that my mother had been planning her trip to my convocation for several years. In any event, all's well that ends well and, with the aid of emergency assistance from the army, we did eventually make it to Toronto. That said, we found that the area of North York around

---

5   Robert McMechan, *Economic Substance and Tax Avoidance: An International Perspective*, Carswell, Toronto, 2013.

Allison's Brain   •   **49**

York University isn't exactly a culinary dream on a Sunday evening, and we ended up dining modestly at Swiss Chalet.

This sort of ties in with the *Allison's Brain* story, so I am reproducing Allison's email the next day.

> **From:** Allison Woyiwada
> **Sent:** April 2, 2012 8:33 PM
> **To:** Allison Woyiwada
> **Subject:** Doctor Bob
>
> *My apologies to those of you who don't know Bob. I'm too lazy and tired to make up a new email list.*
>
> *Bob successfully defended his Phd Dissertation in Tax Law at York U this morning, and the panel members were effusively and unanimously congratulatory! ... I got to sit in and listen to the whole thing. I even got to make comments at the end — told them it was so enjoyable, they were all invited to dinner sometime and they could continue the discussion. I also made them promise to read my book "Living with Bob While He Wrote his Dissertation."*
>
> *Graduation will be in June, so it will become official then, but the champagne can start flowing any time!*
>
> *I think this is right up there with brain surgeon/rocket scientist — a real show stopper at parties :)*
>
> *Cheers*
> *Allison*

Soon afterwards, Allison took me out for a quiet celebratory dinner to the Courtyard Café in the Byward Market in Ottawa. There's an old saying that idle hands make idle minds, and I think in this case that having the Ph.D. thing going on helped to distract us a little bit from the brain surgery business ahead. One other thing I'd like to work in here is that Allison backtracked a bit on her comment about *"Living with Bob While He Wrote his Dissertation."*

From: Allison Woyiwada
Sent: April 3, 2012 9:36 AM
To: McIsaac, Louise
Cc: Sharon Chartier; Bob
Subject: Re: Doctor Bob

Actually, I exaggerated the comment about living with
Bob during the writing. He has a remarkable level of
self-control, discipline, focus, dedication — the list goes on
and on. I have passed on your message Louise. My son said
I deserved a phd for sitting through the defence :)

Cheers
aw

Allison's nurse practitioner Monika passed along the news in early April that she had spoken to Dr. Lesiuk, and learned that he had been in touch with Dr. Kassam's assistant and the Heart Institute to coordinate booking the OR with the schedules of the cardiologist, perfusionist and anaesthesia, etc. Then on April 17th, Allison had an echocardiogram at the Heart Institute. Following this, Allison fired off questions wherever she could to find out what was happening next. The delay was making Allison so frustrated that I even suggested checking with some other neurosurgeons. Allison continued making calls to whoever she could, and a couple of days later she sent out another *Allison's Brain* email update.

From: Allison Woyiwada
Sent: April 19, 2012 4:45 PM
To: Allison's Brain
Subject: upcoming tests

Hi y'all. Been a while since I had any news to share, but
some of the people at the Heart Institute now recognize my
name. If I pass all these tests, we may be able to graduate to
surgery.

Allison's Brain · **51**

*April 17th I had an echocardiogram (didn't see the screen
but heard my heart — that is cool) and, on April 25th and
30th, I will have two tests where dye is injected, one for
the heart itself, and one for the lower abdomen. She said
they would likely have to see the results of these tests before
scheduling surgery — need to know all is in good working
order. I believe I told you that they will be lowering my
body temperature somewhat, and therefore slowing my
heart during this surgery — hence the reason for these tests.*

*I had started making waves (aka calls and emails)
again yesterday and got these calls today. So it may be a
coincidence, or it may help to make waves. Not certain so
obviously, I will continue to make a few waves.*

Cheers
Allison xo

In response to this update, a medical doctor friend assured
Allison that gentle waves are effective. Around this time we were
treated by our friends Gordon and Pamela to a takeout Indian
dinner at home as Allison was concerned about the need to be 100%
healthy if surgery was scheduled and didn't want to be exposed to
anyone's germs. On April 25th, Allison had more tests at the Heart
Institute, and then she diligently researched what things to do and
eat post-surgery to help optimize her recovery.

In early May, Allison emailed Doctors Lesiuk and Kassam,
advising that she was becoming quite anxious about her situation
and desirous of some communication from the hospital. Next
Allison contacted Patient Relations at the hospital and felt that she
got a sympathetic hearing — but nothing happened. So on May
9th, Allison sent a letter to Dr. Jack Kitts, President and CEO of
the Ottawa Hospital through his Executive Assistant. Our friend
Mike Hayes had recommended this step in mid-March, based on
a previous favourable experience that he'd had with Dr. Kitts. But
Allison had not wanted to rock the neurosurgery boat too violently,
so she'd been reluctant to take this step. However, based on the

chain-of-events over the next few days, she might have been better off doing this much earlier.

Allison's communication to Dr. Kitts was quite lengthy, and I am including all of it below, but even by skimming through its contents you'll get the drift of what she was saying about her predicament.

From: Allison Woyiwada
Sent: May 9, 2012 12:02 PM
To: Llafleur
Subject: Allison Woyiwada, Giant Brain Aneurysm

Dear Ms LaFleur:

I am in a difficult situation and wonder if you would be kind enough to forward this message to Dr. Kitts. I am awaiting brain surgery for a giant aneurysm and have been doing so for several months, although I was initially advised that the surgery would be completed in February. I am receiving very little communication from the Neurosurgery Department, and so I am writing to ask if Dr. Kitts can help find a solution to my dilemma.

I authorize you to read the letter and the diary if you wish, so as to help determine the next steps I should be taking.

Thank you for any assistance you can offer.

Sincerely
Allison Woyiwada

Brain Aneurysm Chain of Events:

Note below: Instances where calls and emails were not returned/addressed (italicized and bold) occurred often. However, in many cases, I called several times to try to get an answer to one particular question. In most cases, my question was either ignored in that Dr. Lesiuk didn't receive the message, or it was simply not responded to by his assistant, Carmel McKenna. Twice I called because I

Allison's Brain • **53**

had physical pain (sharp pains in my head — two calls) or abnormalities (numb fingers — one call). I called several times (three) because I had been booked for the wrong test and was anxious that this be corrected. These calls were not returned and the correction in Radiology was not made by Dr. Lesiuk's office. I eventually had to call Radiology to make the change myself. Twice I called/emailed because (1) I had already had test at the Heart Institute; and (2) nitro had not been put under my tongue beforehand. I was unsure if this meant the tests had to be done again. I received no response.

Since being diagnosed with this aneurysm, my life style has changed substantially. I have no projects underway, although I have been involved in directing musicals for my entire adult life. As I was initially told that the surgery was to happen in February, I continued to assume that it would happen shortly thereafter. I did not accept any positions as Music Director, as I assumed that I would have to abandon the process mid-stream. I felt that would have been unfair. However, many projects with which I could have been involved have been successfully completed and I sat and watched them happen, rather than being a part of them.

I have taken steps to prepare well for surgery and maintain or improve my state of health:

1) I take 300 mg of Dilantin daily.

2) I take three tablets of Senotok to relieve one of the side effects of this medication, on the advice of my Nurse Practitioner.

3) I have gradually reduced my daily intake of Nicorette and quit altogether on April 18th.

4) I have reduced intake of red wine as advised by Dr. Kassam.

5) I attend yoga classes twice a week.

6) I walk one hour each day.

7) I practise the piano one hour each day to strengthen my brain and perhaps give me a tool to help with brain recovery post surgery.

8) I read for minimum one hour each day.

9) I play games designed to enhance skills and train the brain (Luminosity etc.)

10) I have done much research on brain aneurysms, surgery and recovery.

11) I avoid crowded places where I may be vulnerable to germs/viruses.

12) I started taking Probiotics to maintain good health.

13) I have willingly informed all friends and family of my situation to provide a support group and to keep them well-informed and no more anxious than necessary.

14) I have agreed not to fly anywhere and, as a result, have missed a friend's wedding and a winter vacation. I may also miss my husband's graduation from the doctorate program at York University

15) If I travel, I have agreed to drive or take the train and to always be close to areas that have large, well-equipped hospitals (Montreal, Toronto).

16) I have maintained my weight within three pounds in spite of the fact that I have been unable to take part in highly-aerobic or weight bearing exercise.

Allison's Brain • 55

If you are able to take the time to read my diary below or simply glance through it, you may understand my growing state of anxiety. Please understand that my anxiety is not due to the surgery, but to the waiting period and to the general lack of communication from the hospital in general. All I have asked for throughout this process is answers to questions. I don't feel that I am considered an important part of this process as very little information is shared with me. In my case, as I'm sure is the case with many patients, communication can relieve anxiety — lack of communication creates it. I have said throughout this process that bad news is acceptable. It is better than no news, but no news has been very common throughout the past five months.

Read on to find out how often no news has been the norm.

Thank you
Allison Woyiwada

Dec 15th CT Scan, scheduled as a result of smelling garbage where the was none

Dec 19th Dr Blake (my GP) told me of the results (giant aneurysm) and told me Dr Lesiuk (neurosurgeon) is assigned to my case)

Dec 22 called hospital and Dr Lesiuk's office re next steps — no answer, no reply

Dec 23rd called Dr. Blake and said I hadn't hear anything from Dr. Lesiuk so he told me to go into Emergency at the Civic and he would alert them that I was coming. 11:30am arrived at the Civic stayed until 9:30 pm for a CT angiogram — home by 10:00 pm for Christmas with my family, was admitted as an in-patient but given a night pass

56 • *Robert McMechan with Allison Woyiwada*

Dec 24 7:00 arrived at Civic for an MRI, left at 10:00pm after having blood test, MRI, and given prescription for anti-seizure meds

Dec 25 vomited because of anti-seizure meds Carbamazepine

Dec 26 arrived at Civic 7:00am — waited all day — no tests — left at 4:00pm, had my medication changed to Dilantin

Dec 27 arrived at Civic 7:00am waited all morning — no tests — left at 11:00am, was released from the Civic as an in-patient

Dec 28 called Dr. Lesiuk's office re results of tests — no answer called Dr. Blake — asked him to request a DVD of the scans and to get me a printout of all tests so far, received an appt for a CT scan in the mail for Jan 19th — called Dr. Lesiuk's office to tell them I had already had this test, no answer, no response,

Dec 29 called Radiology to tell them I had already had a CT scan on Dec 16th — they promised to get a message to Carmel re being scheduled for a test I'd already had

Dec 30 called Dr. Lesiuk's office re wrong test, no answer, no reply

Jan 3 faxed a letter to Dr. Blake telling him of what had happened and what hadn't. He called me back. He will try to get a hold of Dr. Lesiuk and set up an appt for me. Called and left a message, — no answer, no reply.

Jan 5 – called Dr. Lesiuk's office re incorrect test on 19th — no answer, no reply

Jan 6 Dr. Blake called and told me to leave a message with Dr. Lesiuk's office, I called angio department and booked

Allison's Brain • **57**

the test myself for Jan 16th, called Carmel (Dr. Lesiuk's assistant) and left a message saying the angio was on Jan 16th and the CT scan on the 19th was cancelled, — no answer, no reply

Jan 10th received call from Carmel, angio scheduled for Jan 16th and appt with Dr. Lesiuk for Jan 19th instead of Jan 23rd (I already knew about the angio as I had scheduled it myself)

Jan 16th Cerebral angiogram at Civic,

Jan 17 called Dr. Lesiuk (Carmel) re numbness in my fingers, left message — no reply

Jan 19 first meeting with Dr. Lesiuk, said surgery was high risk and scheduling would be completed in a week to 10 days — surgery would occur in February, answered all questions

Jan 23 fax and call Dr. Blake

Jan 25 appt with Dr. Blake, got prescription for dvds of test results, prescription for Dilantin

Jan 26 to Civic to pick up dvd of tests

Jan 27 headache and sharp pains in right temple, lasted most of the day, called Dr. Lesiuk (Carmel), left message — no reply

Feb 3 left phone message and sent fax to Dr. Lesiuk's office asking for date of surgery and to report sharp pains in right temple — left message — no reply

Feb 7 received message that appt was booked with Drs. Kassam and Lesiuk for Feb 14th

Feb 13 looked into health insurance for private room — not guaranteed

Feb 14 meeting with Drs. Lesiuk and Kassam (and Mohammed). First time meeting Dr. Kassam, answered lots of questions, suggested wine and Nicorette be limited or eliminated, had 2nd blood test for Dilantin levels, had prepared long list of questions, got answers to all, asked about communication link and they suggested Nurse Practitioner — I did not know that I was eligible for a Nurse Practitioner until that date

Feb 15 began to limit intake of Nicorette and red wine, bought Thrive 1 mg, 1 every two hours to start, two half glasses of wine per day

Feb 20 down to 6mg of Nicorette per day

Feb 23 received message that blood test had determined that Dilantin levels are high enough, appt at Civic for blood test, met with Monika Pantalone and had a long talk, very helpful, responded to many email over the next while which caused me not to seemingly pointlessly leave messages for Carmel

Feb 27 email Monika re method of dropping body temperature, she asked Dr. Lesiuk and got back to me with the answer

Feb 28 down to 4mg Nicorette per day

Mar 3 email to Dr. Kassam asking if the scheduling is happening yet, response that he is out of the country but copied Dr. Lesiuk to ask for update, no response, 1st day of neck pain, lasted until Mar 12th

Mar 7 purchase probiotics (Monika's suggestion) and start taking them to be healthy when surgery is scheduled

Mar 8th call Heart Institute to find out if there is a date set — they had never heard of me, had dinner with a friend who is an MD who said this is typical for

Neurology, they are the worst department in the system for dropping the ball, letting people fall between the cracks etc. Advised me to continue to contact them on a somewhat regular basis.

Mar 9th called Dr. Kassam's assistant re scheduling (she answered!), she put me on hold, asked Dr. Lesiuk, came back to tell me it would be scheduled within two weeks, called Carmel and left a message saying if I didn't hear back from her, I would assume she is not in charge of scheduling and I would be in touch with hospital admin and the Heart Institute to find out who is, she called back immediately and rather haughtily told me it would not be set for a few weeks, I asked her to call me with even small details, she said the doctors don't share anything with her, putting the team together is Dr. Lesiuk's job, then she is in charge of booking the space, may use Heart Institute or Neurology, undecided even though they told us on Feb 14th it would be at the Heart Institute — Carmel did say she would call every two weeks but never did

Mar 10th wrote a letter to Dr. Lesiuk indicating the delay is causing anxiety, mailed letter xpress post, should arrive Mar 13th

Mar 12 updated my diary so as to have a record of the activity of the Neurosurgery Department to present to Civic Hospital Administration

Mar 16 Dr. Lesiuk called me to answer questions in my letter. He said the surgery would be high risk and would take place within a few weeks, as he stated on March 9th. He also told me that I would be recovered by July 1st in the event that we would be moving to BC. He advised me not to do any of the packing or lifting but I would be ready to fly.

Mar 19 – blood test at Civic — I feel my Dilantin level is too high — got word back that it's normal, continued 300 mg per day, becoming more lethargic and "nappy," plus suffering from short term memory loss and constipation

Mar 30 email from Monika saying no news, will ask Dr. Lesiuk next week

April 5 Dr. Lesiuk's office (Carmel) called saying the Heart Institute wanted to book me for tests, Monika e-mailed saying Dr. Kassam would be back Wed next week and a date would be set then

April 17 called Radiology at the Civic to find if I had been scheduled for a test, they said no but it would be scheduled at the HI, went to HI for echocardiogram, asked about other tests and surgery date, nothing was scheduled but I was told that Dr. Masters was my appointed doctor at the HI (I did not know this) and I was given the number of his assistant. I called her and left a message, no response

April 18 one week after the date that Monika told me Dr. Kassam would be back and that a date would be set then. If one has been set, I have not been told. Received voicemail from Beth, Dr. Master's asst. saying she wasn't sure of my last name. I called her back and spelled my name, asked a few questions but she never got back to me with the answers. Sent an email to Monika asking for details: if the request for the other test has been made, what test it is and if a date has been set for surgery. Also advised her that we may be moving to BC for July 1st and Dr. Lesiuk assured me that I would be fully recovered by then. Monika responded saying that she had been reassigned to ward duties but would forward my questions to Dr. Lesiuk and Carmel. I responded saying I was considering asking hospital admin to help with scheduling.

Allison's Brain • **61**

April 19 Response from Monika saying hospital admin does not usually get involved is scheduling, I researched other neurosurgeons at Civic in case the team could include someone who was available

April 20th received a call from HI asking me to come in for tests (angiography), April 25th and 30th

April 22 Noticing short term memory loss, likely due to Dilantin or stress as it is getting worse

April 25 went to HI for test, they did both heart and lower abdomen but forgot to put nitro under tongue, called Dr. Lesiuk's office once returning from HI, left a message asking if this was critical, no response. Sent email to Monika asking if this is critical and asking Dr. Lesiuk to ask Dr. Masters' opinion. Monika responded copying Dr. Lesiuk and Carmel but neither one responded. She also said she would not have anymore contact with me until post-op

April 29 research necessary diet following surgery

April 30 Email to Carmel re no nitro under the tongue. No response.

May 1 noticed skin is very dry. Researched and found Dilantin may be at fault. Bought and started taking 1mg Folic acid per day.

May 2 email to Drs. Lesiuk and Kassam asking for a date, explaining that I am suffering from anxiety and asking if Dr. Lesiuk still feels that I will be recovered and able to move by July 1st, no response from Dr. Lesiuk, computer generated response from Dr. Kassam saying he was out of the country and returning on April 23rd (today is May 2) I emailed his two assistants and asked for any information. No response.

May 4 Left voicemail for Carmel adamantly asking her to respond and give me information re a date for surgery. She did respond and said she didn't know.

Found patient relations on Civic website and called to explain my situation. Samantha passed the message onto Melanie who called back. She had been in touch with Carmel and gave me the same answer Carmel has — no date. I asked Melanie to call Dr. Kassam's and Dr. Masters' assistants to be sure I am still on the radar.

Email to Dr. Lesiuk asking if he would be able to take care of me following surgery, rather than wait for a period when Dr. Kassam can stay in Ottawa for a full week. No response.

May 7th composed letter to Dr. Jack Kitts, President and CEO of Ottawa General Hospital, asking for advice re scheduling of surgery, brought my diary up to date to also send to Dr. Kitts, sent May 9th, 2012

The following day Allison sent another *Allison's Brain* email update.

From: Allison Woyiwada
Sent: May 10, 2012 3:57 PM
To: Allison's Brain
Subject: no news yet

I think I've had every test they need — had my brain and heart photographed, blood sampled and tested. So I've done my part...

Yesterday I sent a letter to the CEO and President of the hospital, Dr. Jack Kitts, through his executive assistant, asking if he had any ideas for making this happen. Haven't heard back from him yet, but I did hear from the assistant and she had sent it onward to him. I said I was anxious to get this done partly because I had heard such great things about these brain surgeons and was looking forward to having them work their magic on me. I'm trying to remain good friends... very good friends with my surgeons. (I might have a little chat with them after the fact to give them some pointers on how to organize events in a timely fashion.)

I still have a lot of faith in their ability to do the surgery so no worries on that front.

Cheers
Allison

On Mother's Day, we went with Marya to Gatineau Park for brunch at Camp Fortune and then for a walk in the Park. Afterwards Allison sent out another *Allison's Brain* update.

From: Allison Woyiwada
Sent: May 13, 2012 9:05 PM
To: Allison's Brain
Subject: Happy Mothers Day to All You Mothers

Picture of Marya and I in Gatineau park in Quebec today surrounded by fields of Trillium, Ontario's official flower. Bob took enough pics to make a calendar that he would have sent to all of you for Christmas. I think I've talked him out of that idea, so you have me to thank for that.

Re my head, I think I've had every test they need — had my brain and heart photographed, blood sampled and tested. So I've done my part...

I know it's been a while since I let you know what was happening, so I thought I'd update you... still nothing is happening... but I remain hopeful and optimistic, as should you.

Cheers
Allison

64 • *Robert McMechan with Allison Woyiwada*

The next *Allison's Brain* update brought the long-awaited news of a surgery date.

From: Allison Woyiwada
Sent: May 16, 2012 4:43 PM
To: Allison's Brain
Subject: May 28th

Exciting news! I received a call this afternoon saying that May 28th is the date for my surgery to take place. I told them all along, I would be willing to do this on short notice, and they have taken me at my word.

I received a call from Patient Relations yesterday saying that the CEO had "suggested" the team meet this week and choose a date for my surgery. I guess they do what he suggests. (Wish I were a CEO :) Anyway, I love this guy, Dr. Jack Kitts! I wish I'd thought of writing to him a long time ago. Thanks for the suggestion Mike Hayes.

I will send a message on May 27th to remind all of you who promised to send good vibes to me to carry out your promise. Bob will send a message to all of you (along with some jokes he says — no pics for a while — my orders) to keep you updated re my recovery and when I can get to my computer after the fact, I will write to you as well.

Allison's Brain • 65

Having brain surgery may be a funny thing to celebrate, but this is a big relief and long overdue.

Cheers y'all
Allison

xo

ps some people can drive 4 weeks after brain surgery — I'll warn you locals before I do this

Allison then began to attend in earnest to writing out the details she thought would be needed by her family while she was recovering from brain surgery, and although she didn't speak to us about it at the time, she also did preparation for the scenarios where she either suffered irreparable brain damage or didn't survive the surgery. I never saw these latter preparations until after the fact. When I came across them a few weeks later, while repairing and painting Allison's office ceiling and walls, it was a very emotional time. We had put Powers of Attorney in place much earlier when we made our wills, but at that time nothing sinister was looming, and there was nothing distressing about it. After Allison's surgery, when she had serious speech and motor skill deficits that no one could predict would go away, it was very different.

One other thing I should add is that Allison went through the pre-surgery checks, which were very comprehensive, with flying colours. At one point, when Allison was having her blood pressure checked, and the nurse reported that her reading was normal, I was thinking it was lucky that the nurse wasn't checking *my* blood pressure. Once the die was cast, so to speak, Allison was cruising to the finish line.

The Consent to Surgery which Allison signed on May 25th put the whole business in perspective.

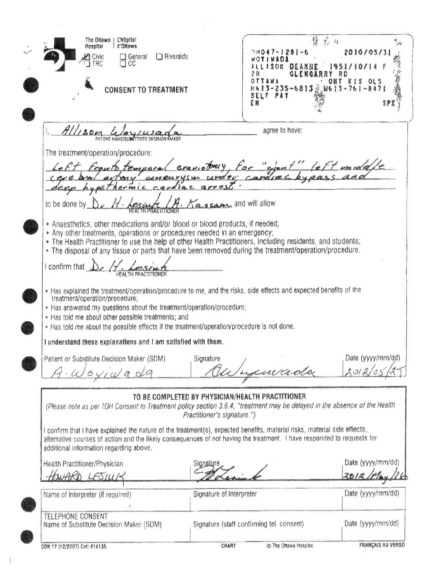

As the surgery date approached, it seemed possible that we wouldn't have the opportunity to spend quality time together for a long time — or perhaps ever again — and we tried to savour the days as much as we could. One thing we did was go for dinner on

Allison's Brain • 67

Preston Street at Il Picolino, and walk through the glorious tulip display at Dow's Lake, but my heart was heavy, and the tulips didn't give it much of a lift.

We had a few kind invitations to spend time with others the day before the surgery, but Allison decided that she would like to spend the day alone with family. I ran the Ottawa Race Weekend Half Marathon in the morning and was pleased enough with the results to send them to Allison, who had been watching for me with Marya from the outdoor second floor patio of the Red Oak Inn at Pretoria and Hawthorne.

From: Robert McMechan
Sent: May 27, 2012 2:45 PM
To: Allison Woyiwada; Marya Woyiwada
Subject: Half Marathon Results

Place:	*3228*
Name	*Robert McMechan*
City	*Ottawa*
Bib #	*13368*
Time	*2:00:28.0*
Chip	*1:58:29:1*
Pace	*5:37*
Category	*M55–59*
Category Place	*96/277*
Gender Place	*2193/4311*
10 km	*0:54:45*

I have been a runner all of my adult life, and have evidently appeared to be so enthralled with my running that Allison gave me a bronzed running shoe as part of the loot for my 50th birthday. I am mentioning this here because running, plus biking and swimming, became my "life savers" in the long weeks ahead. I came to appreciate the therapeutic benefits of swimming late in life, after my daughter Laurie persuaded me to enter the Penticton Ironman with her in 2007. I'm still not a great swimmer, but even a short swim late in the evenings of Allison's most frightening hospital days would calm me down immensely. I often wonder, and still don't know, how people cope with stress without any exercising.

We had a quiet dinner together with Marya in one of Allison's favourite places — outside on the front porch of our home — with Allison giving us her by-then-customary assurances that everything would be OK. She also sent out one more *Allison's Brain* email update the afternoon before her surgery.

> **From:** Allison Woyiwada
> **Sent:** May 27, 2012 4:03 PM
> **To:** Allison's Brain
> **Subject:** one more sleep…
>
> *…and I expect it will be an ok sleep, although shorter as I have to be at the HI at 6:00 am. Slept really well last night. Wasn't sure when the date drew near if my confidence would dissipate but seems to be holding.*
>
> *Met with many doctors last week, all with unbelievably good "bedside" manners —cardiac, anaesthesiology and neurology alike. They gave us the facts as they are, including the potential risks. Dr. Lesiuk was giving us all the possible negative results, as he is obliged to do, so I asked him to give us the possible best-case scenario as well — which sounded excellent. This is the one I'm aiming for, and I encouraged him to do the same! :) He became quite animated when he answered Marya's question re whether a positive attitude*

Allison's Brain • **69**

helps. He said absolutely, both with the surgery and with recovery so I'm sticking to this strategy.

Surgery may start at 8:00am will likely last 12 hours which includes 2 hours to cool the blood and 2 to re-warm it. They may then keep me sedated for a few hours following this so any reports you get from Bob on Monday may be mid-surgery and speculative. However, Tuesday and following may have more details, so be patient.

Having now been through this, I would like to tell you how much better it was for me to have kept you in the loop. You were a wonderful support network. I hope knowing the facts prevented middle of the night dark thoughts for some of you. Loved your emails. Loved this past week of numerous get togethers and good wishes.

Spending today with Bob and Marya and on the phone with Tyler, who is planting in BC, so forgive me for not picking up the phone or responding to email today. I appreciate your thoughts and good wishes. We'll get together as soon as it is practical to do so.

Love
Allison

xo

This elicited a flood of loving and supportive emails, which still choke me up when I re-read them. Here are a couple.

From: Marianna Burch
Sent: May 27, 2012 10:20 PM
To: Allison Woyiwada
Subject: Re: one more sleep…

Hey there Allison — I'm so glad to have gotten this message — figured that these past couple of weeks were

*probably a whirlwind for you for all the obvious reasons, so
we didn't want to bug you too much!!!*

*Anyway, I just wanted to say that I am so optimistic that
all will go well, simply because you are the person you are...*

*I so admire your unwavering positive outlook on every-
thing and the strength/conviction you maintain throughout — without knowing it you have often reminded me
that the "glass half full" philosophy is so much more productive in life, and I want to thank you for that!!!*

*So, just know that I will be sending you and your "team"
constant telepathic signals to keep the ship steady and on
course...*

*Love you and really look forward to seeing you as soon as
you give us the thumbs up!!!!*

Humungous hugs to you and Bob!!!

Marianna

XXOO

From: Marylen Milenkovic
Sent: May 28, 2012 5:57 PM
To: McMechan Bob
Subject: I've been thinking of Allison all day — since
6am this morning

*Just wanted to let you know that although this is a tense
time for all of you that you have a shit load of people
praying, wishing and sending good vibes your way.*

Love Marylen

Many people remarked on Allison's positive attitude, which is
playing a huge role in her post-surgery recovery. I will close this
chapter by saying that, as Allison was being wheeled away very

early the next morning to complex brain surgery, with an uncertain outcome, the last thing she said to me was that everything would be OK. There are some strong people in the world I guess, and then there's Allison.

3.

It's Not Rocket Science

The first thing I would like to say, especially in case I need brain surgery myself someday, is that the title of this chapter is just a joke. It's hard to imagine what sort of people deliberately put themselves into high stress life and death brain surgery operating situations again and again, but as daughter Laurie said at the time of Allison's surgery, it's a fortunate thing for us that some people choose to do this sort of thing. I guess rocket scientists are smart people too, but I wouldn't want them doing my brain surgery.[6]

Allison's was only the second neurosurgery done in Ottawa using the deep hypothermic circulatory arrest technique. The deep hypothermic circulatory arrest was necessary because the aneurysm was located in a hard-to-reach spot. It optimizes conditions for neurosurgery because it reduces brain metabolism. Ordinarily, the brain consumes about 20% of the body's blood flow, whereas when the body is in a deep hypothermic state, blood flow to the brain is stopped. The brain also normally consumes about 25% of the oxygen that the body uses, and the deep hypothermic state dramatically

---

6   Coincidentally, when we were seated beside a young mother on a bus in Antigua in January 2014, she made the point to us that if you want your child to grow up to be a rocket scientist you have to raise the child to do their household chores and homework. Unfortunately she didn't mention anything about what you have to do if you want your child to grow up to be a brain surgeon.

reduces oxygen demand. Without the benefit of the deep hypothermic procedure, Allison would have had a massive stroke.

Dr. Roy Masters, Chair of the Heart Transplant Committee at the Ottawa Heart Institute, carried out the procedure. Allison's blood was withdrawn using a heart and lung machine, cooled and put back into her body. Allison's core was cooled to 16.5°C, and everything stopped including her heart, kidneys, brain and all other organs. The cooling is what caused everything to shut down. Dr. Masters likens the situation to that of someone who is found unconscious in a snow bank and eventually resuscitated, except at the Heart Institute the whole procedure is closely controlled. The biggest risk of the procedure is that there could be brain damage or organ damage while everything is turned off; however, there is no way of knowing whether any damage has occurred until afterwards. This is partly why, in the Intensive Care Unit post-surgery, we were told that "every square inch" of Allison was being monitored.

People can be kept in a cooled down state for a long time without dying; there is, in fact, an old saying that suggests no one is dead until they are *warm* and dead. However, to minimize the likelihood of damage to the brain, the length of time that the body is kept in a cooled down state is crucial. This brings to mind a short story I heard many years ago from a court clerk. As the story goes, one of the court's judges had a heart attack, and when he came to he was concerned about the possible impact of oxygen deprivation on his brain, as he thought that he might have woken up as the associate chief justice—just to be clear, this story doesn't relate to anyone who is presently sitting as a judge and hearing any of my tax cases.

Prior to Allison's surgery, the whole team met a couple of times to map out what was to be done. The team included neurosurgeons, cardiologists, anaesthetists, perfusionists (who operate the heart-lung machines) and nurses. The Ottawa Heart Institute was chosen as the venue for the surgery because the important equipment for a circulatory arrest is not very mobile, and the neurosurgeons were willing to operate at the Heart Institute. When asked to give a description of the surgery that lay people could understand, Dr.

Lesiuk said that it reminded him of a successful military campaign. This is because of the extent of the advance planning involved, and the level of coordination required amongst the members of the large surgical team. Dr. Lesiuk emphasizes that although the aneurysm clipping itself was important, the success of the day was "all about the team."

Dr. Lesiuk had worked with the neuro team for years, and his faith in the team came from familiarity and experience. He also knew Dr. Masters and his team, and he had confidence in the efficiency and skill of all of the people he was working with during the surgery. The advance planning by the team included a mental rehearsal of the operation, and involved planning for several contingencies. The OR equipment request specified the "Kassam craniotomy for aneurysm set up" because Dr. Kassam's was a little more elaborate than Dr. Lesiuk's and included all of the equipment used by Dr. Lesiuk. The OR equipment request also specified a Stryker Neuronav Microscope (Pentano), which provided for magnification and light so the neurosurgeons could see well. It also called for electrophysiologic monitoring equipment, which is used in mapping neural structures to identify areas for surgery, and for piloting safe pathways.

According to Dr. Lesiuk, the first phase of the approximately twelve hour operation was the setup of the equipment for cardiac, blood pressure and neurological monitoring. The positioning of the equipment was critical, so that it would not interfere with the surgery. This was followed by the induction of anesthesia, and a re-check of the monitoring. Then came preparation for the surgery, which included drawing the planned incisions and nurses scrubbing, painting, and draping to isolate sterile areas from non-sterile areas of the body. The draping had to take into account the contingency plans for adopting the second option bypass procedure, in the event the aneurysm clipping could not be accomplished.

Next was the opening of Allison's head by Dr. Lesiuk, to the point where her brain was exposed. As much dissection was done as could be done safely before hypothermic arrest. Concurrently Dr.

Allison's Brain • **75**

Masters did closed-chest-bypass surgery, to connect Allison to a heart-lung machine, so her heart could be stopped. Closed-chest-bypass surgery avoided creating a long incision through the front of the chest, splitting the breast bone, and spreading the ribs to expose Allison's heart. The closed-chest-bypass was accomplished by inserting a large tube through a vein in the groin (the femoral vein) and directing it towards the heart. This was used to drain the blood from Allison into the machine where it was cooled. It was then returned to Allison by another tube also in the groin (the femoral artery).

During the cooling phase Allison's core body temperature was lowered to 16.5°C, after which a standstill blood flow state was accomplished by stopping the heart-lung machine. During the surgery Allison's blood was circulated periodically, to prevent sludge from forming. Then came the dissection and clipping. According to Dr. Kassam's OPERATIVE REPORT:

Once the appropriate temperatures were now reached, as determined by the Cardiac Service, we then initiated a state of low flow and standstill periodically. With the cardiac arrest in place now, we then dissected circumferentially around the aneurysm. The appropriate branches were then identified. The branches were quite adherent to the base of the aneurysm and took some time to separate. An aneurysmorrhaphy was then undertaken and the clot within the aneurysm was now resected, further deflating the aneurysm and collapsing it. The aneurysm was quite sizable, and in fact was partially thrombosed, explaining why perhaps it was even larger than what was seen on the imaging. Eventually we were able to circumferentially dissect around the aneurysm, deflate it. A series of clips were now applied parallel to the aneurysm base, protecting the branch arteries. Eventually we were able to put a set of clips under position. Somewhere in the 28, 29 minute range, the aneurysm was clipped now.

At this point reanimation was now initiated and was started. The flow was now returned and the aneurysm held quite well. There was no evidence of clip migration or shift at this point. We then pursued the appropriate hemostasis. As the patient rewarmed now, and the blood pressure rose, we were met with intermittent diffuse bleeding. This was controlled with serial packing and judicious bipolaring. We took great care not to be overly aggressive with the bipolar in order to avoid the risks associated with injury and retraction. With a packing, we were able to stem this bleeding and irrigation. We waited quite some time for the coagulation indices to return, and allow for this to occur. At this point, the brain looked quite healthy, but despite this, we opted not to put the bone flap back, for fear of postoperative edema that was likely to occur as a result of the reperfusion phenomena. Therefore, we allowed for that to occur. An augmentation large duraplasty was now put into position and held with tack ups. The drains were then inserted and the temporalis and skin was reapproximated after the orbital construct and rim were repositioned, held in place with titanium microscrews. Interestingly, the clips were quite sizable and were actually hanging out from the proximal portion of the defect. This was augmented just purely with an augmentation duraplasty. The skin was closed; the external ventricular drain that had been used throughout the procedure was now closed as well. Dr. Lesiuk and I performed the procedure in collaboration with our colleagues from the Cardiac Service.

The aneurysmorrhaphy involved cleaning clotted blood out of the aneurysm. The calcification of part of the aneurysm made this procedure quite difficult, and the aneurysm had to be squeezed hard, with a pliers-like device, in order to deflate it. The object of the clipping was to reconstruct a normal blood vessel by taking out the blown-out area. For this purpose, four titanium clips (2 x 40 mm and 2 x 35 mm) were put in place, using a clip applier.

The "judicious bipolaring" described in the Operative Report was cauterizing the surgical site, using an electric coagulator in order to stem bleeding. Cauterizing is accomplished by running electric current through forceps that are applied to the affected area. Dr. Lesiuk advises that this system represents an advance in cauterizing, and that it is a mainstay of neurosurgery today.

The closing phase could not be commenced until the warming phase was over. This is because the body's blood clotting system doesn't work well at low temperatures, as the necessary chemical reactions don't take place. During the closing phase the decision was made not to replace the piece of Allison's skull ("bone flap"), which had been removed in order to gain access, as her brain had been badly disturbed by the surgery. This left room to accommodate swelling, and it turned out to be a very wise decision. Allison's eye socket also had to be re-positioned during the closing, as it had been pulled down to facilitate access to her brain.

Dr. Lesiuk ranks the difficulty of Allison's surgery as a 9 or 10 on a scale of 1 to 10. This was because of the size of the aneurysm, and the extent to which it incorporated major intercranial blood vessels. Dr. Lesiuk also says that Allison "went through as big an operation as anyone can go through" and that she "came as close to dying as anyone can without actually dying." We were awfully lucky to have the combined talents of Dr. Lesiuk and Dr. Kassam at work in Allison's case, given that Dr. Lesiuk alone had done more than 4,000 operations in his more than twenty year career as a neurosurgeon

Dr. Kassam did the closing, and that was when I had my first contact from the hospital at around 9:00 p.m. I had deliberately made myself ultra-busy all day, by beginning a kitchen, upstairs office and upstairs bathroom wall and ceiling repair and painting job, that would take me several weeks. I had reasoned that sitting around and fretting all day wouldn't be doing anyone any good, and by at least partially distracting myself, the odds of me surviving Allison's brain surgery seemed pretty good. Marya outdid me here by a considerable margin, as a large group of friends took her out for the entire day.

It was Dr. Lesiuk who called me, and then I penned the first of many *Allison's Brain* email updates.

From: Allison Woyiwada
Sent: May 28, 2012 8:57 PM
To: Allison's Brain
Subject: Update re Allison

Hi: I've just spoken to one of the neurosurgeons who says the operation was "challenging" but it went "fairly smoothly" / "reasonably well" and they are "happy with the way things went." The post-op CT scan "looks OK." I think from Allison's perspective this means the day has therefore been a "roaring success" (my words — the neurosurgeons speak guardedly out of habit me thinks). Allison is being closely monitored in the Heart Institute Intensive Care Unit and is likely to be anaesthetized overnight.

Thanks for your positive thoughts / prayers and I will send you another update tomorrow.

All for now,
Bob

I was pretty happy about this, but I can honestly say now that I had no clue about what lay ahead. The first indication that this weren't no walk in the park came later that evening. I picked up Marya and we went together to see Allison in the Intensive Care Unit at the Heart Institute. Allison was being closely monitored by two nurses and she lay pretty much lifelessly in a maze of strange instruments and wires.

Allison's Brain • **79**

4.

Show Me Two Fingers

The day after the surgery, Allison was moved to Intensive Care at the Civic Campus, for there was no longer any need to have the Heart Institute involved. We had to call ahead to get permission to get into Intensive Care to see Allison, and the waiting room was full of anxious and crying people, some of whom were sleeping, when they could, on uncomfortable chairs overnight. The Intensive Care Unit is kind of a spooky place, as it seems like everybody is hooked up to a lot of machines that are constantly beeping and flashing images on their screens. When I saw Allison, the scene put me in mind of what the inside of a spaceship must look like — so the rocket scientist business was back in play again. Allison was being monitored constantly by a hyper-alert nurse, who always seemed to be making notes and adjusting things. Some of the nurses spent a lot of time with Allison, as they worked in twelve hour shifts for three consecutive days. It seemed like a lonely vigil, and when the nurse got a bit of a break he or she sometimes shot the breeze a bit with us. For the most part the nurses gave us encouragement about Allison, but they couldn't just make stuff up to placate us, and so it was a pretty sober environment.

Occasionally I tried to relieve my nervous tension by telling the brain surgeon / rocket scientist joke, and it usually elicited a bit of laughter. But one day a nurse told me that Dr. Lesiuk was also a rocket scientist, having been an astrophysicist before he became a brain surgeon. The astrophysicist part may have been made up, but it does turn out that Dr. Lesiuk was in Graduate Studies in mathematics and physics, before deciding that brain surgery would be a cool thing to do. So he then embarked on about an eight year course of medical studies, before beginning his career as a brain surgeon. At the time, I figured it couldn't hurt Allison's chances that one of her brain surgeons had also been a rocket scientist.

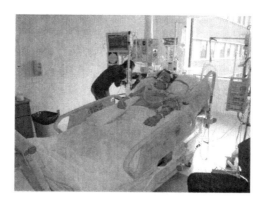

I had gotten a raft of thank-you emails from people who were grateful for my *Allison's Brain* update. This set me on a course of regular updates, which people seemed to want, and which I found were therapeutic to write. My next update, on the following day, was after I had come to appreciate that Allison wouldn't be brought out of her coma until her brain seizure activity had settled down. I will add here that, although for the most part the *Allison's Brain* updates were meant to give people the straight goods, I didn't want to put in words how much of the time I was feeling freaked out. To some extent, you can just go through bad times on autopilot, and that's pretty much how I spent the next few days.

From: Allison Woyiwada
Sent: May 29, 2012 6:15 PM
To: Allison's Brain
Subject: Allison's Recovery

Hi everyone:

It turns out that Allison's recovery isn't going to happen overnight. The neurosurgeon we met today (Dr. Lesiuk) explained that the surgery was a protracted affair (he says he was bent over — doing surgery from 10:00 a.m. until 8:00 p.m. — with a break at 2:00 p.m. for the cardiac specialists to do their work). Four titanium alloy clips were installed: 2 x 40 mm and 2 x 35 mm. The work has caused the brain to become somewhat irritated and Allison has been having some small seizures* because of this irritation. In order to minimize the seizure activity and to give her brain an opportunity to calm down, Allison is being kept in an anaesthetized state. We are told that the first 72 hours are the most crucial; however, the exact time that she will be brought back to full consciousness is unknown, and it could be a few days before this occurs. The good news includes (1) she's been moved to the Civic Hospital from the Heart Institute (where the surgery took place) as there are no problems with her heart; (2) last night, at a point when her anaesthetic was "a little light," she reached for the tubing in her mouth and tried to pull it out — this apparently is a common reaction when coming back to consciousness and a good sign; and (3) the latest anti-convulsant drug they've given to Allison this afternoon seems to be controlling the seizure activity.

Thanks very much for your terrific support, and I'll get back to you when I have anything new to report.

Bob

*"[S]eizures that last a few minutes — which is true of most — generally cause no permanent damage, says Christine O'Dell, R.N., M.S.N., medical advisor, the Epilepsy Institute at Montefiore Medical Center in The Bronx. They're harmful only when they last longer than about an hour, which can exacerbate the brain injury of a previous stroke by damaging the neurons in the brain, or

if the person having the seizure hits the floor or falls onto something hot, like a radiator."

This produced another flurry of email responses, including one from my law school friend Paul McKenzie. It speaks of something that has been a considerable problem for me for a long time.

From: Paul McKenzie
Sent: May 29, 2012 7:29 PM
To: Allison Woyiwada
Subject: Re: Allison's Recovery

Bob

Loss of words for this. Keep me posted. In meantime, I could certainly drop over with coffee and bits of fast food if that helps over next few days. Let me know.

In meantime, treat yourself to some really good quality sleep.

My best wishes to you and family obviously.

I gather some people can get good quality sleep, more-or-less regardless of their situations. But sometime during my adult life the sleep gods deserted me, and once I wake up in the middle of the night, or earlier, I can exaggerate things to worry about on a scale that rivals my mother. However, I have in recent years come across a sleep aid — zaleplon — that doesn't seem to be addictive, and doesn't make me feel like I've been run over. In fact, and I am not kidding about this, I've read that it is sometimes used by astronauts. So with the benefit of a prescription from my doctor, and the assistance of our great Main Street pharmacist Scott Watson and his compounding lab, I was able to get enough sleep. If I had known about this ten years earlier I could have avoided a depression, but that's water under the bridge.

From here on in, I always rose early and called the hospital to get a report from the overnight nurse. On the morning of May 30th, the nurse said there had been a CT follow-up scan late the night

Allison's Brain • **83**

before in which things looked essentially the same; plus the EEG monitoring showed some seizure activity slow down.

Later in the day I sent out the next *Allison's Brain* update.

From: Allison Woyiwada
Sent: May 30, 2012 3:17 PM
To: Allison's Brain
Subject: Three more sleeps

Hi:

Some new stuff to report: if all continues to go well, Saturday is the day that efforts will begin to bring Allison out of her medically-induced coma. The length of time this will take turns on some unknowns — it could be as little as one day or more than several days — that is as precise as things are at this stage.

Nevertheless, it was confidence boosting to visit Allison in ICU this afternoon. The recovery room Allison is in looks like what I'd imagine a couple of combined space ships would look like — there are colour monitors, tubes and pouches of things everywhere. As the nurse we spoke with advised "We are monitoring every square inch of her body." Although Dr. Lesiuk conversed with us in his usual guarded manner, he did say that "there is reason for optimism." He also said that the reason for the go-slow approach is that "we think we are winning," whereas if recovery is accelerated too quickly "we could blow it" (or words to that effect). For those of you with the mind for this sort of thing, we're told that after the brain has been shut down as Allison's has, it would be too overwhelming to have to deal with all of the demands on it at once. So during this go-slow period, during which brain swelling is given time to subside, the brain also resumes some of its automatic functions. We're told that EEG results do not show ongoing seizure activity and that there have been positive signs re motor skills.

My only complaint today is that Dr. Lesiuk offered at one point that he thought tax law would be "boring." In the circumstances though, I chose not to pick a fight with him (although I do have a TaxAssistance.ca cap to present to him when this is all over). As an aside here, we are finding that Dr. Lesiuk and all the staff we have been dealing with (including a dietitian) fit into the "wonderful" category. As my daughter Laurie says, we're very lucky that people choose to do this sort of thing.

À plus tard
Bob

The following morning I sent out what I thought was just a regular update to immediate family.

From: Robert McMechan
Sent: May 31, 2012 5:37 AM
To: Marya Woyiwada; Tyler Woyiwada; Jim Rennie
Subject: Overnight update

Nurse Otto says last night was a very quiet night / nothing untoward happened / Allison is stable.

Allison's brother-in-law Jim, however, managed to find something humorous about it.

From: Jim Rennie
Sent: May 31, 2012 9:22 AM
To: Allison Woyiwada
Subject: RE: Overnight update

Good news! When I read the name "Nurse Otto," I immediately envisioned a woman built like a Germanic soprano who is used to ruling with an iron fist and served as a

Allison's Brain • **85**

Sergeant in the German Army before taking up nursing. Don't tell her I said any of this.

Jim

Then later in the day I sent out another *Allison's Brain* update.

From: Allison Woyiwada
Sent: May 31, 2012 3:26 PM
To: Allison's Brain
Subject: No so fast

Hi:

Today I met three doctors from the Neurology Team (not the neurosurgeons) who were checking in on Allison. They told me that the operation was on a particularly sensitive part of the brain and that the seizures were to be expected. They also said that on Sunday the efforts will begin to bring Allison out from under sedation; however, this could be a long, slow process depending upon how she reacts. If there is an increase in her blood pressure they will back off. They were positive about how well she is doing and when I told them that from a lay perspective what is happening is pretty incredible they said that it was from their perspectives too. It seems appropriate in a way that Allison is a bit of a pioneer.

Nurse Melissa says that Allison's lungs are "pristine" / "amazing" and that she rarely sees lungs in such good condition. She also told me that Allison has "kidneys like a fourteen-year-old." Allison has a "cough reflex" (this is good) and she also opened her mouth today for an anti-bacterial swabbing. Nurse Melissa added that the fact Allison is in such good shape will be a big factor in her recovery.

On a lesser note, yesterday's comment about tax law being "boring" provoked quite an outcry. Three of the choice comments were that: (1) the point about it being "a good thing that some people have chosen to do this" doesn't apply to tax lawyers; (2) tax lawyers don't have to resort to artificial aids to put people to sleep; and (3) my favourite — "Tax law isn't boring. You just make it seem like it is."[7] Whereas my sister Bette-Lou and her daughter Karla say that they can't imagine tax law being boring.

Also, I neglected to mention that while the tax law discussion was taking place yesterday, Marya was humming her Mother a lullaby. Speaking of music, if anyone has the ability to put together some background brain music to be played to Allison, I'll see what I can do about arranging to play it.

Finally, I don't want to bombard you with e-mail updates. If anyone would rather not be receiving such regular updates please let me know and I'll try and decipher/amend Allison's group e-mail list.

Thanks for your support and words of encouragement.

Catch you later
Bob

Marya and I felt pretty helpless in the Intensive Care environment, as Allison was completely dormant, and we doubted that she knew we were there with her, although we couldn't be entirely sure. We got a classical music track to play softly around the clock, and Marya began humming lullabies to her mother. These were especially poignant moments, as Allison had often told the story about how when she was singing to Marya after she was born, a nurse had predicted that Marya would grow up to be a singer.

---

7   John is a funny fellow from Kentucky, who I have had the misfortune of knowing for over 30 years. I have had to organize Derby Parties at his house for him and tried to suppress the fact that he was on the grassy knoll in Dallas. It seems possible that he was responsible for Allison's aneurysm, although this is somewhat speculative.

Allison has a lot of musical friends, and the reference to music for her in Intensive Care prompted a few of them into action. This sort of thing puts me in mind of a comment attributed to Bill Gates, in which he is reported to have said that email is one of the greatest innovations of the 20th century. If I'd had to resort to the telephone for communications, a good deal of what followed wouldn't have happened.

From: Gloria Young
Sent: June 1, 2012 8:43 AM
To: Robert McMechan
Subject: Re: Music for Allison

Hi Bob, several years ago I took a course at Carleton on the healing qualities of music. At that time the research was showing two things. One was that Mozart's compositions seemed the best for patients in pain or trying to heal. The other was that the most effective music to use for recovery and healing was music being played by a harp or a flute/ harp combo.

The professor had CDs of this kind of music… I have looked for my notes but cannot find them, so don't have a list to give you. If you want me to try to find some, I would be glad to do that.

Gloria

Gloria and others then proceeded to donate CDs with various types of music, which we played pretty well non-stop for Allison for the next few months. A couple of weeks later, when Allison had finally been transferred to the Neuroscience Acute Care Unit (NACU), she kept time to music with her left hand, and this became something that she often did, even when she otherwise appeared to be right out of it.

The next *Allison's Brain* update was only four days after the surgery, but it seemed like an eternity.

From: Allison Woyiwada
Sent: June 1, 2012 5:52 PM
To: Allison's Brain
Subject: The Friday Report

Hi

Here's Marya's succinct summary of what Dr. Lesiuk told us about Allison today: They tried lightening up on her sedation a little bit and saw some abnormal brain activity, which can cause damage. Apparently it's not unexpected at this point, but, and I quote, "if we were having this conversation a week from now I'd have good reason for concern." So they've gone a little more aggressive on the sedatives and will re-assess in a couple days.

Marya hummed her Mother a lullaby, and as we were leaving Allison's nurse was quite effusive about how beautiful Marya's singing voice is — ICU doesn't usually have such accomplished performances.

There's unlikely to be much happening over the weekend, so I'll give you all a break.

Thanks again for your terrific support.

Bob

This would be a good place to say that having a wonderful support group is the way to go if you ever find yourself in a situation like this. One of the lessons I learned from this experience is that when you don't know what to do for someone in a difficult situation, you can always take them food. I'm not much of a cook, but with friends like Lorraine, Carole and others, I was well cared for on the nourishment front.

From: Carole Chouinard
Sent: June 2, 2012 5:17 PM

Allison's Brain • **89**

To: Robert McMechan
Subject: Re: Three more sleeps

Have not forgotten about dinner. Chicken is in the oven.
Will bring it over as soon as it is cooked.

After the weekend I resumed *Allison's Brain* updates.

From: Allison Woyiwada
Sent: June 4, 2012 7:24 PM
To: Allison's Brain
Subject: Some new developments

Hi

Allison was kept sedated over the weekend. A CT scan
showed that there is still some brain swelling; however,
today an EEG showed no seizure activity. The result is
that at 5:30 p.m. Allison was taken off the sedative Versed
(midazolam). Because she's been on it for a week, it may be
a few days before its effects are completely gone. But within
a relatively short period, some changes started to occur.
Allison was yawning a bit (even after sleeping for a week)
and Marya saw her swallowing. These are early signs to
be expected when being weaned off the Versed. Dr. Lesiuk
says if there are no setbacks that require more sedation that
tomorrow they will start testing Allison for her neurologi-
cal responses.

Please keep those positive thoughts going Allison's way.

Bob

P.S. Thanks to Carol, Marya and Rick there is now a
16 hour classical music selection playing next to Allison's
bedside. Also to be noted that Dr. Lesiuk came straight
from the OR to meet with us.

Lots of people invited me out for dinner, and it was always great
to have someone's company other than my own. The yeoman duty

on this front was performed by our neighbours Don and Pauline. I recall that one evening, when someone else was also present at their house for dinner and remarked on what an excellent dinner and good time he was having, I explained to Matt that "You get used to it."

From: Pauline Lynch-Stewart
Sent: June 04, 2012 8:55 PM
To: Allison Woyiwada
Subject: RE: Some new developments

Allison is never far from our thoughts these days, Bob. We'll be beaming over lots of happy, healthy vibes in a north-westerly direction tomorrow!

Let us know if you'd like to come for dinner on Thursday night. We won't keep you waiting as long this time. :) You could come at 6:30 for a 7:00 dinner (we promise!)

And big hugs for you too!

Pauline

The next three days brought daily *Allison's Brain* updates.

From: Allison Woyiwada
Sent: June 5, 2012 7:26 PM
To: Allison's Brain
Subject: Still more tests

Hi

Allison had an MRI late this afternoon. If the results are good the propofol sedative will be lightened up on Wednesday and it's possible that Allison will be awakened. The MRI was too late in the day for Dr. Lesiuk to have studied the results; however, Allison's nurse told us that he thought that if there was a problem with the results, the neuro team would have been visiting Allison and switching some of her medicines. In her present state, she is

Allison's Brain • 91

coughing a fair amount — this is expected — and she has been moving her toes. Allison's nurse also noted that she "looks symmetrical" although he cautioned us that we won't know her condition until she's been awakened. And even then there can be ongoing change.

We also noted that the visible swelling on Allison's face / left eye has lessened substantially. If there is a problem with the MRI results, there will be another EEG tomorrow. One other point is that my friend John has explained that the reason Allison was yawning yesterday was because I was in the room and I am a tax lawyer. In any event, it seems we are getting closer to having Allison awake.

Cheers
Bob

From: Allison Woyiwada
Sent: June 6, 2012 10:52 PM
To: Robert McMechan
Subject: June 6th Update

Hi

Allison had good MRI results, and so the remaining sedation is being very gradually reduced — with an overnight pause — it therefore looks like Thursday will be the day that all sedation will be eliminated. This is, of course, subject to the usual caveat that if there are any untoward signs it will be continued.

We're also told that, because of the large amount of sedation Allison has had over the last 10 days, it isn't possible to know when she will resume consciousness; however, it looked to us this evening as if she was valiantly trying to open one eye.

One other point is that, when I repeated Allison's rocket scientist joke to a couple of the nurses today, they told me that Dr. Lesiuk is also a rocket scientist. Apparently he was an astrophysicist before he became a brain surgeon. John has suggested that he will likely try to become a tax lawyer next.

All for now,
Bob

P.S. Tomorrow is an all day visit to the hospital so if there's an update it will likely be a late one.

From: Allison Woyiwada
Sent: June 7, 2012 9:43 PM
To: Allison's Brain
Subject: Very Slow Going

Hi

Today the remaining sedative (propofol) was reduced to a very low level — at which it will remain overnight. Because the breathing apparatus is so intrusive and causes a fair amount of coughing etc. the plan when we left today was that Allison would likely have a tracheotomy tomorrow. We are assured that this will be a simple matter and that it will substantially lessen Allison's discomfort.

In terms of responsiveness, for the first time today, Allison's right eye (the left one is still swollen) would occasionally engage with us and she squeezed my hand with her left hand a couple of times. The nurse also got Allison to squeeze with her left hand and to release her hand on request.

We are advised, however, that since the surgery was "as big as it gets" (Dr. Lesiuk describes the aneurysm as "the size of plum") recovery will be long. The matter of how long is an

Allison's Brain • **93**

*open question although Allison's nurse told us today that it
often takes brain surgery patients a year to recover.*

*All for now,
Bob*

*P.S. Allison's nurse says that this evening she has also
opened her left eye to a degree, wiggled her toes on her left
foot on request, indicated with a shake of her head that she
isn't in pain and also nodded assurance to the question "Are
you sure?" Her breathing is to some extent unassisted, and
so the question of whether a tracheotomy will be necessary
is to be addressed again on Friday morning.*

The following day Pauline wrote a letter to Allison that she asked
me to read to her.

From: Pauline Lynch-Stewart
Sent: June 8, 2012 8:59 AM
To: Robert McMechan
Subject: Notes on my garden for Allison

*Bob — thought I'd write a short note for you to read to
Allison when you think she's up to it. Pxo*

Hello Allison!

*I was just out in my garden this morning and missing your
happy company and your delight in the spring progress, so
I thought I would write and let you know how things are
coming along.*

*The carpet of thyme along the walkway has never looked
better. It is blooming in several shades — from a pale lav-
ender to a rich magenta purple — interspersed with a few
patches of white. Those gorgeous colours are also blooming
in the spikey flowers of the salvia, with their delicious sage*

fragrance. In fact, the garden is all dressed in purples, pinks and white right now except for those scrappy red columbine that are invading every nook and cranny they can. But best of all, in honour of the early signs of your awakening, the irises that you have enjoyed for years have popped into full bloom in the last 24 hours. And they are spectacular. I will send you some soon.

Our family is thinking and talking about you every day, and sending you the best healing vibes we can, Allison. Wake gently and well from your long sleep, my friend. I'll write again soon,

Love from Pauline

I tried reading Pauline's letter to Allison and got choked up. Marya told me this was because I'm "a suck." The good news on June 8th was that, when Dr. Lesiuk loudly asked Allison to show him two fingers, you could tell she was making a valiant effort. Dr. Lesiuk said this implied that a high degree of brain circuitry was working. After Dr. Lesiuk left the room, Allison managed to hold out two fingers.

The Friday *Allison's Brain* update was the best post-surgery update yet.

From: Allison Woyiwada
Sent: June 8, 2012 10:22 PM
To: Allison's Brain
Subject: Friday Night Update

Hi

The big news today was that Allison managed to hold up two fingers on request — Dr. Lesiuk says that there has to be a lot of brain circuitry operating in order to do that. Allison was also quite interactive with us at times through her facial movements. She also tried to respond to the doctors by answering them orally but she was thwarted by

Allison's Brain • 95

the breathing apparatus that she's had for the past twelve days.

Dr. Lesiuk told us that we might not see Allison without the effects of sedation until next week. He also mentioned that his concerns are regarding speech and right side motor control but that it is too early to make any informed judgments. In his words Allison's recovery "is a process not an event."

Late today the breathing apparatus was removed and the doctors performed a tracheotomy. They say that this approach will be much easier for Allison to deal with than having the breathing apparatus. Allison was sedated with propofol again for the tracheotomy so she was quite dozy late this evening.

I'll sign off for the weekend and thanks again for your support,

Bob

This two fingers episode with Dr. Lesiuk was a new beginning for Allison, and we were now anxiously waiting to see how she had come through the surgery.

5.

The Last Fifty Cases Don't Matter

It looked like Allison might be transferred out of Intensive Care at the beginning of week three, but a decision was made to keep her there as she had a slight temperature and was drifting in and out of wakefulness a lot. My *Allison's Brain* update went out on June 12th, which was also my 60th birthday.

From: Allison Woyiwada
Sent: June 12, 2012 11:48 AM
To: Allison's Brain
Subject: Week Three Update

Hi

Allison is continuing in the Intensive Care Unit although she is approaching the time when she will be transferred to a neuro observation unit with a 2 patient to 1 nurse ratio as her condition is quite stable. She has been breathing on her own for a few days and although she has a slight fever at times she has not gotten any infections — this is being monitored closely and she will be treated with antibiotics if it occurs. She was the most alert this a.m. that I've seen her to date and moving her head side to side. Her cognitive gains are mainly evident from facial gestures and this a.m. she identified Dr. Lesiuk's watch for him. She is now moving her left arm and hand a good deal when

97

she is awake — we think this is because she knows it's a good thing to do. Although her right side is considerably less active than her left side, she has occasionally managed to squeeze with both her left and right hands. There is also some left leg movement on request; plus, right leg movement when encouraged with stimulation. The three doctor neuro team visiting her yesterday say that patience and time will be the two main requirements on a going-forward basis. They mentioned that her progress to date is better than in the case of the only other brain surgery patient in Ottawa who has had such major surgery. There remains a possibility that she will have to have a shunt installed for drainage of cranial fluids to her abdomen.

For those of you who are doctors / medically savvy — please forgive my lay person's descriptions.

I won't be sending daily (as opposed to weekly) updates any longer as the critical period has passed and daily changes are likely to be very gradual — I am assured with setbacks occurring along the way.

Thanks for all of your support.

Ciao,
Bob

P.S. I've read some of your e-mail letters and cards to Allison and that has seemed to capture her attention.

Regarding the P.S., I received an avalanche of cards and letters to Allison over the next few weeks. I read these to Allison every day, and she seemed to pay attention, although I can't say she understood. Once again lots of people responded to the update.

From: Sandra Graham
Sent: June 12, 2012 4:36 PM
To: Allison Woyiwada
Subject: RE: Week Three Update

*I was thinking that if you have any recordings of Allison
singing or a recording of her own performances of Gilbert
and Sullivan in which she is conducting, this might be
a good thing to play because her mind will know that
she is conducting and singing and those parts of her body
and mind which were involved with these past musical
experiences will most likely react instinctively (on one level
or another) to her own music making.*

*kind regards,
Sandra*

We thought this was an excellent suggestion and managed to put together some of Allison's recordings from her performance days, which we added to the collection of music that we were playing for her.

That evening Don and Pauline hosted a 60th birthday party for me. That sort of thing went a long way towards keeping me on an even keel. Lots of laughs and silly gifts, including a pair of Ph.D. socks from Janice and Mike. I had come across a stash of birthday presents from Allison while moving the furniture in her office, which shook me up when I saw it, and I promptly put it away without looking at anything.

Although at one time Allison and I had considered it possible that she would be out of the hospital and able to attend my convocation in Toronto, we had agreed that if she couldn't be there I would go ahead with it as my mother, sisters and son were coming from Western Canada. Since it would be unrealistic for Marya to do full-time hospital attendance while I was in Toronto for a couple of days, I called upon a group of close friends who agreed to divide up the hospital visits while I was away. When I got to the Ottawa Airport, I sent them an email.

From: Robert McMechan
Sent: June 13, 2012 8:59 AM
To: Carol Anderson; Sharon Chartier; Joan Duguid;
Pauline Lynch-Stewart

Cc: Marya Woyiwada
Subject: Thanks!

As I travelled in a cab to the airport I reflected on what a brilliant group has taken up the mantle of helping Marya. Don't hesitate (and please do) send me your comments, observations etc when you are able to do that. As Allison was constantly saying before her surgery, any news is better than no news at all.

You are a terrific "bunch"!

(Almost) "Dr. Bob"

P.S. "Dr. Bob" is a name Allison coined for me a while ago and it got a smile from her on Tuesday.

We had a pretty good time for the next couple of days at my convocation, at which I got to sit for several hours, in a hot red robe, with a funny hat. My son gave me a t-shirt that reads "Not that kind of doctor." The best story I can tell you is that, as we were driving away from York University, my mother asked me from the back seat "So what's next, Bob?" When I told her that was the end of the line, she said, "Can't you be a Chancellor or something?" As it happens, I am pretty happy being a writer in the Caribbean.

Marya tells me that she and her mother sort of watched the convocation on her laptop in the hospital as it was being broadcast live. All I can say is that must have been a pretty exciting time for them.

During the time I was away, there were a lot of reports from Marya's backup group about positive changes in Allison's condition, so maybe all it took was for me to get out of town. She was moved out of Intensive Care into NACU. Here are some of the email reports I received.

> **From:** Pauline Lynch-Stewart
> **Sent:** June 13, 2012 6:59 PM
> **To:** Robert McMechan
> **Subject:** Re: Thanks!
>
> *Well, I was so impressed today Bob by how bright and focused and attentive Allison was.*
>
> *Not initially, for the first hour she was very dozy, and I just let her sleep. But then the nurse cleared the trach (I left for that!) and positioned the bed like a chair so she was sitting up, with her feet down. When I came back in the room she greeted me with a look of recognition and a small smile. We proceeded to have a long (90 minute) conversation including reading bits from* Maclean's *and the* Citizen, *during which she responded pretty quickly*

Allison's Brain • 101

and appropriately to what I said — although as I said to Marya, sometimes she looked at me like "whaddya think?" or shrugged like "who cares and why the heck are you telling me this anyway?" Good to see her no nonsense personality shining through. To me, she also seemed frustrated about her situation, particularly not being able to talk, but as the nurse said, it's all on the schedule.

Dr Kassam stopped by and was fairly beaming about her progress and reassuring that the right side would come along. He asked me if I'd had a conversation with her, in much the same way a new mum would ask if you'd seen her child walk. As if to say "pretty good eh?"

Must go, on our way to the gats [Gatineau Hills] for a picnic. Hope all is well with the family reunion for the big day!

Talk soon,
Pxo

From: Joan Duguid
Sent: June 13, 2012 8:14 PM
To: Robert McMechan
Subject: Allison

Hi Bob

In visiting Allison in neuro obs. Nice young man is her nurse tonight. She is a little groggy, spacy is a better word. You described that look to me. I don't know how different this setting is for her from ICU but it may be slightly noisier.

Hope your time with your Mum et al is going well and that you can relax and enjoy this occasion. We will keep you updated. All seems well.

Joan

From: Sharon Chartier
Sent: June 15, 2012 12:30 PM
To: Marya Woyiwada; Robert McMechan
Cc: Pauline Lynch-Stewart
Subject: Today with Allison

Hi Marya and Bob,

Pauline was here earlier, and I am with Allison now. Her color is really good today, her vital signs (especially heart rate) are even better than yesterday.

While Pauline was here, they got her up in a chair!!! Lots of other activity earlier, so Allison is resting for a few minutes now.

I told her about Alexander's school gr 8 grad which we all attend (even though he is in gr 7). Went for 2 hours and Allison gave me a great big grimace at the thought.

She seems much more alert than yesterday. I imagine progress will not be even. Some days show greater improvement, others less.

So, congrats again Dr Bob! All is good here. Marya is really excellent with her mom and we are taking our lead from her.

Sharon

Helen Tabara, the Occupational Therapist assigned to Allison, did an initial assessment on June 15th. The OCCUPATIONAL THERAPY ASSESSMENT has the following description of her functional mobility.

Pt was able to move her left hand. Slight edema noted to the left hand, and arm elevated on pillow to assist with decreasing edema. No active movement noted to right arm during assessment. Pt's nurse Jen, indicated pt was able

Allison's Brain • **103**

*to grip slightly with right hand earlier in am. Jen also
reported family indicated pt was able to shrug shoulders
2 days earlier. Able to obtain full PROM of right U/E,
no hand splint required at this time. Pt was able to move
left toe slightly, but no other active movement noted. Tone
present in right leg, at pt's feet positioned in plantar flexion
and inversion. A foot drop splint was provided, to position feet in dorsiflexion (when in bed), for passive stretch.
Recommend Q2 hrs, alternating between right foot and
left foot. Pt's nurse informed re foot drop splint schedule.*

No one told us that Allison would eventually be able to walk.
Using a ceiling lift, Allison would be transported to a Broda geri-
chair, and put in a supported seated position, tilted towards the rear.
On one memorable occasion, after Allison had been in the chair
for a while, a nurse came along and asked "Allison, would you like
to be in your bed or the chair?" There was no response, so the nurse
repeated "Allison, would you like to be in your bed or the chair?"
After a considerable delay, Allison said "It's six of one, half a dozen
of the other."

The week four update shows Allison was beginning to rally,
although it was slow-going.

From: Allison Woyiwada
Sent: June 18, 2012 5:02 PM
To: Allison's Brain
Subject: Week 4 update

Hi

*Allison has been transferred from the Civic Hospital
Intensive Care Unit to the Neuroscience Acute Care Unit
(NACU) as her condition has been stable for some time
now. Today I spoke with a doctor in NACU (who works
with the neurosurgeons) who told me that it is still "early
days" in terms of analyzing Allison's progression given how
major the surgery was that she's been through. Yesterday*

*she was grooving to some tunes from "The Big Chill"
and Queen with her left hand — including snapping her
fingers and mouthing lyrics. Her right side movement is
very limited at present although she can squeeze a bit with
her right hand, and I'm told she has also lifted her right leg
slightly. Her facial swelling has largely subsided, and when
she smiles it is a full smile. She sometimes tries to mouth
words to us, but we mostly can't make them out except for
easy words like "bye bye."*

*The speech therapist who visited today says that the doctors
are holding off for the time-being on down-sizing the trach
because of the amount of secretions Allison still has (she
coughs them up — we're told this is very good); however,
after the trach is down-sized she expects that Allison will
be able to begin speaking. As with all of the other care she
is receiving, there is a "go-slow" approach with the speech
therapy so that Allison can gradually adjust. Today she
swallowed some coloured ice chips and also some pudding
on request; however, she doesn't have the reflex yet to
protect her airway. Even sticking out her tongue is behaviour to be gradually re-learned.*

*An occupational therapist and a physiotherapist also visited
at different times today. The physiotherapist is working
gradually on having Allison be able to sit up on her own
and says she was stronger today than on Friday. I noticed
that when Allison was being helped to sit up she was
clearly pleased with not lying down.*

*Although we haven't been able to hear Allison speak, it
seems plain that she understands us a good deal of the time.
At other times she lapses into a non-attentive state but
this, we're told, is consistent with post-surgery confusion
and fatigue. This will take an unknown but presumably a
lengthy period of time to overcome.*

Allison's Brain • **105**

*For those of you who have sent cards to Allison, I've read
them to her and she clearly appreciates them!*

All for now,
Bob

The clearing of Allison's trach was an ongoing challenge because
of the level of her secretions. Trach clearing isn't for the faint-
hearted, and we almost always left the job to the nurses. There were
stories about how an uncorked trach can produce projectiles which
hurtle across the room. Allison having to re-learn the swallow reflex
was new territory for me. One of the nurses told us that after your
brain has been shut down it's like being a newborn, and you have
to re-learn everything. I didn't take that as great news, but it was
encouraging to have Allison back amongst us again, so it wasn't the
end of the world. Seeing Allison being assisted to sit in an upright
position was also a bit of an education. I'd never been around anyone
who was attempting to regain enough strength to sit up, and I didn't
know what was a reasonable expectation. We'd been told early on in
Intensive Care that the three big concerns with extended bed rest
are blood clots, pneumonia and muscle loss. It was pretty clear that
Allison had already lost a lot of muscle, although the protein she
was getting through the NG tube (nasogastric intubation) in her
nose — which she pulled at whenever she could — was meant to
combat loss of muscle.

The importance of re-orienting Allison was raised with me by
the occupational therapist. I explained this to the ladies who had
been assisting Marya with hospital visits.

From: Robert McMechan
Sent: June 18, 2012 7:26 PM
To: Carol Anderson; Joan Duguid; Sharon Chartier;
Pauline Lynch-Stewart
Cc: Marya Woyiwada
Subject: Hospital visits

You are all more than welcome to visit with Allison anytime. One of the therapists was telling me today that at this stage "re-orienting" Allison is big on the agenda. Seeing you certainly helps with this. Anything that helps to "ground" her so that she regains a good understanding of what she knows is apparently good. When she starts to speak (the speech therapist actually said that she thinks there will be "rapid progress" at some stage) she'll let us know what she thinks. If there any times you'd like to visit let us know — you've already done a lot!

Bob

At this stage my daughter Laurie in Calgary, who was having a very tough time of her own with a difficult pregnancy, came up with a reason for Allison's non-attentive states.

From: Laurie Souchotte
Sent: June 18, 2012 7:54 PM
To: Allison Woyiwada
Subject: Re: Week 4 update

Hard to believe it's week 4 already! All the news sounds positive. I remember the ICU being a pretty intense place… good care obviously, but lots more distraught families etc. NACU will hopefully be a comfortable place.

Do Allison's non-attentive states happen to coincide with tax discussions by chance? :)

Another insightful email came from JoAnne Sulzenko, who Allison had collaborated with for a few years to produce *Welcome Winter*, featuring a reading of Dylan Thomas' *A Winter's Tale* by Rob Clipperton.

From: JoAnne Sulzenko
Sent: June 18, 2012 8:09 PM
To: Allison Woyiwada
Subject: Re: Week 4 update

Thank you, Bob. Some good news about things Allison is beginning to do.

I recommend Abba for Allison. Mama Mia. I have the CD if you would like when I'm back after the 25th.

The program for Allison sounds like a good route, but I am sure it is hard for you and for Allison to be patient.

Andrei says he read an amazing book about how the brain rewires itself after trauma of some kind. Here is the reference in case you haven't read it or heard of it:

The Brain That Changes Itself: Stories of Personal Triumph from the Frontiers of Brain Science *by Norman Doidge (James H. Silberman Books)*

I see that you welcome cards from folks for Allison. Perhaps what I will do is buy some postcards in Picton and put a couple of lines from my line-a-day project that is on my website on one and then the next, etc... I'll omit the ones that are too dark, but it may be fun to chart the progress of the verses. If you think that's likely not to prove interesting to you or Allison, then please be honest, and I'll do something else.

We think of you every day and hope for progress every day, even if it is slow. With affection, JoAnne and Andrei

We had read the Doidge book about the phenomenon of neuroplasticity before Allison's surgery. I kept it by my bedside and looked back at it from time to time for encouragement. For those of you who are not familiar with the concept, there is a body of evidence supporting the view that other areas of the brain can take over the functions of an injured part of the brain, given enough prompting and time. This isn't possible with all brain injuries, but we held out great hope for Allison's brain. One of the favourite instances that Allison gives of this happening involves her niece Kelsey in Alberta.

Kelsey was a victim of seizures, which she experienced several times a day. In her early twenties, a doctor froze the part of her brain causing the seizures and found that all of its functions had already been transferred to the other side of her brain. So the problem part was removed and Kelsey stopped having seizures.

The brain is a funny thing, and although Allison was now alert at times, she suffered from lack of right side awareness. The therapists told us that when visiting we should sit on Allison's right side, as this would help her understand that she had a right side, which in turn would cause her to move it. This didn't sound far-fetched, as during our reading before Allison's surgery we had come across the notion of learned non-use. Experiments have shown that when some stroke victims have lost the use of a limb, it can be coaxed into moving again by restraining the good limb. But for those who assume that the useless limb is permanently lost, the brain will become accustomed to not trying to move it. This is an undoubtedly simplistic description, that may cause experts to shudder, but it's my understanding.

Around this time, we began responding to requests from friends who wanted to visit with Allison. Many friends were keen to visit, but uncertain about what to do. My general advice was that people should tell Allison what they had been doing, play music to her, read to her, show her pictures and the like. We didn't like to leave Allison alone during the day, and Marya and I welcomed the stimulation that fresh faces could provide, as well a bit of a break. This was a tricky business though because sometimes when people showed up to visit, Allison would be sleeping or just ignore them.[8]

Here's a response I sent to Jill Berry, one of Allison's school teacher friends.

> **From:** Robert McMechan
> **Sent:** June 20, 2012 5:27 AM

---

8   Mike Hayes has also reminded me of "the look." Allison would sometimes open her eyes, give her visitors an "are you still here" look, and close them again.

Allison's Brain   ·   **109**

To: Jill Berry
Subject: Sunday a.m. visit

Hi Jill,

Sense of humour is good — her personality doesn't seem to have changed. The memory stick of photos from your retirement event including songs by and for Liz sounds great. So far we've found that her memory of friends is unimpaired; however, some past events don't seem to resonate. We won't really know what the situation is until after she can speak / has been "assessed." In any event, subject to her having had more surgery this week before you visit (to install the shunt), I think you will find her fairly easy to entertain. As I mentioned, she does sometimes still lapse into periods of inattentiveness — Dr. Lesiuk says these will diminish over time. As to how long you stay that's up to you. If you leave before I arrive and tell her that I'm coming for the afternoon she'll understand.

Thanks again,
Bob

P.S. There is a CD player in the room. Short stories are also good — we have some books in Allison's room, but if you have any different ones that's excellent. I don't think her co-ordination is up to sign language yet although she is getting fairly proficient with her left hand.

On June 20th I sent an update to our immediate families.

From: Robert McMechan
Sent: June 20, 2012 11:44 AM
To: Tyler Woyiwada; Jim Rennie; Laurie Souchotte; Phil McMechan; Bette-Lou Paragg; Joan Veselovsky
Subject: Allison Today

Her trach was finally downsized, and we are hearing her first words today. On Thursday a.m. the speech therapist will be checking her vocal cords and if she is protecting her airway yet when she swallows. Language assessment will take place on Monday. I've understood a few words so far like "interesting" (not in relation to tax) and "wheelchair" (which she sits up in for a couple of hours each day). Pretty good left side movement. Right side is much behind but we hope that it will improve a lot with rehab.

Bob/Dad

P.S. It's been a big day and she's sleeping quite a lot for the time-being.

This prompted more comedic responses.

From: Laurie Souchotte
Sent: June 20, 2012 1:51 PM
To: Robert McMechan
Subject: Re: Allison Today

Did you ever teach her Pneumonoultramicroscopicsilicovolcanoconiosis? :)

If she is protecting her airway they will be able to take the trach out all together?

From: Jim Rennie
Sent: June 20, 2012 1:57 PM
To: Allison Woyiwada
Subject: RE: Allison Today

Linda hopes that Allison's vocal cords are OK because she doesn't want to take over the role of "the sister that sings."

Jim

Coherent sentences from Allison were few and far between, but Marya recalls that, when Allison's trach was removed, she said, "I used to be able to do that," when she saw someone stand up in her room.

Allison's Brain • **111**

The next family update came the following day.

From: Robert McMechan
Sent: June 21, 2012 2:58 PM
To: Tyler Woyiwada; Jim Rennie; Laurie Souchotte;
Phil McMechan; Bette-Lou Paragg; Joan Veselovsky
Subject: Allison today

The speech therapist assembled a team this a.m. to check Allison's vocal cords and swallowing reflex with a camera. It was uncomfortable (or worse) to have the camera sent down through a nostril although beforehand Allison was keenly watching the screen for images and seemed to know she was going to get a look at her vocal cords. Unfortunately her epiglotus (sp?) and aritenoid (sp?) are quite swollen, obscuring the view, and the test had to be abandoned. Another test is set for Friday a.m. this time using barium (sp?) and X-rays. The best story from today is that one of the women who came to help put Allison back into bed is also a (Russian I think) violin player. She recognized Allison as her orchestra conductor from Centrepointe Theatre and described her to us as "amazing."

Bob/Dad

It has been a standing joke between Allison and I that we couldn't go anywhere without someone recognizing her. This even happened in London and Paris, so the Russian violin player wasn't a total surprise. My favourite story about this relates to a visit I once made to Westcoast Video near Hopewell School. It was the end of a school day, and one of the mothers there gave me an "I think I know you" look. I explained that I was Allison Woyiwada's husband, and I was then told that I was "really famous by association." I have since tried to capitalize on this, but many Allison supporters still don't know me.

On June 22nd Allison pulled out the intracranial pressure (ICP) measuring device that was used to monitor the level of drainage of cranial fluid. Allison had begun saying a few words by then, and she told the nurse that "shit happens." However, she didn't remember her name was Allison. I recall asking Dr. Lesiuk whether, if the ICP readings got low enough on their own without external drainage, Allison would need to have a shunt installed. His response was that it was too risky to take the chance to see where the cranial pressure levelled off, and the installation of a shunt was the only prudent alternative.

Sharon Chartier provided an update later that day.

> **From:** Sharon Chartier
> **Sent:** June 22, 2012 5:16 PM
> **To:** Robert McMechan; Pauline Lynch Stewart; Joan Duguid; Marya Woyiwada; Carol Anderson
> **Subject:** I met the Man!!
>
> *Hi all,*
>
> *Just left Allison. Dr. Lesiuk came in to see Allison and said that they are expecting to take her to surgery to install the shunt within the hour. He said that, on the spectrum of things they do in the brain, her surgery on May 29th was an engine re-build, and what they are going to do later today is an oil change.*
>
> *She flexed all the toes of her right foot up once which was great to see. The Nurse had asked her to move her foot a few times and Allison hadn't responded but did it a few minutes later for me. Okay, I don't shine a flashlight in her eyes every so often so maybe she felt like co-operating with me!*
>
> *Hugs to all,*
> *Sharon*

Flashlight checks had been a phenomenon from the moment Allison entered Intensive Care. Every so often a nurse would open Allison's eyelids, and shine a flashlight in her eyes. This was an

Allison's Brain • 113

ongoing neurological assessment, which could help detect increased intracranial pressure and seizure activity.

Because Allison was now sitting up in her wheelchair and had a plastic tray in front of her, it looked to me like she could begin doing things with her hands. I borrowed a bunch of kid's activity things from Pauline and took them to the hospital. It soon became apparent that any activity Allison undertook would need to be pretty basic, so I gave her a zebra puzzle in four pieces. Allison only got two of the four pieces in the right place, and she couldn't figure out how the zebra's hind end fit. Within a short time, she gave up and looked quite forlorn. It's hard to describe how crummy I felt. One thing that really impressed me, however, was that nurse Michael, who had looked after Allison in ICU, came for a visit.

From: Robert McMechan
Sent: June 23, 2012 12:13 PM
To: Pauline Lynch-Stewart
Subject: Activities for Allison

Even the simplest is too daunting for her now. She tried her hand at putting the 4 pieces of zebra together but didn't get it right and stopped doing anything at all. She just likes listening to music / stories.

Bob

From time to time, Allison's school teacher friend Donna Walsh made what I will call "stealth visits" to Allison; we coordinated everyone else's visits, but Donna always dropped by unannounced from Christie Lake. Donna noted in a diary entry on June 23rd that Allison was looking quite alert in her chair, moving her hands, saying some words, and smiling.

Around this time Pauline had done a bunch of research to find an Internet-based platform to use for booking hospital visits and keeping track of things generally. She came up with Lotsa Helping Hands, which turned out to be an invaluable resource in the months ahead. Once someone registered as a member on the site, they could go to a calendar which showed them the times available for visits and then book them. I could also send requests to the group when something unusual came up. About 25 of Allison's friends signed up to use the site, and I kept them updated with developments and photos.

From: system-messages@mail.lotsahelpinghands.com On Behalf Of Pauline Lynch
Sent: June 23, 2012 2:36 PM
To: Robert McMechan
Subject: Lotsa Helping Hands site

I like this site a whole lot more! No worries, we can delete these sites once we figure out which is best — it's just that one has to create the site to actually see how it works. This one is much easier to use, offers a lot more web-based practical advice about using the site, and gives us the opportunity to easily create numerous repeating "shifts" per day. Makes it a lot more convenient to offer various time slots in a day. Only thing I'm concerned about is this. I don't get it... no cost for these services and no advertising on the website. So how do they sustain the operation I'm wondering? I've read through "about us" and "terms and conditions" but would like you to review as well because you need to be completely comfortable about the use of this too. However, also note the number of articles that have been written about it in major newspapers across the U.S.

You have been added as a Member of our Community web site, Team McMechan/Woyiwada, powered by Lotsa Helping Hands.

To sign in and join the Community go to the address below to set your password.

Allison's Brain • 115

https://www.lotsahelpinghands.com/c/659213/login/reset/
ba37a3436679548284a2ac8bd92f8716/

If you need any help using the site, you can contact
support@lotsahelpinghands.com.

Powered by Lotsa Helping Hands

I did some due diligence on the site at Pauline's suggestion and found that it had been set up by a bunch of altruistic, smart people for cases such as ours. I was also amazed that the website is free.

Pauline also came through with some good video clips describing Congresswoman Giffords' recovery after being shot in the left side of the head. She too suffered from loss of motors skills and a speech deficit, and made remarkable progress, partly through the benefits of music therapy. This planted a seed about trying music therapy for Allison, which turned out to be one of the keys to her recovery.

From: Pauline Lynch-Stewart
Sent: June 24, 2012 9:47 AM
To: Robert McMechan
Subject: Giffords footage

Bob,

This is a link to a good montage of clips of Gabrielle Giffords' recovery. I am sending this because I think that it has some hopeful and inspiring, if difficult footage, but mostly because it shows the power of music in recovery! And it also shows that even though there are hard days, ultimately strength of character and determination will prevail to achieve amazing things.

http://abcnews.go.com/US/gabby_giffords/humor-determination-key-congresswoman-gabrielle-giffords-recovery/story?id=14944407#.T-cKUrX8t2A

See you this evening,

Pauline

Jill Berry sent an interesting update on June 24th about her visit that day with Allison.

From: Jill Berry
Sent: June 24, 2012 1:28 PM
To: Donna Walsh
Cc: Robert McMechan; Marya Woyiwada
Subject: Re: Saturday afternoon visit with Allison

Hi Donna, Marya and Bob,

I just got back from visiting with Allison. I was so surprised that she was sitting up in a chair! Her eyes were closed, and she was listening to CBC classics radio. I brought in Bernie's laptop to show her the photos of the Mill St Pub retirement celebration for Roxanne and me. She wanted to push the arrow button to advance the pics with her right hand but had her left hand taking over. It was a lot of effort so I advanced the pics. We laughed that she uses her left hand to lift her right hand to her face to scratch her itch. Her nose was itchy constantly. I think it's the adhesive of the bandage holding her feeding tube. The nurse, new to Allison, went on break. Then the shenanigans began. She was trying to remove the feeding tube from her nose, so we had a hand battle! I won! I told her that I think this was the first time that I was more stubborn than her. I want this on record! She also was pulling on the trac tube to the machine, but I talked her out of that with a firm voice: Allison, STOP THAT! She laughed! She was curious as to how everything worked. Tried to open her seat belt and at one point move the chair table. I asked her if she was trying to escape. She said, "Aren't you going to help me?" I said that I thought I better not. At one point she grabbed me with both arms and pulled me to her and we kissed. We held hands a lot. One time she initiated it. Not always could I hear her. I wished I'd known there was a "volume switch"! Not always was she coherent but she has her pet phrases. She was using the fingers of both hands. I mentioned maybe she should use a keyboard and make her own music. She said it was worth a try. She has strength in her left arm, as she moved books on the window ledge, she pushed herself closer to the machinery. She wanted to touch the buttons but I dissuaded her. She also used her left foot to propel herself in the wheelchair. She was lifting her right foot as if she wanted it on the foot rest. I asked her if that's what she wanted, and she said she was still deciding and laughed. It'll be good when she gets a PEG tube for feeding. Having that tube hanging from her face is distracting for her. I asked the nurse to cut off part of the bandage holding the feeding tube as it kept going into the corner of her mouth. I was constantly moving it aside but it kept going in. I left some CDs for her in an envelope. Use if wanted. She'd been up for 2 hours, so they put her back to bed as I left. It'll be interesting to know if she remembered my visit. I was soooooooooo glad to see her.

Jill

Allison didn't remember Jill's visit later that day, or that her friend Donna Walsh had visited on Saturday afternoon. However Jill's email brings a couple of things to mind. The first of these is what both Jill and I would call shenanigans. Whenever Allison could she pulled medical lines and tubes out of her body and pulled things apart. The second is known as perseveration. Allison would become fixated with something, like the underside of the clear plastic tray on her wheelchair, and spend great amounts of time investigating it. This pattern also showed up in her speech, when she would use a word and then use the same word again repeatedly in place of other words. No one could predict this would stop.

Amidst the anxiety and stress of daily hospital visits I managed to take in the Perth Kilt Run with Carol Anderson. Carol found some of her kinfolk at the run, and I just enjoyed the break from everything. I tried my hand at the haggis toss, and I think I was the only contestant who heaved the haggis into the Rideau Canal.

Carol visited Allison on Sunday afternoon, and said that Allison was conversing with her when she was telling her stories, but she couldn't understand what Allison was saying. This is hugely ironic, because much of the time we don't know what Carol is saying, especially on Robbie Burns Day. It did seem clear to Carol though that Allison loved interaction and stories. Carol had Allison write her name, and reports that Allison wrote "Woyiwada" without any coaching. Carol also tried to explain to Allison that she was about to become a grandmother, aided by a brilliant bit of drawing which is reproduced below.

Allison's Brain • 119

My week five update dealt with some of these things.

From: Allison Woyiwada
Sent: June 25, 2012 3:14 PM
To: Allison's Brain
Subject: Week Five Update

Hi

Allison has begun week five in a fine fashion, having made quite impressive cognitive and physical gains in the past week. Although she is easily fatigued, her Allison-personality shines through and her humour is fairly often evident. Today, having been asked twice by a nurse how many "kids" she has, she replied "two and two others" (Tyler, Marya, Laurie and Phil). When asked what their names are she replied both times "Is there money in it?" Phil says it is now obvious that cash bonuses will be the key to her ongoing rehabilitation.

Attempts last week to check her swallowing reflex with a miniature camera were thwarted because her epiglottis and arytenoid were badly swollen, obscuring the view. Today, however, she passed the barium / x-ray tests with flying colours (swallowing small amounts of liquids, pudding, sandwich, cookie, peaches) with no difficulty and as of today she will begin eating solid foods. This means that the dreaded nose / protein feeder tube which she has pulled out and fought over pulling out for several days will now be phased out subject to the dietician's need to do a "calorie count" (although off-the-record if she pulls it out again it will likely stay out this time). It also means that the efforts to wean her off the trach begin today — by removing the trach "cuff" and installing a cork.

Physically, she is managing much more right side move- ment to the point that today the physio called her "a new woman." She is very diligent about repeatedly pulling herself up on the left and right hand sides of her bed to build strength. Because of her growing strength, today for the first time she was transferred to her wheelchair without the use of the lift (and she even stood for a short while for the first time in a month albeit supported).

On Friday evening Dr. Moulton[9] did the shunt operation and said it "went fine" — the next day there were no evident ill-effects from the operation although the back of her head where the shunt was installed is still sore.

Tyler has returned from western Canada, and Allison was regularly asking for him this morning before he arrived at the hospital. Her ability to identify people by their names (Marya, Tyler, Bob) has been improving although she is still often confused and has a memory deficit.

Yesterday though, when I told her that a helicopter had landed across the street from the hospital, she told me that "there are a lot of northern residents." She is likely to be moved out of the Acute Care Unit within the next while as her condition continues to be good and stable.

Allison really enjoys the cards you are sending to her, and today she actually opened a card for the first time.

All for now,
Bob

I missed the occasion, but Marya describes her mother's reaction to her first hospital meal of meatloaf. Apparently Allison was ecstatic about having real food, and was telling Marya that she shouldn't have gone to so much trouble. This level of enthusiasm for hospital food petered out though, and at times it was hard to

---

9   I insisted on meeting Dr. Moulton before signing the consent for him to do Allison's shunt surgery as I didn't know who he was. It turned out that he was the Chair, Division of Neurosurgery, University of Ottawa and Ottawa Hospital with more than 30 years of experience.

Allison's Brain • 121

get Allison to eat anything. Meal times were always quite an experience, as Allison had lost the ability to feed herself, and she did not understand how to use cutlery. I always looked for a towel to serve as a giant-sized bib and hoped for the best. I also removed anything like salt and pepper, packages of sugar, and little milk containers from Allison's tray, as she would eat them or make a mess. We always knew when Allison was finished eating, as she would pile up everything in one big heap.

Marylen Milenkovic sent an email, on June 25th, with a musical twist to it. Marylen has a background as a performer and music director, and she and Allison had collaborated as directors for the Savoy Society.

From: Marylen Milenkovic
Sent: June 25, 2012 8:07 PM
To: McMechan Bob
Subject: For Allison

Bob, Can you please print this off for Allison to read, and I hope you've got an iPad so you can play the two songs at the end.

Allison, Bob has been sending us regular reports about your recovery. Bravo dear friend, you're recovering as you should and you will be well 'cause you're strong, disciplined and surrounded by love.

Chuckle Homework for Allison,

Allison if you get these jokes, your brain is in fine form as you recover.

Q: Why are conductors' hearts so coveted for transplants?

A: They've had so little use.

—

Music: A complex organization of sounds that is set down by the composer, incorrectly interpreted by the conductor, who is ignored by the musicians, the result of which is ignored by the audience.

—

A young child says to his mother, "Mom, when I grow up, I think I'd like to be a musician."

She replies, "Well honey, you know you can't do both."

—

Here's one of my favourite oldie goldie songs that I think is appropriate for the both of us: http://www.youtube.com/watch?v=9SxToTUoWGM

I've also included Desperado (Linda Ronstadt), in memory of our little trio in Wpg: http://www.youtube.com/watch?v=oAK5Ids7l5g

Love ya Marylen

The following day Allison got out of the Neuroscience Acute Care Unit and into the Neuroscience Inpatient Unit, where the ratio of nurses to patients is more like it is in a regular hospital ward, unlike the two patients to one nurse ratio in NACU, and the one to one ratio in ICU. This was definitely progress, and in the early days in the Inpatient Unit, Allison got along pretty well. The nose feeder came out, and her trach was corked. Allison told her nurse that she thought she was in Waterloo, but she knew her name was Woyiwada.

Jane Mahoney, the social worker assigned to Allison's case, told us that this was Day 0 for rehab, because all of Allison's tubes were out. Allison was fitted for a helmet, and managed about 200 meters of walking with Christine Moore, her physiotherapist, using a walker on wheels. Jane and Christine were two key players in

Allison's Brain • **123**

Allison's post-surgery team, and a more expansive description of their roles is fitting.

Christine was Allison's first physiotherapist. She loves working with people, and gets up every morning with a bounce in her step. Becoming a physiotherapist now requires a two year Master of Health Science in Physiotherapy post-graduate degree. Christine has been a physiotherapist for eighteen years, with the last twelve years working in the neurosurgery area. Every case is different, and no two days at the hospital are the same.

The post-surgery work done by a physiotherapist is done as a member of a team of clinicians who work in NACU, as well as on the wards. The physiotherapist works very closely with the occupational therapist, and together they determine how far they can progress with patients. Almost everyone is assessed after neurosurgery, and at the initial assessment it is necessary to look at the patient as a whole, rather than just focusing on his or her mobility. This is because when there are cognitive issues, such as an inability to remember, the approach taken to a patient's physiotherapy is different. Ordinarily, for example, we do not think about walking, and when it has to be re-learned, the way it is "taught" depends upon the individual patient. Some patients have the ability to be analytical in re-learning how to walk, whereas for others who have difficulty remembering, the focus is on repetition.

Ultimately, the acute care therapist's role is to get the patient ready for the next step. Ideally, the patient can be gotten ready to go home. If this is not possible, the team investigates other options such as rehab. One example of this is the Acquired Brain Injury Care Stream at the Rehabilitation Centre of the Ottawa Hospital. In order to accomplish this, and because of funding cutbacks, family is now playing a more significant role than it has in the recent past. The physiotherapist shows family members how to help with the reacquisition of physical skills, and the family members then assist the patients in doing the exercises that are prescribed.

Christine says Allison initially had no right side movement, but this eventually came back over time in spurts. She also exhibited right side "neglect" as she didn't know her right side was there. As Allison had been bedridden for an extended period, the first step was to help her find "verticality," i.e. to help her realize what sitting up straight was like. The method was to prop up Allison in her bed with support and to gradually increase the duration of the supported sessions. Next the support was withdrawn, and with assistance Allison was able to sit up in a chair on her own. In the beginning, the transfer from bed to chair was accomplished with an overhead lift. Once again, the duration of the sitting sessions was gradually increased, until Allison could sit up for an extended period. Next involved having Allison on her feet, fully supported at the outset. Eventually, with Christine and the physiotherapist's assistant's support and the aid of a walker, Allison was able to take a few steps.

Different walkers were tried out, and Christine recalls that Allison rammed the walkers into everything she could as she began re-learning how to walk. Christine also recalls that Allison's progress was often interrupted by medical complications, and that the clock didn't really "start ticking" on her recovery until she was stable. Initially, Allison's level of physical impairment was severe; however, it was the level of Allison's cognitive impairment that kept her from moving to the rehab centre earlier than she did.

Christine's description of what she does is that it is definitely a vocation and "not a job." There are times where her work leads to a complete recovery. There are others in which the patients are unable to recover, and her work is targeted at helping the patient and family adjust to their new circumstances. Her experience is that a patient's attitude and determination often play a big role in the extent of recovery and that family can play a role in helping a patient to recover mobility after neurosurgery.

Jane Mahoney also has a Masters degree, and she has worked in the neuro field for sixteen years. She says the social worker is a respected member of the post-neurosurgery team at the Ottawa Hospital. There is a structured environment for the team members, with well-established role clarity. The social worker is consulted

Allison's Brain · 125

in the case of more complex discharges. In the neuro area, a social worker's goals include helping to see that patients are "in the right place at the right time" and moving them through the hospital as efficiently as possible. There is enormous pressure to move people through the system, as there are always other people waiting for hospital beds, and discharge planning begins when a referral is made to the social worker.

A psychosocial assessment is done when a referral is made, and the social worker then helps the patient and the patient's family set goals appropriate to the patient's circumstances. The work can include crisis counselling, and one of the social worker's key jobs is communication. Family members can very often be in a high emotional state after a patient's brain surgery, and communicating information to the family helps to reduce anxiety, and to increase satisfaction. We found that Jane was our main source of information about where Allison stood, and she always helped us to stand back and see the big picture.

As Jane works in the acute care and inpatient units, she often doesn't see the end product. Sometimes patients recover quickly, sometimes slowly, and sometimes not at all. There is no way of knowing how much time will be required for recovery after neurosurgery — or the extent to which there will *be* a recovery. In Allison's case, as she had a number of medical setbacks post-surgery, her discharge was substantially delayed. The extent of Allison's cognitive deficit was also a big factor in the timing of her discharge. Jane also says different neurosurgeons have different comfort zones when it comes to discharging patients and that Dr. Lesiuk is cautious in his approach.

Jane loves what she does. She finds that every day at work is different, and she greatly values being a member of the neurosurgery recovery team. Jane also feels that the longevity of the service of team members at the hospital is an important factor in what it accomplishes.

At around this time, once again through the magic of email, our friend Annemieke Holthuis in Victoria put me in touch with someone in Ottawa who could speak to the matter of recovery from a brain injury, from a patient perspective. I met with Cynthia Taylor, heard her story, and jumped at the chance for her to meet Allison, which happened within a few days. It was fascinating to see Cynthia interact with Allison, and to hear her explanations of what Allison was probably feeling.

We also benefited from advice from Pat MacDonald, who was visiting her mother in California. Pat is another singer and director, who Allison had collaborated with for the Savoy Society. Pat's brother-in-law had suffered a stroke about five years earlier and had fought his way back to recover his speech.

> **From:** Pat MacDonald
> **Sent:** June 27, 2012 3:07 PM
> **To:** Allison Woyiwada
> **Subject:** RE: Week Five Update
>
> *Again, thanks for keeping us in the loop. Never imagined there was so much to it. She is one feisty lady, and I can just imagine her trying to pull that awful thing out of her nose! Hope it is gone by now. Not sure if you know Bob, but Allison and I had various conversations about my brother-in-law who had brain surgery (tumour) about 5 years ago now, and some of the things he had to go through. We all said it was like playing Taboo when it came to speech because there were words that he could not remember, so, being smart as is she, he worked around them and we played guessing games and finally came up with them. There was definitely a learning curve and various plateaus, but he is now pretty good. No, it will never be totally the same, but the blanks are much better. He just has to think some things through.*
>
> *He forgot various concepts like how to add a tip, but when coached on it, it came back. The brain is an amazing thing. Lots of noise and hubbub bothers him; a crowded room with lots going on. I think it is the sensory overload thing.*

Allison's Brain • 127

Everyone is different obviously as are operations, but I just wanted you to know that with time things do reorganize. Personality is the same; sense of humour is the same; intelligence is the same. Hang in there.

Sorry this isn't a card, but you can read it to Allison if you want:

Hi Allison,

Pat here. I don't know if you remember now, but you and I had some discussions about my brother-in-law Raymond and his brain surgery, and you asked what effect it had. I told you that he forgot words for a bit but that they came back over time. It was like playing the game Taboo where you are not allowed to say some words while you make the other people guess what you mean. You probably have lots of things inside you that you want to say but are not sure how to say them yet. Please don't get too frustrated because words will come back to you. It just takes time.

You sound like a tiger working on your strength, and I could just see you trying to pull out the nasty nose tube. You also have lots of friends rooting for you, and one who will be happy to help whenever we can. Hang in there baby! Doug says hi too.

A lot of the stuff that Pat said was encouraging. I had no idea what to expect in terms of Allison's recovery of her ability to speak, and no one would ever promise anything. In fact, Dr. Lesiuk told us a couple of times that the last fifty cases don't matter, as everyone is different. We considered ourselves fortunate that Allison's personality hadn't changed, as I had read some horror stories on that front, including Terry Evanshen's. Terry was a famous wide receiver in the Canadian Football League from 1965 to 1978 who was badly injured in a car accident. Among other things, he lost all of his memories and had a dramatic personality change. I had mentioned this sometime earlier at dinner to my friend Max from Vancouver and said that I hoped Allison's personality wouldn't change, as I liked it the way it was. Max responded to this by saying I married above my pay grade. Well I can say the same for Max.

On the night of June 27th, Allison got out of her bed during the night and was found on the floor by her bed at around 3:00 a.m. She was restrained afterwards and disliked the experience a great deal — to put it mildly — whenever that took place. Restraints had to be used often, for Allison was often trying to get out of bed when alone. She was also fitted for a helmet because she was at risk due to the missing bone flap, which was taken out for the surgery.

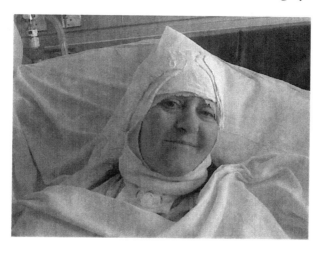

The doctor from the rehab centre who evaluated Allison on June 28th determined that she would not benefit from aggressive rehab. The notes from his assessment include "Draws a face when asked to draw the face of a clock. Recalls 0/3 objects. Ø insight into recent surgeries." Later Allison had visitors who gave us favourable reports about their visits.

> **From:** Lynn Graham
> **Sent:** June 28, 2012 9:01 PM
> **To:** Robert McMechan; Marya Woyiwada
> **Subject:** My visit this evening
>
> *Hi Bob and Marya,*

I certainly appreciated spending time with Allison. After you left, Marya, Allison stayed awake until around 7:30 and then she began to doze. During the time she was awake, we looked at photos in Maclean's, and then I read her two or three articles in it. She had moments of real awareness, such as observing the two front covers that comprise this week's edition and commenting that one side must be French and the other English — not the case but still a pretty smart observation! She is good at counting — I certainly noted that as she looked at the photos.

Janice and Mike arrived at 8, and I left soon after.

All in all, a good experience for me and I hope for Allison.

Take care,
Lynn

From: Mike Hayes
Sent: June 28, 2012 10:32 PM
To: Robert McMechan
Subject: Visit with Allison

Bob,

Janice and I had a nice visit with Allison. She enjoyed having her feet rubbed by both of us, told me "don't make me laugh." And I told her laughter is good for her.

She was tired, but was onto something about Friday, doing something special because it's Friday, so expect a surprise.

We were both taken by her great progress, had both arms going, thumbs up, wave, and the legs too. In fact she was sliding down the bed, but told me she was comfortable and didn't need to be propped back up. I think she had a plan to get out of there! We had the nurse and helper come get her moved back up the bed, and she was really helping them.

What we noticed right away were all of her funny facial expressions, those looks she gives, a sigh, and she says "whatever" with a thumbs up. It was great to see her making great progress.

We stayed until 8:45, think we were getting the "I'm getting annoyed look and I'm trying to rest" when she opened her eyes and saw we were still there.

Mike

The following day was a very big day for Allison; I wrote all about it on the morning of June 30th.

From: Robert McMechan
Sent: June 30, 2012 6:42 AM
To: Jim Rennie
Cc: Marya Woyiwada; Bette-Lou Paragg; Ben and Joan; Phil McMechan; Tyler Woyiwada
Subject: Photos of Allison

Yesterday was a big day for Allison as she finally got her trach out, got her new (blue) helmet (she commented on the blue accent), and we were able to take her outside (in her wheelchair) for the first time since May 28th. She loved feeling the breeze and seeing something new! Allison loves photos, so don't hesitate to send us some of you and your family — it also helps to re-orient her. Don't hesitate to come for a visit sometime as there is plenty of room in our house!

Bob

p.s. She needs to wear the helmet for walking (yesterday was her third day up with the walker), and any other time she could be in danger of falling, until the piece of her skull on the left side that was removed for the operation is replaced sometime down the road.

Allison's Brain • **131**

Later on the 30th, when Allison was alone for a while by herself, she managed to get out of her chair and take her helmet off, ending up on the floor again. Two of the solutions for countering Allison's growing but self-destructive strength were to give her a lower hospital bed, and to surround it with mattresses. We also often told Allison that the helmet and the wheelchair seatbelt were for her own safety, but that didn't seem to register.

A remarkable thing happened that evening, as I was sitting with Allison on the side of her bed. Out-of-the-blue, although she made little sense before or after, she asked me if I was checking her email. This sort of lucidity presented itself very rarely, but it gave us hope that Allison wasn't totally gone. Dr. Lesiuk explained to us that people recovering from brain injuries who display moments of lucidity typically settle over time at their peaks, rather than in their valleys, and so we had cause for cautious optimism.

Allison has always been a big fan of Canada Day in Ottawa, partly because she enjoys a party. It fell on a Sunday, and it was another big day for Allison. Tyler took her for a long wheelchair ride around the block, and I did the same later. We then had a "picnic" in her room with things I'd brought from home. We also managed to see fireworks from a hospital window, although Allison fell asleep. The fireworks clearly had an impact though, as she was able to tell the nurses about them the following day. I was also impressed with the fact that, when we went for a wheelchair ride outdoors, she remembered the Heart Institute building. Later in the week Allison also managed to walk without a walker while supported.

The week six update recounted lots of good news.

From: Allison Woyiwada
Sent: July 03, 2012 7:43 PM
To: Allison's Brain
Subject: Week 6 Update

Hi

Allison continues to make good progress. During the past week she was moved out of the Acute Care Unit to the Neuroscience InPatient Unit. She has had her trach removed and she has resumed eating regular meals. Her stitches are now all out, and she has a blue helmet (see attached photo) that she will have to wear whenever she is in any danger of falling — until the section of her skull which was removed for surgery is eventually replaced. The filter installed in her ICU days to prevent the migration of blood clots from her legs was removed today. Her alertness and mobility took a bit of a swan dive in the last day or so, but late today she was diagnosed with an infection which is now being treated with antibiotics. So we are hoping for good form tomorrow.

Allison's strength (both right and left side) continues to grow, and she can now take wheelchair rides (including outdoors around the hospital grounds) without being propped up with a head rest. She has also begun some

Allison's Brain • **133**

modest walking attempts with a walker — supervised by her physiotherapist — which we expect to result in her eventually (although we don't know when) being able to walk on her own again. For the time being, however, she has to be reminded to keep both hands on her walker (however this isn't always her first choice and she has "developed" a little stubbornness!) and to keep her head up / look straight ahead. This can be quite challenging.

On the cognitive front her periods of alertness are expanding although she still needs pretty regular snoozes — especially after big days like Canada Day. We had a Canada Day picnic in the hospital which included toasts (with 0% Becks for the worry-warts amongst you) which she instigated several times and clearly enjoyed — it was almost like she'd done toasts before?). We also watched the 10:00 p.m. fireworks from a 7th floor window.

When asked how the fireworks were she commented that they were "right up there" — although she fell asleep during the later stages. My daughter Laurie says we now make quite a couple, as previously I was the only person she knew who could fall asleep during fireworks. Allison's speech is often quite jumbled, although sometimes out-of-the-blue she makes very coherent statements like "Have you been checking my e-mail?"

Another favourite moment of mine occurred after she'd advised her nurse that her surname is Ukrainian. When the nurse queried me about this I responded that the name was her former husband's name. Allison promptly added that she has "only one ex." This same exchange also involved Allison saying that "Bob is a pretty solid guy." (I swear). Those of you who prefer lame tax lawyer "humour" will no doubt resent this development.

134 • *Robert McMechan with Allison Woyiwada*

Dr. Tse checked Allison's epiglottis and arytenoid area with a camera (this doesn't look like fun) and advises that things are looking to be getting back to normal. Speaking of the vocal cord area Allison's sister Linda says she hopes that Allison's vocal cords are OK as she doesn't want to have to become known as "the sister who sings."

Your cards continue to delight her and, although I usually end up reading them, she is taking a crack at it herself these days. Her comprehension of conversation is generally at a high level, but her reading needs lots of work.

Thanks for all of your good wishes and support!

Bob

Catherine Chubey, Allison's first speech therapist, and her assistant tried cognitive testing with Allison on July 6th but gave up because, although Allison initially co-operated, her attention span and focus were too limited. We found this quite discouraging. Discouraging too, was the news from Jane Mahoney that Allison would not be going to the rehab centre for aggressive rehab, but to Saint Vincent's, a less challenging environment. However, after speaking with Dr. Lesiuk, and Dr. Lyla Graham who had worked at Saint Vincent's, we realized there was no alternative. The bottom line was that it is only possible to go to aggressive rehab if you can optimize the time you spend there, and in order to do that, you need to be able to concentrate and remember.

I will also mention that Marya and I tried to overlap our visits a bit around this time, so we could both assist Allison with walking. This could be quite a challenge, for Allison didn't often want to walk straight down the hall. Besides stopping to inspect things along the way like garbage cans, she leaned to one side. On the 6th, we were having a walking session, and Allison got really angry with me for insisting that she walk straight ahead and down the hall. She called me a "dick" and refused to kiss me goodbye. I found this really upsetting. When I look back, I think that was because I was walking a pretty thin line.

However, the next day she had forgotten that I was a "dick," and we had another hospital picnic dinner. Allison was putting lots of words together in sentences, and nurse Carolyn told me that she had seen Allison walking and standing by herself, and that she could get out of bed by herself. I have also noted that Allison corrected my pronunciation of Sigourney, although I don't recall what the context was.

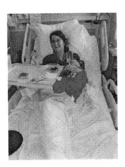

Pat MacDonald returned from California, and she took Allison to a piano in the hospital to work on playing songs. Pat says that Allison's left hand was better than her right, and that she had trouble with her fingering, especially with her thumb. Allison, she reported, had the counting and timing and was reading the music to a good extent. Pat also tried to help Allison choose from hospital menu options, but noted that was a problem for Allison. The menu options became a daily event with Allison, trying to have her decide what to order. Usually we made the choices for her because she couldn't decide.

Allison became quite sick on July 9th, and a nurse suggested that her course of antibiotics may have ended too soon. The occupational therapist told me that Allison was having trouble understanding things out of context and suggested that we keep things basic and simple with reminders of the context, such as pointing out things to her during wheelchair rides. I recall doing this with Allison on many wheelchair rides, taking her through the long hall on the main floor and talking as we went.

Allison was back on antibiotics on the 10th and seemed better than she had been a day earlier. Allison's ex in-laws Diny and Kevin from Alberta visited with Marya on July 10th, and Diny gave Allison a bracelet with lots of dangling things on it. This turned out to be a source of endless delight for Allison, and she spent countless hours examining it. Christine said she was going to try a two wheel walker because Allison didn't pay enough attention with the four wheel walker and just shoved it ahead of her. I have also noted that Allison knew her first and last names, but always also said "Woyiwada" when asked what city she was in.

On the night of the 10th, Allison was once again found on the floor, but a CT scan showed everything was OK. My week seven update to the *Allison's Brain* group was a bit of a mixed bag.

From: Allison Woyiwada
Sent: July 10, 2012 9:55 PM
To: Allison's Brain
Subject: Week Seven Update

Hi

Allison is still in the Neuroscience InPatient Unit at the Civic Hospital. The plan has been to have her move to a rehab centre; however, she's had a couple of setbacks with infections treated by antibiotics that have slowed her progress. Her physical strength continues to grow, and she now sits up by herself and even stands occasionally; plus, she can walk short distances with assistance and wearing her helmet — which isn't always her first choice!

On the cognitive front there continue to be flashes of coherence / normalcy (such as calling me a "dick" for trying to have her walk with my support when she clearly had other intentions that I couldn't discern!). A good deal of the time, however, her speech is jumbled and her writing

Allison's Brain • **137**

is too. In Dr. Lesiuk's words, she is having trouble with "word processing." The attempted "assessments" by specialists to date have all ended on the basis that Allison is not able to concentrate long enough to stay on task. This means she will likely be sent to a slow rehab setting at least initially (Saint Vincents) as she couldn't derive the optimal benefit from more aggressive rehab at this point.

Allison's memory has been poor although, there too, there have been occasional glimpses of its return. Today, for example, she studied photos of her Manitoba family at length and appeared to be piecing things together. Later when I took her out for a wheelchair ride and suggested that we look at the houses on the street adjacent to the hospital, she told me that we'd done that before and that we could go around the block again (which was true).

Using Dr. Lesiuk's recent words (despite his misgivings about tax law) Allison's recovery is "a process not an event." If I have this correctly, he also says that it takes six months to achieve 90% of one's overall recovery. He also advises that "the last fifty cases involving recovery from a brain injury don't matter, as everyone is different."

Through all of this, Allison keeps a positive demeanour nearly continuously, and she is quite a joy to be with.

Thanks to all who have sent cards to Allison, and thanks also to the many who've given "Bob support"!

All for now
Bob

P.S. Cynthia Taylor's visit last week was a big success, and after I left the two of them alone, they bonded splendidly. I could tell from Allison's expressions that she was fascinated by Cynthia's stories regarding her own recovery.

The reference to photographs in the update prompts me to recall that, many times, I took photos of our home and neighbourhood to Allison, explaining that was where we lived. She looked at these with no hint that she recognized anything. We had decorated her room with photos of our family, so she could see us all every day. I also wrote out our address and our family relationships and left this with her.

This brings me to a funny story that is worth sharing. Our neighbours, Carol Alette and Jim Fraser, always have a raspberry patch, and they gave me some raspberries to take to Allison. These were a big hit with Allison, and so the next day I told them, and they gave me a much larger bowl. At the time they said that I could also have a couple, and I told Allison this when giving her the bowl, taking a couple of raspberries as I did. Allison polished off the entire bowl of raspberries with great relish, and looked up when she was done to say that I was "an honest fellow." I assume she meant that by only taking a couple of raspberries, in accordance with Carol and Jim's instructions, I had been an honest fellow.

I noted the next day that Allison lifted her bowl underneath her spoon when eating soup to prevent spilling and used her fork to eat her macaroni and cheese. This was quite an event because when Allison fed herself, she generally just grabbed the food with her hands, including things like mashed potatoes and roast beef with gravy. This was quite indelicate, and we always encouraged her to use the utensils.

Marya and I went to see the Saint Vincent Hospital on July 11th and were given a wonderful overview of its restorative care program by Wanda Assang, RN. In the end, Allison went directly to the rehab centre, but we thought that if Allison wasn't ready for aggressive rehab, Saint Vincent was a good place for her to be. It has a large airy open area as you enter the building, grounds with picnic tables, and Wanda told us that we could bring in outside therapists to supplement the local therapy program.

This was about the time it really hit home that our costs for Allison's rehabilitation could represent a great deal of money.

Allison's Brain • **139**

Allison had taken a basic package for her post-teaching health coverage, and we found that the maximum benefits for therapy were $750 per annum. It would be easy to spend that much in a week on occupational and speech therapy, even if you only had a few sessions in the week. No one thinks about having a catastrophic injury when they are healthy, but we are all just moments away.

By mid-week, Allison was in high form and is reported to have talked about a vacation in the Okanogan (which we'd been on the year before); done some hand jiving, whatever that is; looked spiffy in her new La Senza pyjamas; sang a few lines with Carol and Gerald when they sang some Gilbert and Sullivan tunes; and "listened politely and expressed support and excitement" at Gerald's explanation about the discovery of the Higgs boson particle. I have my suspicions about the Higgs boson story, but then I am generally suspicious when people claim to see invisible little particles.[10]

I explained to Allison that her new pyjamas were a gift from my mother and she wrote the following thank-you note.

---

10 Although Gerald is now the Chair, Department of Physics, Carleton University, and I certainly don't mean to be disrespectful.

However, later that week Allison became completely non-responsive. She began shaking and was suspected of having a seizure. Then the nurse told me that her Dilantin level had been found to be much too low. Allison had a CT scan which fortunately showed no stroke. When she returned to her room, she was still trembling, and this continued the following day. The advice I was given initially by Allison's nurse was that she would continue to tremble until her Dilantin got back to a proper level.

The following morning, I got a call from the hospital and sent out a family email update.

From: Robert McMechan
Sent: July 16, 2012 7:13 AM
To: Marya Woyiwada
Cc: Tyler Woyiwada; Jim Rennie; Laurie Souchotte; Phil McMechan; Bette-Lou Paragg; Ben and Joan
Subject: Dr. Alcatani Called at 7:00 a.m.

Dr. Alcatani called to give me a "quick update" because of my e-mail early this a.m. to Jane the Social Worker. Allison is back in the Neuroscience Acute Care Unit on the 2nd Floor. She had a seizure yesterday because her Dilantin level was too low (6 instead of 40). The CT scan last evening showed some ventricle enlargement. This is a possible indicator of early shunt failure. Today the medical team is working on three issues (a) seizure; (b) possible shunt failure — she is to be tested today regarding this; and (c) the source of her abdominal discomfort. Please keep me posted — I can get to the hospital today for our 1:30 meeting with Jane and the therapists.

Bob

P.S. No explanation from anyone yet why the Dilantin level was too low.

The next update came from Marya.

From: Marya Woyiwada
Sent: July 16, 2012 12:29 PM
To: Robert McMechan
Subject: Re: Update re Allison

The shunt is infected and will be replaced. Dr Lesiuk has yet to talk to the infections specialists regarding the exact plan and timeline. She will be put on antibiotics asap. They will either wait for the infection to clear before they replace the shunt, or do it immediately. They will also either do it in one surgery or 2, the latter meaning she would go back to the temporary external drain. The swelling can be due to the combination of seizure activity and the infection. They are working on finding the right dosage of dilantin, and Dr Lesiuk assured me that missing a dose or 2 is not the reason for the low dilantin level. Could be metabolic. Seizures can cause damage, but a number of doctors have assured me that it's atypical. At this point Dr Lesiuk still sees this as a setback. No results from the ultrasound at this point, but Dr Lesiuk suggested that the pains in her belly could also be due to the infection.

I followed up with the week eight *Allison's Brain* update, without much lilt in my prose.

From: Allison Woyiwada
Sent: July 16, 2012 12:29 PM
To: Allison's Brain
Subject: Week Eight Update

Hi

Allison appeared to be making good progress and was in very good form all day Saturday. She was putting more words together sensibly in a sentence than I'd heard since pre-surgery. Unfortunately she crashed (my word) on Sunday afternoon / evening and is back in the Neuroscience Acute Care Unit. What we've been told is that her Dilantin level (anti-seizure med she's been taking since December) got down to "6" from the "40" level that it's supposed to be kept at. I'm only a tax lawyer but monitoring Allison's Dilantin level doesn't sound like rocket science. In any event she's had some seizures and has had her brain fluid tested — her brain is swollen again — and an ultrasound today. This is compounded by the fact that she has also been experiencing abdominal pain from some as yet undiagnosed source.

The meeting with the Neuroscience InPatient Unit social worker and Allison's therapists that was to be held today has been cancelled. I was hoping to find out whether supplementing Allison's therapy with outside therapists (she receives limited physiotherapy a few days a week and it appears to me no speech or occupational therapy at all) would be beneficial. In any event, Marya and I have visited Saint Vincent (her likely destination when she is no longer in need of hospital care) and we think it will be an excellent venue for her. The administrator we met was extremely helpful, and she explained that we can arrange to supplement the therapies that Allison will receive there with outside therapy.

Allison's medical costs are mounting (Ontario teachers amongst you please note that the basic post-teaching benefits are completely inadequate for coverage in the event of a serious medical problem). In light of that, Marya is organizing a benefit concert which will likely be held sometime in September. We are also going to set up a trust fund for Allison so online donations can be made for her benefit.

Hopefully there will be much better news in the Week Nine Update!

Allison's Brain • **143**

All for now,
Bob

P.S. Thanks to everyone for their support and especially to
Marylen and Pat for their attendance and vigilance with
Allison on Sunday evening.

Medical costs had already become an issue because we had at first opted for a private room for Allison, thinking that, after brain surgery, it would be a good idea to have some peace and quiet. Allison's basic insurance coverage provided up to $100 per day for a room, whereas a semi-private room was $180 and a private room was $220. We were also anticipating a $1000 monthly charge from Saint Vincent's. At that time Robert Borden set up a trust account for Allison at TD Canada Trust which we still use today.

Allison had her infected shunt removed on July 17th when the priority surgery backlog cleared up. In the meantime, she was on antibiotics again and feeling much better. When I visited her in OR recovery and the nurse was occupied elsewhere Allison said, "Now's our chance to get out of here." This was the first of many occasions on which Allison told visitors that they should help her get out of the hospital.

Dr. Lesiuk's Neurosurgery Operative Report includes a Clinical Note.

This 60-year-old right [sic] handed musician was well
known to the Neurosurgery Service. She had undergone a
huge left frontotemporal craniotomy under deep hypother-
mic arrest for a giant left middle cerebral artery aneurysm.
At the time of that procedure it was elected not to replace
the bone flap for fear of uncontrollable postoperative
swelling. She had a protracted convalescence complicated
by shunt dependent hydrocephalus, and a variety of
infectious complications, the most recent now being an
infection and associated malfunction of her current VP
shunt. Arrangements were accordingly made to remove the

infected shunt and replace it with a temporary external ventricular drain.

This external ventricular drain caused lots of excitement (or rather Allison did) in the days ahead.

For the following couple of days Allison was pretty much out of it. She knew her name was Allison, but did not know her surname or where she was. She didn't know my name — but that was still better than being called a dick. But the thing that took the cake is that, when Pat and Doug MacDonald dropped by and sang, "Why was she born so beautiful," Allison didn't respond. This song is a roaring favourite of mine, and I never miss a chance to sing it with Allison when I can. The lyrics can be off-putting — "Why was she born so beautiful, why was she born at all, she's no bloody use to anyone, she's no bloody use at all" — but when it is sung in harmony, preferably en masse, it is a thing of great beauty and brings tears to your eyes.

At around this time, an ultrasound was done because of Allison's complaints about pain in her abdomen. The ultrasound turned up a tumour in Allison's liver, which had to be investigated further by an MRI. At one point, Dr. Lesiuk took me aside and told me that the results were consistent with the possibility of colon cancer. This led to a long saga involving colonoscopies, a biopsy and other medical tests. The finding was that Allison has neuroendocrine cancer, for which she had surgery in 2013, to remove a malignant tumour from her liver. As of the time of writing Allison's oncologist Dr. Rachel Goodwin has recommended a wait and see approach, as no other cancer has been detected.

From: Robert McMechan
Sent: July 20, 2012 10:17 AM
To: Marya Woyiwada
Subject: Friday a.m.

Nurse Bram says a signature is required re sedation for the MRI to be done today re your mom's abdomen. I told her you would be in this a.m. — she says there's no rush as

Allison's Brain • 145

the doctors are now in OR. She says your mom knows her name this a.m. but not her last name or where she is. She pulled out her nose tube and so she is restrained again. Yes I will send you the blurb I've been writing.

Bob

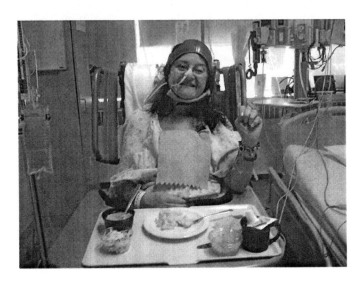

The reference to "the blurb I've been writing" was a small contribution to the blogspot that Marya and her friends were creating for Allison. Marya did a fantastic job of arranging and putting together the publicity for a benefit concert for her mother, and the work of putting it together began around this time. The blogspot scored a phenomenal number of hits when it was created — see *woyiwada.blogspot.com*. It's hard to overestimate the power of the Internet, and the incredible communications abilities that go with it. People from our neighbourhood told me they heard about Allison from their daughter in Asia.

You will recall that earlier I extolled the heroism of Lorraine England for having provided Tuesday and Thursday dinners for seventeen successive weeks. Well it turns out that Lorraine also has a dark side, and I think it only fair that I explain what I mean by that. Quite a few friends were riding a 170k biking event on July 21st, and I was able to join them. Our friends Joan and Warren hosted a dinner afterwards, which was capped off by a friendly boating competition in their pool. I had made it clear that my boat would be the "Allison" and that any result other than me winning would be pretty lousy. Lorraine didn't ride in the 170k biking event, and generously I thought offered to visit with Allison. But Lorraine then used the occasion to nefariously secure Allison's "endorsement" of her boat AWYN4ALLISON II.

I will let Lorraine's account of the evening speak for itself, but you have to ask yourself what sort of person would sneakily seek an "endorsement" from a patient in a neuroscience acute care unit?

> **From:** Lorraine England
> **Sent:** July 22, 2012 11:25 PM
> **To:** Various Henchmen; Allison Woyiwada
> **Subject:** Fwd: Re: Boat
>
> *Hello Boat fans.*
>
> *Thank you for asking how she did, Stephanie.*
>
> *The AWYN4ALLISON II did quite well yesterday. She shot out of the starting blocks super propelled by the retractable clothes line cord, made it to the end and was turned around successfully. At this point the competition got over their rude comments that her propulsion technique may not be within the rules and unfortunately some came with ammunition (Chris's wife Katherine didn't understand why he was buying Campbell's soup last week when it was 32 C and besides they never eat it). It became apparent when several Campbell Soup can depth chargers were thrown at the AWYN4ALLISON II… and eventually these depth chargers sank her when she was 3/4 of the way back down the pool by fan power. I jumped into the pool and rescued her… many other captains were also in the pool by this time, so that rule seemed to have been equally not applied to contestants. I righted her, poured the water*

out… and the fans were still happily spinning. She made it to the finish line on her own steam!!! (almost)

The prize of two Dollar Store silver rabbit book ends was won for Most Original Boat (or something equally prestigious).

It was a great regatta.

Allison… don't listen to any of Bob's recounting of the race. He won… but it is questionable about the fair and square part.

Thank you for all your encouragement, support and suggestions. This win would not have been possible without you!

Love Lorraine/Mom

The next few days were a pretty mixed bag. On the 22nd Allison sang "The Policeman's Song" with John Forster and Ruth McEwen, who had both performed for Allison with the Savoy Society. The next day Allison sat up when she wasn't supposed to and a lot of brain fluid drained out. Louise Hall and Susan Smith tried to get

Allison to take her meds by likening them to shooters, but Allison wasn't going for it.

Then came my Week Nine *Allison's Brain* update.

> **From:** Allison Woyiwada
> **Sent:** July 23, 2012 9:51 PM
> **To:** Allison's Brain
> **Subject:** Week Nine Update
>
> *Hi*
>
> *Allison remains in the Neuroscience Acute Care Unit at the Civic Hospital. Her shunt was removed early last week, and Dr. Lesiuk has confirmed that it was infected. Allison has been on a course of antibiotics, and Dr. Lesiuk says there need to be "a couple of negative cultures" before a new shunt can be installed. There are two sets of results pending, and the prospects appear to be promising, so the shunt surgery could take place this week.*
>
> *Allison's overall complexion and demeanour have improved markedly since the events of mid-July involving the drop in her Dilantin level and the infection from her shunt. Allison's nurse Jennifer says she likes having Allison as her patient as there is always an element of humour involved ("she rolls her eyes appropriately"). I witnessed this humour recently when Jennifer was asking Allison if she would take the rest of her Dilantin and Allison said, "No thanks, that will be good for now." I was quite buoyed up when Allison announced to Gloria Fox when I arrived on Saturday afternoon, "That's my husband." This has been somewhat diminished by Allison asking me this evening when I left, "When will I have to see you again?" (much to the delight of Louise and Susan I'm sure). As I left and explained that I would be doing her weekly update, I asked Allison if she had any message for you. Her response was, "Tell them how fantastic it is." (I am not kidding about*

Allison's Brain • **149**

this.) Although Allison is from time-to-time putting words together in a manner that can be understood, this is not too frequently the occasion. Dr. Lesiuk says this is not the result of post-surgery confusion, and that it will need to be addressed by rehab efforts.

Speaking of rehab, a number of you have asked about the funding gap I mentioned in last week's update. We are advised at Saint Vincent's that we can bring in outside therapists to work with the Saint Vincent's therapists. The cost of this is basically $150 per visit whereas Allison's total insurance coverage for therapy of all kinds (physio, occupational and speech) is $750 per annum. There is also a very significant monthly fee for staying at Saint Vincent's; plus, given that Allison's tolerance for noise has substantially diminished post-surgery, we have not opted for standard 3-4 bed per room accommodation, and insurance pays for less than half of her room costs.

In light of this, Marya is putting together a benefit concert to be held at Southminster Church at 7:00 p.m. on Sunday September 23rd. She has assembled a stellar cast of performers — more details re this will follow. A trust account has also been established at TD Canada Trust for anyone who wishes to make a donation. In the coming days a blog will be released with more details regarding all of the efforts to raise funds for Allison. It presently appears that a great deal of rehabilitation work will be required to get Allison back up to snuff. The good news in this is that Allison is displaying the same doggedness and good nature that has made her famous!

All for now,
Bob

P.S. There are far too many of you to name individually — thanks to you all for your terrific ongoing support!

P.P.S. Fittingly, my vessel named "Allison" prevailed in a fierce nautical competition held at Revelstoke Drive on Saturday evening. When I explained this to Allison there may have been a bit of eye rolling on her part.

The following day Allison had a telephone conversation with Marya. This was her first telephone conversation since before surgery. Months later, when Allison was back home, the telephone was a problem for us, as Allison would answer calls when I wasn't around, and then not remember there had been a call, or not have any idea what the call had been about. I did my best to ensure that important hospital calls would only be to me, but on a few occasions I found myself calling around to various places, to try to find out what was what. Fortunately, this problem has abated as time has passed.

The same day Allison wasn't cooperating in taking her medication, and this became a fairly frequent behaviour. Marya suggested at one time that her mother, having been accustomed to being a strongly independent woman, might be refusing to take her medication because it was one of the few things that she could have any influence on. Whatever the case, nurse Cathy commented that she liked to see Allison's strong-mindedness, as it is a good sign in patients. Looking back that was pretty sage advice, as it seems quite apparent that a fighting spirit is a key ingredient for recovering from a brain injury.

Allison's memory was showing flashes of improvement at this time, and when I showed her photos of our home she appeared to recognize the place. I also showed her photos from Canada Day three weeks earlier, and at first she didn't remember, but then thought she might have some recollection. When I showed her a photo of us on a bus in Athens, she mentioned Sayulita, which was a place we had stayed in Mexico, but then she agreed with me that the photo was taken in Athens. One earlier story about Allison's memory, from which I was spared by Marya and didn't find out about until later is that, as I approached Allison and Marya one day, Allison didn't know I was her partner.

Allison's Brain • 151

Another good memory story from the time is that when a nurse asked Allison if she knew her name, Allison responded that it was Anne. When the nurse responded, "No it's Jen." Allison replied, "That's what I meant." When Allison was on her game, which wasn't always, her humour was very often evident.

The following day, when a physiotherapist came to see Allison, she was unable to follow instructions. Christine Moore was on holidays at the time, and it may have been the case that having someone else take Christine's spot was too much for Allison's brain to process. We have come to learn that people with brain injuries cope well in familiar situations, but changes in the environment can be challenging.

Next Allison was placed in quarantine, as it was suspected that she might be harbouring a virus. Hospitals can't be too careful in trying to prevent the transmission of viruses to other patients, so anyone entering Allison's room had to don a hospital gown and gloves. Allison's friend Ruth McEwen came for a visit, and Allison managed to convey to both of us that she was tired and wanted to be alone. Ruth got pretty excited about this, as she said it showed that Allison was back to being herself. Ruth also pointed out that

Allison found it easier to make conversation when there was no music playing.

While Allison was in the hospital, Ruth's father died. I brought Allison a sympathy card, and explained to her what had happened. Allison appeared to think for a moment, and then wrote Ruth a message.

The following day, Allison was apparently dancing briefly with the physiotherapist and knew her name and the hospital name — but not the month or the year or my name. Allison managed to tell Marya she was feeling overwhelmed, so we scaled back the visitors. The next day the quarantine was lifted, and Allison showed some cognitive gains. She remembered JoAnne Sulzenko had brought her a Musician's Dictionary and spoke quite clearly to Dr. Lesiuk, introducing me as her husband Robert. This made such an impact that Dr. Lesiuk saw signs of progress and said Allison would "definitely" benefit from rehab.

However, while Allison was waiting for shunt surgery, she took another nosedive.

> **From:** Allison Woyiwada
> **Sent:** July 30, 2012 9:42 PM
> **To:** Allison's Brain
> **Subject:** Week Ten Update

Hi

Allison remains in the Neurosciences Acute Care Unit after an up and down week. For a few days early in the week, she was quarantined on a suspected basis that turned out to be a false alarm. By Friday and Saturday, she was in high form and becoming quite loquacious (although a fair bit of the time we didn't understand her). On Friday afternoon she introduced me to Dr. Lesiuk as "Robert" and he assured her that we'd met before. She then proceeded to work very hard to string words together in sensible sentences and managed to get out a few. This was such a success that Dr. Lesiuk announced that he saw progress and he agreed that Allison was "definitely" going to benefit from rehabilitation therapy (this was a marked departure from his normally guarded comments).

Friday evening also produced a bright "Hi Gord" when Gordon and Pamela came to visit followed by a couple of gems. When I asked Allison whether she remembered the restaurant where we sometimes go with Gordon and Pamela her reply was, "When you were invited?" Following this I said that I was going to Carol's for dinner whereupon Allison immediately said, "so much for us then." I am advised that this level of gaiety continued on Saturday evening and that Allison was at some points requesting assistance to leave and giving out instructions.

Unfortunately, Sunday and Monday have seen Allison become quite inactive and uncommunicative for reasons that are not yet apparent. Dr. Lesiuk says "the usual causes" will be investigated. Allison has had her new shunt installation postponed a few times already, and Dr. Lesiuk advises that the OR logjam of emergencies is about the worst he has ever seen. We are nevertheless still hoping the shunt will be installed soon and that Allison can exit Acute

*Care, move into the InPatient Unit, and then proceed
before long to Saint Vincent's.*

*Quite a few of you ask me how I am doing, so here is a shot
at that. It is quite an adjustment, to say the least, to live
alone after having lived with such a full-of-life person for
sixteen years. Coupled with Allison's ups and downs in the
hospital, the best description I can think of is an emotional
roller coaster ride. Fortunately, thanks to exercise, nose-
to-the-grindstone work habits, and the support of friends,
there are far more ups than downs.*

*Don't forget to circle Sunday, September 23rd on your
calendars for attendance at Southminster Church in
Ottawa for the evening benefit concert for Allison. If you
have questions about the concert please send them to Marya
directly as I am not involved with the concert at all.*

*All for now,
Bob*

*P.S. I'm advised that Allison's new blog site will be live
soon and based on a sneak preview I can tell you that it is
going to be really terrific. Also, Allison continues to enjoy
old-fashioned "snail mail" and you have been great to send
her so much of it.*

Allison had to be restrained a good deal of the time while
waiting for shunt surgery, for she was hooked up to a brain drain
and had no concept of the harm she could do to herself by moving
about. This made her very unhappy and she lobbied a lot to get out
of the hospital. It felt awful visiting with Allison when she had to
be restrained, and most nurses would let us remove a restraint if we
were sitting beside her. Removing the restraints was no easy task
though, and I think even Houdini would have been challenged.

Then there was a frightening period when Allison became completely non-responsive. I happened to have ridden with a neurologist during the 170k biking event, and having found that Allison's

Allison's Brain • **155**

Dilantin level was much too high, I emailed him to ask whether it could be responsible for her comatose state. Dr. Sitwell replied that it was possible and that the only way to tell was to bring down the level a bit. I roused Allison a bit by showing her some coverage of Canada's first medal in the Summer Olympics, and she gazed intently at the *Globe and Mail* for a long time, although for part of the time it was sideways. She finally smiled at me when I tried to take the paper from her so she could eat dinner. However, she barely spoke a word to several of her visitors, to the point where some of us thought she was depressed.

Sharon Chartier notes that on one of her visits Allison had a bed bath and then had lunch, whereas the two events should have been in the reverse order. Allison finally had her shunt surgery on August 2nd, but remained non-communicative after the surgery. Friends who visited during this period mainly noted that Allison was sleeping a lot. The only sign of any life was that the fingers on her left hand were keeping time to Beatles songs. When I visited on August 4th, I said hello several times and sat by her side holding her hand, but she didn't look at me or show any sign of recognition. I was advised by nurse Bella that the neurologists couldn't identify a problem. Fortunately, on the weekend she rallied a bit.

> **From:** Allison Woyiwada
> **Sent:** August 06, 2012 9:31 PM
> **To:** Allison's Brain
> **Subject:** Week Eleven Update
>
> *Hi*
>
> *Allison remains in the Neuroscience Acute Care Unit at the Civic Hospital. She had a new shunt installed on Thursday a.m. and her external drain was removed; however, her non-responsiveness, which began a week ago, continued on Thursday and Friday. A neuro-team visited her on Friday afternoon and said they couldn't detect any neurological (as opposed to neurosurgical) reason for Allison's downturn (beginning on Sunday July 29th).*

After this period of non-responsiveness, this past Saturday brought a somewhat brighter day for Allison, which fortunately continued on Sunday. Allison was also in quite good form at dinner this (Monday) evening, sitting up in her chair and eating on her own for the most part (albeit a bit indelicately at times). She was also fairly talkative during dinner, although I can't really say about what. Also, as is often the case when she isn't laid low by one thing or another, she appeared to understand pretty much everything said to her, and she also appeared to remember the events / scenes in some photos I showed her on my laptop before dinner (although she did nod off periodically). Deirdre was greeted warmly by name when she arrived during dinner, and it's also possible that Allison had some instructions for me when I was leaving (although once again, I can't really say about what :)).

The recorded highlight of the week from my perspective (the unrecorded highlights being, of course, much more difficult to relate), was the MacDonalds' afternoon visit with Allison this past Sunday. Pat wrote in Allison's journal, in part: "Allison is enjoying the music and does a bit of conducting. When Doug and I tried singing some G&S we got conducting and even a cut-off — very precise and on the beat. ... Music gets Allison engaged. I encourage anyone who comes to bring some music, G&S or whatever, show Allison the book while you sing it to her. She really focuses on it for a long time. We brought a book of songs from the 50s (That's Amore, Fly Me to the Moon stuff) and even when we stopped singing she was still responding and engaged. I always remind her when I am there that I know words are hard but that they will come like they did for Raymond. Allison did attempt a few words here and there and was answering yes..." Also, in a less notable matter, Allison chose a peach for dessert (that I had brought

Allison's Brain • **157**

*for her), over the hospital's strawberries, pronouncing the
word "fresh."*

*We continue to hope that Allison will not need to be in
the Neuroscience Acute Care Unit much longer and that
she can be moved before very long to the Neuroscience
InPatient Unit, and then to Saint Vincent's where her
rehab work will begin in earnest. As I've mentioned
previously, there will be a benefit Concert at Southminster
Church at 7:00 p.m. on Sunday September 23rd to raise $$
for Allison's uninsured medical and rehabilitation expenses.
Tickets will be available at the Ottawa Folklore Centre
(and online when her blog site is completed).*

*As many of you suggested, I've registered Allison's Yaris
lease with leasebusters. It's not official though until lease-
busters gets back to me.*

*All for now,
Bob*

*P.S. Donations towards Allison's uninsured medical and
rehab expenses can also be made by cheque payable to
Robert McMechan. Cheques should be marked "in trust for
Allison" and will be deposited in her trust account.*

On August 7th, Marya got Allison back outside with the assistance of nurse Ratna, and on August 8th, Allison was moved back to the Neuroscience InPatient Unit. We spoke on the phone in the morning, and she sounded quite perky. Unfortunately she had a very troubled roommate, which was very distracting.

Also on August 8th Marya sent out an email regarding the benefit concert.

> **From:** Marya Woyiwada
> **Sent:** August 08, 2012 5:14 PM
> **To:** multiple contacts
> **Subject:** Benefit Concert for Allison Woyiwada

Hi All,

As you may or may not know, my mom has been recovering from an extensive brain surgery since May 28th. Although the surgery very likely saved her life, my mom now has significant cognitive and physical deficits that require extensive rehabilitation therapy. To relieve some of her rehabilitation and related medical expenses, I'm hosting a benefit concert to raise funds. Details below. Please visit the web woyiwada.blogspot.ca, and help spread the word about the concert and donations. See attached poster if you're able to print and post.

I'm also looking for volunteers to help with dropping off posters door-to-door in Old Ottawa South and the Glebe, and going to businesses in the area to see if they'll put up a poster.

Thank you for your support,
Marya

WHAT: Benefit concert to raise funds for rehabilitation and related medical expenses

WHEN: September 23, 2012, 7:00 p.m.

WHERE: Southminster United Church , 15 Aylmer Avenue, Ottawa.

WHO: Host Rob Clipperton

Singers Isabelle Lacroix, Marya Woyiwada, Sandra Graham, Dillon Parmer, Fraser Rubens, and Denis Lawlor with pianist Jean Desmarais;

Pianist/organist Matthew Larkin with trumpeter Nick Cochrane;

Hopewell School Jazz Band conducted by Blair Smith;

Members of the Savoy Society of Ottawa, featuring Shawne Elizabeth, accompanied by Robert Palmai;

Southminster United Church Choir conducted by Roland Graham.

Tickets are available at the Ottawa Folklore Centre or online at woyiwada.blogspot.ca

A Celebration of Music

Help raise funds for rehabilitation and related medical expenses

from extensive brain surgery for award-winning music teacher Allison

The next few days involved lots of sleeping when noise levels permitted; listening to music; looking at the *Globe and Mail*; and receiving visitors with varying levels of enthusiasm. Marya took a photo of her mother in bed on August 13th with a blanket on her head.

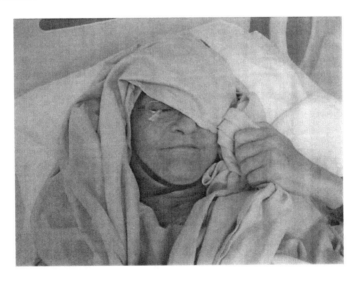

The Week Twelve *Allison's Brain* update came next.

From: Allison Woyiwada
Sent: August 13, 2012 7:54 AM
To: Allison's Brain
Subject: Week Twelve Update

Hi

The highlight of the past week is that Allison has been moved out of Acute Care back to the Neuroscience InPatient Unit. However, Allison has not recovered the enthusiasm and steam she had before her recent setbacks, and we are looking for this to occur in time. In the words of our friend Cynthia Taylor, who has been more than around-the-block with this type of experience (and even stayed in the same InPatient Unit room when she had a serious brain injury two plus years ago), it is extremely important to emphasize to Allison that she will be able to speak clearly in time, and that she will eventually be able to resume activities she loves. Cynthia also points out how difficult things are when one's brain is in such a fragile state, and she puts it very helpfully when she says that the things we normally take for granted in our lives as part of the background are all part of the foreground after a serious brain injury.

Dr. Lesiuk has mentioned that he is not certain the ventricle drainage level is correct yet, and he says there is some expert judgment involved in determining this level. His plan is to keep monitoring the size of Allison's ventricles (as I understand it) and he says that if the drainage level is not correct, this will affect her progress. Dr. Lesiuk has now gone for a richly-deserved two week vacation, and Dr. John Sinclair (who also has a wonderful reputation) is the neurosurgeon standing in for Dr. Lesiuk during his vacation.

Allison's Brain • **161**

Allison's blog has been released (woyiwada.blogspot.com) and it generated more than 2,000 visits in a short time. In a similar vein, more than 50 people signed on to attend Allison's September 23rd benefit concert in Ottawa within 48 hours of being invited (and this before the publicity for the concert has been much yet in the public domain). Several people have also left splendid tributes on Allison's Facebook site, speaking of what a wonderful music teacher she has been and how lucky they are to have had her as their teacher. When I read tributes of this kind to Allison she is clearly moved by them and she truly appreciates what's being written.

The donations towards Allison's uninsured medical and rehabilitation expenses have been arriving and they are being deposited in her trust fund. We plan to put this money to very good use, when Allison is in a position to begin receiving regular speech and occupational therapy. She is now once again receiving physiotherapy, although her movement is restricted by medical machines. Courtesy of Pat MacDonald, the primary offender has been decorated with a drawing by the name of "Bob," and I confess to now sometimes feeling at least a little bit useful.

Thank you for your support!

All for now,
Bob

P.S. Allison has not been able to watch the Olympic Games (apart from part of the closing ceremony with Marya which she enjoyed) but she has shown quite a lot of interest in the photos in the Olympic section of the Globe. I recorded the closing ceremony for her as the music and theatre were often quite spectacular, and she will love watching it when she is back home.

P.P.S. My friend Ian McNaughton has dedicated his upcoming Ironman at Mont-Tremblant to his Mother and to Allison!

Later on the 13th Allison had a visit from Marianna, Micheal and Stefanie Burch. Stefanie had made Allison a huge get well card, and Marianna had scored two pair of New York pyjamas for Allison.

Then Marya had an illuminating telephone conversation with a speech therapist in Montreal.

From: Marya Woyiwada
Sent: August 20, 2012 9:13 PM
To: Robert McMechan
Subject: speech pathology

Jean's sister is a speech therapist, and I had the honour of having a 45-minute long conversation with her on the phone today. Since she did not see mum in person, she cannot do a proper analysis (she lives in Montreal) but based on the extensive details I gave her, she was able to give me a number of suggestions, that I thought I should share with you.

1) I mentioned that mom is not good with choice, i.e. when I ask her if she'd prefer salmon or steak for dinner, she has difficulty with that. Chantal indicated that we should work with brain injured patients the same way we work with children, in that we have to access all of their learning styles. The best approach is a multi-modal one. So when asking her which dish she would prefer, Chantal suggests we draw in and write it, as well as say it. She thinks that mum doesn't understand as much of what we're saying as she lets on.

2) Chantal uses iPad applications that have nice pictures of things with one word underneath, in her current therapy. It's like a more sophisticated, less demeaning version of flash cards, also stimulating multi-modally. She highly recommends this.

3) She suggested that, in spite of the fact that mum knows what order numbers go in, when taken out of context and when adding more complex elements, she may need some assistance. I'm going to make her a number strip to put on her wheelchair tray.

5) An easy thing to do about the dictée is to make 5 squares so that she knows to stop.

6) If we do choose to use flash cards, they should be meaningful for her. Something that represents things that interest her. She might find regular flash cards boring and irritating. We can also get her to write using the flashcards.

7) Chantal understands why they're not doing thorough evaluations at this point. There is clearly a lot of healing happening, and things are continuously progressing. This is good because it means that she hasn't hit a plateau!

8) Mum has access to words but words are stored according to 2 rules 1) sound, 2) meaning. Sonological rules are a little jumbled up for mum. Chantal thinks with practice that can get sorted out.

9) For reading, newspapers are ideal because of all the pictures and such. Either way, whether or not she's understanding the content, she's likely enjoying the act of scanning the letters. When you're reading something with her, write the word on a separate piece of paper and draw it also. It's all about multi-modal.

10) For someone in her situation, it's more likely that the reading and writing are more impaired than listening and talking.

11) Keep reading sentences short.

She said to try these things and call her in a couple weeks, and let her know how it goes. At that time she'll give me more advice.

This was a lot of good advice and it helped a lot. Marya had begun doing dictées with her mother and she was having a bit of success. Marya also began posting a daily events calendar for Allison, and we crossed off events as they occurred throughout the day, so she would know what was happening. I also began doing simple iPad exercises with Allison, with varying degrees of success. She got quite good at identifying the object out of four that didn't match the other three, but another exercise involving dragging objects from the left to match the related object on the right didn't go well, as she kept using her right hand to try to move the stationary object. I would explain to Allison why this didn't work, she would appear to understand, and then she would do it again.

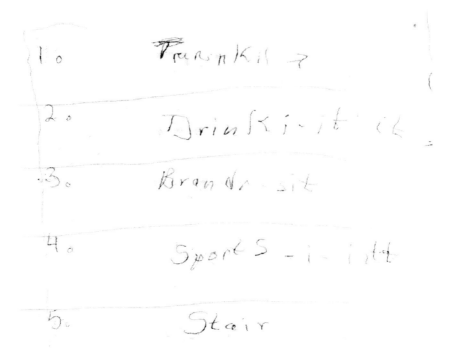

The Week Thirteen *Allison's Brain* update was pretty positive.

From: Allison Woyiwada
Sent: August 21, 2012 6:56 AM
To: Allison's Brain
Subject: Week Thirteen Update

Hi

Allison has had a good week and seems to have regained the ground she'd reached before her various medical setbacks (described in week seven to nine updates). Her tolerance for noise has improved, and she is now in a standard room with two roommates in the Neuroscience InPatient Unit. Having roommates has for the most part been a success, although the first night involved a lot of commotion and shrieking until the offending roommate was removed. Since then Allison has had a variety of roommates, including an otherwise nice lady by the name of Gloria, who inquired as to whether I was Allison's father. Gloria was removed shortly afterwards.

When Allison is alert, she has become quite chatty again although her speech is very often mixed up and she has difficulty finding the right words. One evening last week, after I opened the wrong end of Allison's milk carton, I asked her how she'd gotten hooked up with such a doofus, and she was unable to explain this. (My ego is in no way assisted by reminders that Allison has taken quite a shine to the male physiotherapist!) Marya has gotten valuable suggestions (we think) from a friend's sister, who is a speech therapist working in Montreal, as to how to encourage Allison's progress with language. However, Allison's responses are not always off-the-mark, and she remains possessed of determination and a positive attitude. This determination sometimes results in her being restrained again, as her growing strength exceeds her judgment. On the positive attitude front, Marya says that when she told her mother "life is tough" in relation to a relatively minor matter Allison responded, "no it's not."

We continue to hope that all of the medical hurdles Allison is dealing with will soon be overcome and that she will be able to benefit before long from regular, organized occupational and speech therapy, etc. In that regard we are very appreciative of the enthusiasm being shown for Allison's benefit concert at 7:00 p.m. on Sunday September 23rd at Southminster Church in Ottawa and for the extremely generous donations to her trust fund.

We are also very grateful to those of you who have been able to visit with Allison (and do your best to lift up her spirits when she seemed to be depressed — we now speculate this had to do with meds or brain-fluid level, etc). Music

Allison's Brain • **167**

*continues to be a constant companion and joy for Allison,
and she would be very badly off without it.*

*Allison's blog is located at Allison's Brain woyiwada.
blogspot.com/*

*All for now,
Bob*

*P.S. In yet another remarkable illustration of the brain's
recuperative powers, David Palamar tells me that he spoke
with an airline pilot in Tulsa recently. She told him that
she had suffered a serious brain injury in an auto accident
which left her in a state of confusion for two years. She
is now back working as an airline pilot. This afternoon
Jim Wegg also told me that the ABI clinic at the General
Hospital does remarkable work with people who have
brain injuries. We expect Allison to go to this clinic after she
has progressed through Saint Vincent's.*

The daily hospital visits coupled with full time tax practice were
quite draining, and I accepted an offer from Sharon Chartier and
Dan Hermosa to stay at their cottage at Lac Xavier and watch the
Mont Tremblant Ironman, in order to get a bit of a break. I left on
a Saturday after visiting in the morning and returned on Sunday
evening. After I'd been home for a couple of days, I got this email
from Mary Wilson.

From: Mary Wilson
Sent: August 21, 2012 7:30 AM
To: Allison Woyiwada
Subject: Re: Week Thirteen Update

Hi, Bob

*Just a follow-up from my visit with Allison on Saturday.
At one point she said to me very clearly. "People become
invisible, you know. Even you. It happened to Bob."*

I think that meant she missed you!

Mary Wilson

Evidence that Allison's form was improving was starting to show up once in a while. I sent this update to the family on August 24th.

> **From:** Robert McMechan
> **Sent:** August 24, 2012 6:00 PM
> **To:** Tyler Woyiwada; Laurie Souchotte; Phil McMechan; Jim Rennie; Bette-Lou Paragg; Joan Veselovsky
> **Cc:** Marya Woyiwada
> **Subject:** "It comes and goes"
>
> *Allison used this phrase to describe how she feels when we were talking about her level of understanding this P.M. She is now, again today, perusing the Ottawa Citizen with great interest after dinner. Her sense of reality, e.g. that we're not going out this evening, still needs work!*
>
> *Marya says she actually heard the word "discharge" used today. We are having a meeting with the social worker Monday.*
>
> *Bob*

It's difficult for Allison to pinpoint any memories she has from the preceding three months. However, Allison recalls a visit from Alastair Green and Carol Anderson on August 26th. Alastair and Carol are very memorable people, but it seems that there may also have been things percolating in Allison's brain.

Allison's Brain • **169**

6.
Beethoven's Sonata Pathétique

An amazing development out-of-the-blue on August 27th seemed to be a springboard for Allison's progress in the weeks ahead. I describe the events of that day in the Week Fourteen Update.

From: Allison Woyiwada
Sent: August 27, 2012 8:41 PM
To: Allison's Brain
Subject: Week Fourteen Update

Hi,

The most remarkable thing happened today! Allison has been weaned off the IV that's been administering blood thinner, and so her mobility is greatly improved. Marya took her mom to a piano at the Civic which happened to have a piece of sheet music on it. Allison proceeded to sight-read and play the 2nd movement of Beethoven's Sonata Pathétique. *None of us expected her to be able to do this. The rest of this update pales in comparison.*

Allison has had another good week in the Neuroscience InPatient Unit. She continues to become physically stronger and is often quite talkative, although understanding what she means to say is not without difficulty. Her comprehension generally seems to be quite high, and in her own words with respect to how things are going on the cognitive front, "it comes and goes." One among many examples of this is that while one day she was talking about accessing the second and third floors in our house, days later my reference to our house appeared to leave her bewildered. Steady work with elementary iPad games has resulted in good improvement in her results. Marya has also had good success giving her mom some simple dictées. We are hoping this bodes well for her upcoming work with skilled occupational and speech therapists when she is moved to a rehabilitation centre.

In that regard, we met today with Jane, the social worker at the Neuroscience InPatient Unit, to discuss the next steps. Dr. Lesiuk is back at work, and the first order of business is that he is planning to replace the missing skull piece. When one sees the great concave on the left side of Allison's head and compares it with the large swelling at that point previously, there is no doubting the wisdom of the neurosurgeons in leaving the restoration until now. Following this procedure, which we are told is uncomplicated and can be day surgery for outpatients, Allison will be evaluated again by doctors from the Acquired Brain Injury Clinic. If she is ready for aggressive rehab at that point, she will be re-located to the ABI Clinic. If slower rehab is required initially, an application will be made to Saint Vincent's and the Civic doctors will do a comprehensive neuropsychological evaluation to identify Allison's rehabilitation needs. In either case, this will be a giant leap forward on the rehabilitation efforts front. Jane also tells us that Dr. Lesiuk emphasizes that these are "early days" in Allison's recovery.

Lately a visit with Allison is rarely a dull affair. Alastair Green reports that when he asked Allison what meals the hospital prepares best her response was "they don't." Then Allison reflected a bit on this and added "no they don't."

Allison's Brain • **171**

This was while she was eating. Allison's good humour and positiveness are front and centre although occasionally (this will surprise you) she likes to have her own way. The nurses say that a degree of feistiness, which is sometimes evident, is better for Allison's progress than complacency — which we don't see.

Publicity for the benefit concert at 7:00 p.m. on Sunday September 23rd at Southminster Church is making its way into the public domain. I am including a copy of an article from an Ottawa community newspaper below.*

All for now and thanks for your terrific support!

Bob

P.S. Methinks I would be remiss if I didn't tell you that Allison called Marya a "brat" today. I take some delight in this, having myself been called a "dick" a few weeks ago. Although I wasn't present for the occasion, my understanding is that the "brat" business had to do with Marya declining to pack up Allison and bring her home.

[*Some parts of this article have been omitted to avoid repetition of content.]

The OSCAR — OUR 40th YEAR SEPTEMBER 2012
Chance to give back to community builder
By Kelly Ray

Allison Woyiwada has been front and centre in the music education and performing arts fields in Ottawa for almost three decades. Well known in Old Ottawa South as Hopewell Avenue Public School's music teacher from 1982 to 2008, she spent thousands of volunteer hours directing extra-curricular school bands, leading school band trips, and staging student musicals. As a recent-retiree, Allison has continued to touch lives through music through work

172 • *Robert McMechan with Allison Woyiwada*

*with the Savoy Society of Ottawa and has performed in
'Le nozze di Figaro'.*

*Things changed for Allison, however, in late in 2011 when
she was diagnosed with a "giant" brain aneurysm. Allison
had a ten-hour "clipping" operation at the Heart Institute
in Ottawa on May 28, 2012.*

*Although the surgery very likely saved Allison's life, she
now has significant cognitive and physical deficits that
require extensive rehabilitation therapy. Allison's basic
post-teaching insurance coverage only provides limited
benefits for rehabilitation therapy. There will also be a
significant monthly fee once Allison reaches the stage when
she can be released from hospital and accommodated in
the restorative program at the Saint-Vincent Hospital in
Ottawa.*

*The Ottawa music community is hosting a benefit concert to
raise funds for Allison's rehabilitation and related medical
expenses. "For a woman who has been so instrumental in
the community," said Nick Cochrane, former student and
trumpeter at the Benefit Concert. "It is a pleasure to have
a tangible way to give back in this way. I encourage all to
attend the concert, donate online, or see how they can help
out."*

It would be hard to overstate the emotional and psychological impact of Allison's piano performance. Marya showed a video of it to Jane Mahoney, who then showed it to Dr. Lesiuk. It seemed incredible that Allison could concentrate for such an extended period when playing the piano, given her difficulties with attention span and focus. Allison's playing wasn't perfect, but it was a very moving and uplifting few moments. Later the CBC did an outstanding eight minute segment, in advance of Allison's benefit concert, which included this incredible story. I have to warn you though that it's a real tear-jerker.

Allison's Brain • **173**

http://www.cbc.ca/player/Radio/Local+Shows/Ontario/ID/2282127708/

Late in 2013, while preparing to write *Allison's Brain*, I was going through archives and came across the original video. Allison saw it then for the first time. She pointed out that when she was seated at the piano she recognized that her hand position was incorrect, and so she moved them down an octave. This just reinforces the view that we began to formulate at the time. Despite Allison's deficits, her brain was high functioning in some respects, and we could hope to see improvements in her given time and lots of work. As Allison had never been shy about lots of work, the prospects for recovery were there.

The following day, after taking Allison for a wheelchair ride in one of her fancy new sets of New York pyjamas, I did some Internet searching on the iPad. I don't know why, but Allison suggested searching for "George." Then Allison became quite fascinated by how her bed moved up and down just by pressing some buttons. She talked quite a lot, but also used a lot of words that didn't fit very well.

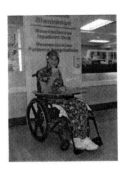

On the 29th I emailed the family with some fantastic news.

From: Robert McMechan
Sent: August 29, 2012 11:38 AM
To: Laurie Souchotte; Phil McMechan; Kristie McMechan; Bette-Lou Paragg; Joan Veselovsky; Jim Rennie
Subject: Fantastic news!

Allison just accepted into the Acquired Brain Injury Institute for aggressive rehab. This means she is not going to Saint Vincent's for slow recovery and likely advances the time that Allison can come home by a few months!

Dad/Bob.

P.S. She is supposed to have bone flap surgery this week or next and is now on a waiting list to go to the ABI Clinic.

The therapists considered that Allison had made large progress in the past week, and that was the reason for the reversal of the earlier decision that she was not ready for aggressive rehab. The nurses also determined that Allison didn't need her wheelchair anymore, but said she should use a walker to go to the bathroom. Well guess what — sometimes Allison decided that she didn't need to use a walker. Soon afterwards, Allison insisted to me that she didn't need to use her walker, and then she promptly fell in the bathroom. This brought a trio of nurses running; however, fortunately Allison wasn't injured.

Allison was, by now, refusing to eat many of the hospital meals, but loved our neighbour Maryna's fresh tomatoes, and said that Maryna's dessert was "awfully good."

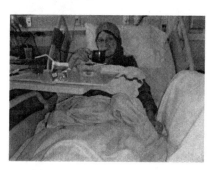

Allison had a visit from her friends Louise and Susan that went well.

From: Louise Hall
Sent: August 29, 2012 8:51 PM
To: Robert McMechan; Susan Smith

Subject: Emailing: Susan_Allison_Louise-Aug29_2012, Susan_Allison_Louise-Aug29_2012-2

Hi Bob and Susan,

Here are the pics from our visit this evening. We truly enjoyed our time together — looking forward to the next visit.

Louise

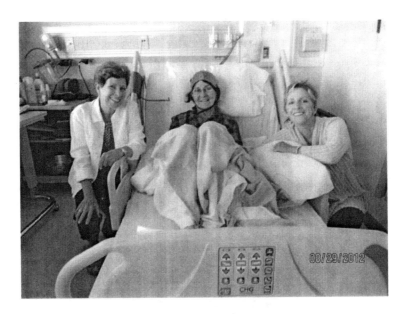

On August 30th, Allison ate her roast beef dinner with cutlery for the most part and then put on her socks and shoes, and we went outside for a walk after dinner. We walked all the way down Melrose Avenue and back, and Allison asked to stop for a rest before we got all the way back. When we returned to her room Allison said, "I should say goodbye.", and then she lay down to sleep. Allison remembers this walk and recollects that it was very frightening to be walking outside on such uneven surfaces. She also recalls thinking that she would never make it back to her bed. I recall thinking that while it was great to get out walking together again, Allison had lost so much weight and was so frail that she seemed like a very different person.

Around this time I had done some research about music therapists and sent this email to Marya.

From: Robert McMechan
Sent: August 31, 2012 3:00 PM
To: Marya Woyiwada
Subject: Music Therapy for Aphasia

There is a huge body of literature about this — I'm copying one article below. I took a look at TalkRocket, and I'm not convinced that it is what your mom needs at this point. Music therapy, on the other hand, looks to me like something we should be starting ASAP. The article below about Congresswoman Giffords is very interesting — it speaks about music therapy and "neuroplasticity" — this is something your mom read a lot about before her operation. Cheryl Jones in Ottawa has very impressive music therapy credentials — Cheryl Jones MMT, NMT-F, MTA, works as a music therapist in brain trauma and neurodegenerative disorders. She holds her Masters of Music Therapy from Wilfrid Laurier University. She has advanced training in Neurologic Music Therapy from the Bio-medical Research Centre at Colorado State University. She is a fellow of the Robert F. Unkefer Academy of Neurologic Music Therapy, is a member of the Network of Neurologic Music Therapists, and of the International Society of Clinical Neuromusicology. Cheryl is a researcher for the Conrad Institute of Music Therapy Research. She is accredited by the Canadian Association of Music Therapy. She currently resides in Ottawa, Canada, where she maintains a private practice Con Brio Music Therapy. Let's meet her.

www.cbc.ca/news/canada/story/2011/11/18/f-vp-bambury.html

I recall thinking when I came across Cheryl's website (http://conbriomusictherapy.com/) how fortunate we were to have someone with her credentials living in Ottawa. After meeting with Cheryl and seeing her work with Allison, it seems much more than just fortunate. Cheryl is now working on a Ph.D., and she has kindly contributed *The Power of Music Therapy* appendix. I'm not a rocket scientist, but I think Cheryl's work with Allison, and her explanation of it, is a real eye-opener.

Also on the 31st, I accompanied Allison and Marya to the piano in the hospital, where Allison proceeded to sight read some music. There was no problem with concentration and no sign of perseveration. In retrospect, I shouldn't have been surprised that sight reading was a strength for Allison, as she had been sight reading music for fifty years and had said that she could read music faster than the written word. I had looked at orchestra scores for performances Allison conducted and found them incomprehensible.

On September 1st, Allison was outfitted with an electronic bracelet because she'd been found wandering around the hospital. Marya took her outside in the afternoon, and she sat and lay down on the grass on the hospital grounds. I also took her outside for a walk after dinner. She again sat in the grass but couldn't get up by herself. We returned to her room, and she was happy with the paper and Mozart.

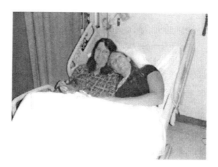

Over the next couple of days we went for walks outside and had telephone conversations with my mother, my son Phil, his wife Kristie, and my daughter Laurie. These went OK although Allison was asking Kristie about her pregnancy, and it was my daughter Laurie who was pregnant. Each night at dinner, Allison enjoyed Maryna's fresh tomatoes, and fresh fruit that I brought for dessert. I also read some Garrison Keillor stories, which Allison also seemed to find funny, and Allison played the iPad matching game in which she did well, although she couldn't remember the names of many objects.

The next *Allison's Brain* email update was quite positive.

From: Allison Woyiwada
Sent: September 4, 2012 5:44 AM
To: Allison's Brain
Subject: Week Fifteen Update

Hi

Allison has had another good week in the Neuroscience InPatient Unit. Because of the large gains she's made in the past while, she's been accepted into the aggressive rehab program at the Acquired Brain Injury (ABI) Clinic (connected to the Ottawa General Hospital) and she is on a three week waiting list. Allison will be evaluated when she arrives at the clinic and a therapy program planned for her. We visited the clinic last week and in Marya's words it looks "hardcore." There were therapists doing various kinds of therapy when we visited.

We are expecting that Allison's bone flap / skull surgery will take place sometime this week, although it remains subject to scheduling. Allison has recently been walking up a storm — to such an extent that she has to wear an electronic bracelet so the nurses can keep track of her. Before the bracelet, someone found Allison wandering around the main floor of the hospital. When leaving the 7th floor with Allison, we have to check in with the front desk so the alarm can be turned off when she goes by. A couple of evenings ago, Allison asked the staff at the front desk if it would be better if she just took the bracelet off permanently. This occasioned some mirth.

Allison has been playing the piano a fair amount lately. Although her playing doesn't meet her own exacting standards, it sounds pretty darn good to us. It is also thrilling to see her able to concentrate on something for such extended periods; plus, the problem we've been witnessing with "perseverance" seems to be diminishing.

All of this is, of course, very positive; however, there is a considerable distance to go. Allison's conversation is quite often difficult to follow (yesterday afternoon Allison chipped in with some directions to a fellow asking how to leave the hospital parking lot — this was fairly priceless), her memory is a work-in-progress (we hope), and although she is physically stronger, she has balance and stamina issues which we expect to fade with time.

Thanks so much for your wonderful support!

All for now,
Bob

P.S. Allison updates, tickets for the September 23rd benefit concert and details re donations to Allison's trust account are at http://woyiwada.blogspot.com

September 5th also brought good news, as Allison had surgery to replace the missing piece of her skull.

From: Robert McMechan
Sent: September 5, 2012 8:28 PM
To: Tyler Woyiwada; Laurie Souchotte; Phil McMechan; Jim Rennie; Bette-Lou Paragg; Joan Veselovsky
Subject: Titanium mesh installed!

Allison is back on the 7th floor this p.m. not very long after the surgery today to replace her missing skull section. She is still under anaesthetic and dozing, but when she wakes she is often smiling. I think she knows this was the last step before she can be released from the hospital! Dr Lesiuk told me yesterday that she'd be ready to leave in a couple of days; however, we have to wait for a bed to open up in the ABI Clinic. We were 3rd on the waiting list last week and the RN we met estimated 3 weeks.

Onwards and upwards!

Allison's Brain • **181**

Bob/Dad/Almost Grandpa

This next email might be overkill but what the hell ...

> **From:** Pauline Lynch-Stewart
> **Sent:** September 5, 2012 8:49 PM
> **To:** Robert McMechan
> **Subject:** RE: Titanium mesh installed!
>
> *I think she's smiling because her favourite tax lawyer is sitting there.*
>
> *Congrats to both of you for jumping yet another hurdle!*

For the next couple of days following surgery Allison slept a lot. She also made it difficult for the nurses to clean the incision from her surgery, as she didn't want them touching her head. I remember at the time thinking that the nurses were really earning their money. I went over a calendar with Allison and showed her the weeks that she was expected to be at the rehab centre. She was not happy about this at all, and thought she should be going home. We also watched some movies on a mini DVD player.

On September 8th, Cheryl Jones came to meet Allison at the hospital while Marya and I were there, to explain the music therapy she was offering. It seemed to me that Allison liked her instantly, and her fondness for Cheryl has only grown over time. Cheryl sent us a written proposal the following day.

> **From:** Cheryl Jones
> **Sent:** September 9, 2012 8:54 PM
> **To:** Robert McMechan
> **Subject:** Music Therapy
>
> *Dear Mr. McMechan,*
>
> *In follow-up to our meeting yesterday, I would recommend Allison participate in two 30-minute Neuro Music Therapy sessions per week.*

The primary goals would be: 1) to support Allison to initiate and speak specific phrases. The NMT objective for this goal will be Melodic Intonation Therapy (MIT), using melodic fragments to cue word access and support word fluency; 2) to provide opportunity for word access, fluency. The objective used for this goal will be singing of familiar songs.

Allison will also be encouraged to continue playing the piano, reading previously learned pieces and sight-reading new or less familiar pieces. Playing the piano will serve to provide a multi-site neural stimulus, provide opportunity for Allison to be non-verbally self-expressive, and to affirm and celebrate her skill and what she can do.

Please feel free to contact me with any questions.

Sincerely,
Cheryl Jones

We learned on September 10th that a room had come open at the rehab centre on the 13th.

From: Robert McMechan
Sent: September 10, 2012 10:53 AM
To: Jane Mahoney
Cc: Marya Woyiwada
Subject: Hi Jane

Hi Jane,

We've just been informed that the ABI Clinic has a bed for Allison beginning Thursday this week, and we'd like to thank you for all of your excellent help! There is a benefit concert being held at 7:00 p.m. on Sunday September 23rd at Southminster Church (Bank Street at Aylmer — near Sunnyside) and if you are able to attend we are delighted to give you a couple of complimentary tickets. In other news, we've met with a music therapist who we are

Allison's Brain • **183**

engaging to help with the restoration of Allison's speech. She has asked whether it is possible to have a copy of the speech therapist's report and any other document that will help her understand the extent and exact location of Allison's brain injury? Also, if she is able to do a (30 minute) session with Allison before the move to the ABI Clinic, she is wondering if there is a room available that will be private?

Thanks again,
Robert

From: Jane Mahoney
Sent: September 10, 2012 11:10 AM
To: Robert McMechan
Cc: Marya Woyiwada
Subject: RE: Hi Jane

HI there,

Now how did you hear that so quickly!!??? I just got the 'official' bed offer a few minutes ago!! She is going to Room # 2204-2 under the care of Dr. Marshall on Thursday. They would like her there around 9:30, so we will book the ambulance around 9:00'ish.

Thank you for your kind words… and the offer of the tickets… I'm out of town that day, visiting my daughter at Queens! But it looks like an amazing event!

I can print off the speech assessment for you and see what other documents there may be that would be helpful. Just as an FYI, if the therapist comes here, she will need to jump through a few hoops with our manager with respect to getting access to Allison, i.e. proof of insurance and a few things like that. Sue Longbottom is our manager at ext. 13259.

Take good care. It has been a real pleasure working with you guys... I wish only wonderful and great things ahead for all of you. I will leave the papers that I print off at the nursing station for you. Just tell the clerk there is an envelope in the 'social work box' for you.

Jane

Marya sent me a funny email in the evening on the 10th that led to a colourful (depending on your point-of-view) exchange.

From: Marya Woyiwada
Sent: September 10, 2012 7:22 PM
To: Robert McMechan
Subject: She just saw a guy walking alone...

And thought to herself, 'I'm gonna be that guy someday'

From: Robert McMechan
Sent: September 10, 2012 7:27 PM
To: Marya Woyiwada
Subject: She just saw a guy walking alone...

She's a constant riot — even funnier now than she used to be. Please tell her I'll be in to see her again as soon as my cold germs are gone and that I miss her a lot!

From: Marya Woyiwada
Sent: September 10, 2012 7:37 PM
To: Robert McMechan
Subject: Re: She just saw a guy walking alone...

She said 'aw', giggled, and called u a sweetie. Gag...

The Week Sixteen Update to the *Allison's Brain* group had lots of good news.

From: Allison Woyiwada
Sent: September 10, 2012 8:00 PM

Allison's Brain • 185

To: Allison's Brain
Subject: Week Sixteen Update

Hi

Allison has had another good week, and events are finally moving quickly! Allison had her missing skull piece replaced with titanium mesh last week, and she is no longer required to wear a helmet. Plus, the ABI clinic where she is going next for aggressive rehab has had a bed open up much earlier than expected, and Allison is moving this Thursday. She isn't thrilled about not coming home at this juncture, but she understands that the therapy work now begins in earnest and that there is a ton of work to be done to re-establish her speech, etc.

In that regard we met on the weekend with Cheryl Jones, a music therapist who has excellent credentials and a wonderful manner. Allison was going to start music therapy sessions with Cheryl right away but now we'll wait and see how the music therapy fits in with the comprehensive ABI program before proceeding.

...

Cheryl established a rapport with Allison in a short time and Allison is keen about proceeding with the music therapy. Marya was initially concerned that someone with so many academic qualifications might be "nerdy" but this wasn't the case.

We are very pleased to be receiving such a great response for the benefit concert and generous donation support!

Details about the benefit concert and Allison's trust fund are found at woyiwada.blogspot.com

All for now,
Bob

P.S. It has been reliably reported today by Jill Berry that Allison has solemnly pronounced that "Bob is a fine fellow." I thought I should mention this in light of all of your serious concerns about the "brat" business that I mentioned last week.

The next email from Sharon Chartier on September 11th came as a surprise. Unfortunately because of my cold, I missed the excitement of the next few days.

From: Sharon Chartier
Sent: September 11, 2012 12:30 PM
To: Robert McMechan
Subject: Do you know Allison is heading to the General today at 2 pm???

Sharon then emailed us again in the mid-afternoon.

From: Sharon Chartier
Sent: September 11, 2012 3:03 PM
To: Robert McMechan; Marya Woyiwada
Subject: Room 2204, bed 2

Ward C Physio and occupational therapist are here seeing what Allison can do.

Dr Lesiuk came in just before she left the Civic and gave her the green light.

She is to see him in 4 to 6 weeks for a checkup.

Sharon

I asked Sharon by email how Allison was responding to the sudden change.

From: Sharon Chartier
Sent: September 11, 2012 3:17 PM
To: Robert McMechan
Subject: Re: Room 2204, bed 2

Allison's Brain • **187**

She is talking quite clearly, but it doesn't necessarily make a lot of sense. She is tired, and I have told them she normally naps a good 2 hours in the pm, so we will get her in bed very soon.

Marya arrived shortly afterwards and was briefed by the nurses. I sent out a family update.

From: Robert McMechan
Sent: September 11, 2012 8:09 PM
To: Laurie Souchotte; Phil McMechan; Bette-Lou Paragg; Joan Veselovsky; Jim Rennie; Tyler Woyiwada
Subject: Allison's New Quarters

Allison was moved ahead of schedule today to the ABI Clinic where she will be getting lots of therapy. The staff told Marya today that a normal stay is 8–12 weeks but that Allison's stay may be somewhat longer. I haven't gone to the Clinic yet as I am nursing a cold.

Acquired Brain Injury Program

http://www.ottawahospital.on.ca/wps/portal/ Base/TheHospital/ClinicalServices/DeptPgrmCS/ Departments/RehabilitationCentre/

The Ottawa Hospital Rehabilitation Centre's (TOHRC) Acquired Brain Injury Care Stream provides a range of patient-centered care from the acute stage to the community. It delivers goal-oriented therapeutic assessment and intervention that address cognitive, behavioural, psychosocial and physical needs. The goal of the care stream is to maximize function in individuals with a brain injury.

It seems like a long haul but at least the rehabilitation is finally getting started!

Dad / Bob

I will add here that throughout Allison's more than three months at the Ottawa Hospital Civic Campus we could see that she was being looked after by a terrific bunch of nurses. It can't be easy to work with brain-injured patients on a regular basis, and it takes a lot of patience and skill to do what they do. The handwritten notes that the nurses make though are another matter. I've always taken it as a given that doctors have horrible handwriting, but it seems that most nurses are not outdone in this respect. Having tried to decipher a few hundred pages of hospital records, which include a lot of nurses' notes, I am sort of an expert in this regard. However, for the months of June through August, I did make out a number of recurring entries.

I've excerpted a bunch of these entries from the hospital records, as they show a good deal about Allison's cognitive state. Beginning in June in NACU, it was noted: "Patient mouthing words at times but incomprehensible." Throughout the summer there was a similar refrain. "Patient gets distracted easily." "Not answering questions correctly or even appropriately." "Patient is verbalizing but presents with cognitive deficit." "Patient remains pleasantly confused." "Patient confused and disoriented." "Remains pleasantly disoriented and very talkative." "Ø orientation to place, time. Often drifts to other subjects, confused when speaking." "Patient confused and answers questions inappropriately." "Responds to questions with inappropriate words." "Word salad persists." "Confused to place, year and reason for admission. Surprised to hear that she had brain surgery." "Patient having animated conversations but not always making sense." "Speech continues to be confused." "Confused and disoriented, inappropriate speech." "Difficult to communicate with patient due to expressive aphasia."

However, the Occupational Therapist's notes on August 27th foreshadowed what was just ahead for Allison. "Patient continues to be pleasant, cooperative and motivated to participate in therapy."

Allison's Brain • **189**

7.

ABI Rehab and the Benefit Concert

Allison wasn't a happy camper on her first day in rehab. We were aware there could be adjustment problems, as people with brain injuries do not adapt quickly to change and are typically happier in a familiar environment. In retrospect, Allison recalls being upset because someone started taking stitches out of her head. I'm guessing that taking time to discuss this with Allison would have helped to make her feel better. In any event, we were very happy that Allison was at the rehab centre because she would finally be getting an extensive program of various types of rehabilitation therapy.

Another reason we liked having Allison in the rehab centre was because of the environment. Patients are treated more like residents than patients, and the residence-like atmosphere was greatly aided by the absence of the constant and sometimes excessive noise plaguing the hospital. I should also add that the staff at the rehab centre does wonderful work with brain injured people.

In the early going there were assessments of Allison to see what she could and couldn't do. The SPEECH LANGUAGE PATHOLOGY ASSESSMENT was pretty grim. The September 14th report contained the following:

> *Clinical Impression:*
> *To confirm the data from the previous assessment on file…*
> *the CIHI screening for communication variables was*

administered. This was supplemented by informal diagnostic therapy tasks.

She was unable to follow instructions for more complex formal testing.

Ms. Woyiwada continues to show a severe aphasia affecting her ability to read, write, speak and understand language. In addition, she is not oriented to person, place and time. She seemed unaware of her communication breakdowns and showed no distress or memory of these difficulties.

She was able to point to some common objects in her room and follow some simple familiar instructions.

She could not follow a two stage instruction without repetition and gestural cues.

She could not consistently identify everyday objects from coloured photographs when they were named for her or when she was given the printed words. Sometimes she read the word aloud correctly but did not match it with the correct object. She seemed unaware that she was unable to do this task.

She tried to read a single sentence [phone message] but read it incorrectly and could not say who the message was for, nor what the topic was.

Her speech is inappropriate and verbose. She will repeat phrases and sentences and may give tangential comments, without self-monitoring. The responsibility for communication rests with her communication partners and requires gestures, repetition and simplification.

She was able to write her name but was unable to write words to dictation. Some spontaneous writing was spelled correctly but the words were unrelated and she would perseverate on a single word before continuing.

Allison's Brain • **191**

Recommendations:
Ms. Woyiwada will be scheduled for 4 sessions of cognitive communication therapy a week. Therapy will be aimed at comprehending and using a basic, functional vocabulary to meet her everyday needs. Additional strategies will be used to supplement spoken/written language as needed.

The OCCUPATIONAL THERAPY ASSESSMENT done at the same time was much to the same effect.

Perception/Cognition:
No formal testing completed because of severe communication difficulties. She has severe receptive and expressive aphasia which has a significant impact on her ability to understand and follow instructions given by therapists. On daily tasks and on functional activities, she does show orientation difficulties to her surroundings, memory issues and difficulty in managing two tasks at the same time. Client does not seem to understand that her communication difficulties affect her ability to communicate with others. The language difficulties are a barrier to fully understand her cognitive strengths and weaknesses.

Allison was quite chatty Friday evening and Saturday, and her visitors Joan Duguid and Lynda Rivington both noted this. Allison's word selection was often problematic, but she was very determined and remained positive. She asked me how she got into the situation she was in and was very interested to hear the story. This didn't stick with her though, and afterwards I explained it again to her many times.

Allison also showed a lot of interest in the entries in the diary we kept in her room and made her own.

Allison also kept an agenda of her activities at the rehab centre. Here is a typical week.

Allison's Brain • **193**

One hundred and eleven days after Allison had gone for surgery, she was allowed out of the rehab centre on a day pass and made her first trip home! I had to do a massive cleanup job before Allison came home because, living on my own, I had stuff piled up everywhere. Part of this story is pathetic, but I'll tell it anyway. Having won the nautical competition in July on Revelstoke Drive, I was awarded a frog that croaked whenever I walked by. I had stationed the frog on the dining room table, amongst a lot of other things, as it broke the solitude and kept me company. It also had a brilliant unintended side effect — by scaring the bejesus out of Marya one day, when she was at the house by herself looking for music.

In any event, Sunday September 16th was a momentous day, and I'll reproduce my whole diary entry. We were very curious to see how Allison would react to being home given her memory difficulties.

> *Allison's first trip home in 111 days! She was waiting for us when we arrived and had packed her laundry to wash, hairbrush and sunglasses. When we drove home we passed by 23 Centennial [our rental property at the time] and Allison was interested in the "roof" although that might have been the wrong word. When we arrived home Allison inspected the back yard — which is in awful shape. Then*

walked into the house, had a cookie, looked around the main floor, and then sat in her pink chair with the new blanket from Jennifer and Max, and looked through her box of cards. Then up the stairs to the 2nd floor deck for a chicken and wedges and coleslaw lunch by Marya. After lunch Allison rearranged the furniture on the deck so she could nap in the sun, but then decided at about 1:00 P.M. to nap in the 2nd floor guest bedroom. Allison napped until 3:00, decided not to try the stairs to the 3rd floor, walked back downstairs to her pink chair, and Marya did her nails (after Allison had another cookie). While watching TV as Marya does her nails Allison is distracted and does not concentrate well on anything else. We downloaded the iPad applications recommended by Mary Pole (speech therapist). Allison got a little concerned as she thought she had to teach with it but we explained she didn't have to teach. Allison went for another nap and then got up for dinner. We had a great dinner courtesy of Don and Pauline, and chatted a lot about Allison's recovery. Then sorted out some clothes to take back to the rehab centre. Allison was fatigued around 7:00 P.M. A great day!

The next day, my sister Joan and brother-in-law Ben arrived, having driven all the way from Manitoba to help out. We had a brief visit with Allison at the rehab centre in the evening, and Allison was in good form as, when I asked her to identify a pen, she told me to fuddle-duddle off. Fuddle-duddle is a good choice of words to use here, as the *One Hundred Years* musical that Allison wrote, and produced many times over the years at Hopewell School, has a song called "Fuddle-Duddle" that represents the 1970s.

The same day, I sent out the Week Seventeen Update to the *Allison's Brain* group.

> **From:** Allison Woyiwada
> **Sent:** September 17, 2012 9:14PM
> **To:** Allison's Brain
> **Subject:** Week Seventeen Update

Hi

Allison has had yet another good week, and there is a lot of good news to report. On Tuesday last week she moved from the Neuroscience InPatient Unit at the Civic Hospital Campus to the ABI Rehabilitation Centre at the General Campus. A special thanks to Sharon Chartier for being on hand and giving up her day to help this move go smoothly. After a short transitional period during which Allison wasn't totally convinced that the ABI Rehabilitation Centre was the right place for her (as compared to home, for example) she now seems to be quite on board with the ABI program, which typically includes several different therapy sessions in a day (Hallelujah!).

Then on the 111th day Allison actually came home for a few hours! She walked in as if she owned the place, looked around a bit on the main floor, and then promptly sat in her favourite chair with her new blanket from Max and Jennifer, looking through the box of cards you've sent her over the course of the last three months. She then went upstairs to enjoy the sunshine on the second floor deck, worked in at least 2 1/2 hours of nap time, and enjoyed the lovely dinner that Don and Pauline had prepared. One of the highlights, from my perspective, was that although for the last several weeks Allison hasn't been able to tell me where her passport was in the house, when I asked her about it again on Sunday she walked over to and pulled it out of a vase in the living room. This was quite timely as I need the passport in order to renew Allison's Ontario health card very soon.

This P.M. I dropped in to see Allison with my sister Joan and brother-in-law Ben who have just arrived from Manitoba. As we were commenting on how well Allison is doing on the speaking front after only a couple of speech therapy sessions, I held out a pen and asked her

Allison's Brain • **197**

what it was. In response to this I think Allison may have said "fuddle duddle" or something like that. There is a lot of work to be done by Allison in re-establishing her understanding of how words relate to objects and the like; however, there is no evidence of her being daunted.

The Sunday benefit concert at Southminster Church is fast approaching. Marya and company have done a tremendous amount of work organizing, preparing for and publicizing the concert. The Ottawa Citizen carried an article about it this past Saturday, which I have copied below. We hope to see many of you at the concert.

Thanks again for all the terrific support including your very generous donations to Allison's trust fund!

*All for now,
Bob*

P.S. Last, but certainly not least, Allison and I became the proud grandparents (for the first time) this week of Blake Matthew Souchotte, son of my daughter Laurie and her husband Joel Souchotte, who reside in Calgary.

—

*Benefit concert to assist beloved music teacher's recovery
Allison Woyiwada taught at Hopewell public school*

Ottawa Citizen September 15, 2012

The Ottawa music community is hosting a benefit concert to assist in the recovery of award-winning music teacher Allison Woyiwada. This exceptional teacher has been at the forefront of the music education and performing arts fields in Ottawa for almost three decades. Well-known in Old Ottawa South as Hopewell Avenue Public School's music teacher from 1982 to 2008, she spent thousands of volunteer hours directing extra-curricular school bands, leading school band trips, and staging student musicals.

Late in 2011, Allison was diagnosed with a "giant" brain aneurysm and is now recovering from her May 2012 surgery. Although the surgery very likely saved Allison's life, she now has significant cognitive and physical deficits that require extensive rehabilitation therapy. Allison's basic post-teaching insurance coverage only provides limited benefits for rehabilitation therapy. ... To raise funds for Allison's rehabilitation and related medical expenses, a benefit concert is being held.

WHAT: Benefit concert to raise funds for rehabilitation and related medical expenses

WHEN: Sunday, Sept. 23, 7 p.m.

WHERE: Southminster United Church, 15 Aylmer Ave., Ottawa.

WHO: Host Rob Clipperton;

Singers Isabelle Lacroix, Marya Woyiwada, Sandra Graham, Dillon Parmer, Fraser Rubens, and Denis Lawlor with pianist Jean Desmarais;

Pianist/organist Matthew Larkin and trumpeter Nick Cochrane;

Members of the Savoy Society of Ottawa, featuring Shawne Elizabeth, accompanied by Robert Palmai;

2011-2012 Hopewell School Jazz Band conducted by Blair Smith;

The Southminster United Church Choir conducted by Roland Graham.

Tickets are available at the Ottawa Folklore Centre or online at woyiwada.blogspot.ca.

Allison has been recognized for her work in the community on many occasions, including as recipient of the Whitton Award (1993), Arts Advisory Award for Innovative Programming in the Arts (1997), Community Builder Award (2000), Hopewell School Music and Drama Award (2006), Capital Critics Circle Award as Best Director (community) (2006-2007) and Lifetime Achievement Award from Hopewell School students (2008). Upon her retirement from teaching, a wing of the Hopewell School was dedicated to Allison and the "Allison Woyiwada Music Award" is presented annually to a student at Hopewell School.

A trust account has been established for Allison. To make a donation, send a cheque payable to:

Robert McMechan, marked "in trust for Allison"

Donations can also be made online.

© *Copyright (c) The Ottawa Citizen*

The following day, Mary Pole called to say that Allison had done quite well identifying body parts, but was having a lot of trouble with words using the iPad program. The magnificence of this 4-in-1 Language TherAppy program is unmistakable. There are exercises aimed at comprehension, naming, writing and reading which begin at the most basic level, and then become increasingly more difficult at higher levels.

It would be safe to say that Allison has spent at least hundreds of hours doing these exercises, and she still does them regularly. Allison found that if she worked hard her cognitive gains were evident, but if she stopped doing the exercises she slipped. This type of at-your-fingertips therapy has to represent a huge advance over what was available pre-computers, and Allison has benefited enormously from it.

I was asked for permission to do an emotional assessment of Allison, the results of which are reported in NEUROPSYCHOLOGY — SUMMARY OF INVOLVEMENT, based on an interview conducted on September 18th.

Summary of Involvement:

Mrs. Woyiwada was referred to determine her affective function and neuropsychological follow-up during her inpatient ABI admission. She was interviewed on September 18th, 2012, however, given the extent of her aphasia, communication was limited. She showed some fluctuation in her verbal responses. At times, her responses seemed appropriate and comprehensible though brief, and moments later, her speech would become incomprehensible with significant jargon. There were also elements of perseveration. Not surprisingly, assessment of her mood was limited. Nonetheless, she showed consistency in her responses to simple closed-ended questions about her mood (i.e. happy?; sad?; wish you were dead?; want to be alive?) and essentially, appeared to deny low mood and suicidality. Her behaviour was consistent with this. She was cooperative and showed initiative for daily activities. Her progress was monitored through the team. There appeared to be improvement in her recall of daily processes (procedural learning?) and familiarity with staff. However, she remained with persistent functional and communication difficulties. As such, the team felt she would need ongoing daily supervision to ensure her safety post-discharge. Formal neuropsychological testing was deferred given the extent of her aphasia, however, she could be referred for an outpatient assessment should she show significant improvements. Should there be concerns about her affective function, her mood could be further assessed using behavioural anchors.

Nesrine Awad Shimoon, Ph.D., C.Psych.

Allison told me before bed at the rehab centre on the 18th that it had been "a good schooling day." When she caught the drift of it, she buckled down and seemed to enjoy the day-to-day challenges.

Allison began coming home every evening for dinner. My sister Joan took over the kitchen and we ate very well, even after I fired Lorraine. Allison was always social at these times, but she was ready to go back to bed at the rehab centre at around 7:00 p.m. When she returned to the rehab centre, she was to locate her name in a book and sign in. This often wasn't successful, but she was encouraged to do it on her own. As with other things, Allison wasn't devastated by not being able to do this, and persisted.

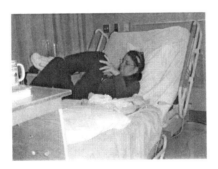

On the 20th, I attended a meeting with the rehab centre social worker Susan Lindsay, and I was very surprised to hear that an October 23rd discharge date was being planned for Allison. Allison called home on the 20th for the first time, and when I told her a plumber was coming to fix a leaking faucet at our rental property on Centennial Boulevard, I think she told me that I should handle it because she found it too stressful. I had taken over the management of the rental property when she went for surgery, and coupled with tax practice and attendance to Allison, I also found it stressful, although I had absolutely no expectation that Allison could continue to manage it. Perhaps owing to Murphy's Law, the issues with the rental property escalated dramatically, to the point where I found that the best course was to sell it.

When Allison came home on the 20th for my sister Joan's birthday dinner, she did some "cleaning," which consisted of banishing things to the basement, and throwing things in the garbage including one of my cherished running medals. The following day we had a quick dinner at home and then went to part of the rehearsal for the benefit concert at Southminster Church. Allison saw some people there that she hadn't seen for a long time and was pretty happy to be sort of back in circulation. We came home when Allison got tired, and she went to bed at home for the first time since May 27th. I had taken a lesson in giving needles to inject a blood thinner, so Allison was able to stay home for the weekend.

Allison came downstairs from the third floor on her own on Saturday morning and asked for "bran snakes" for breakfast, but really wanted toast. This was one of many occasions when Allison had us looking for something she wanted, but described it with a different word. We had a tight schedule that morning, as we were going to the Farmers Market in Metcalfe, stopping at the Red Dot Cafe in Osgoode for lunch, and returning home in the early afternoon to meet Cheryl Jones for the first music therapy session. When we were ready to leave the house, I called upstairs to Allison, and she said she was just brushing her hair and would be down in a few minutes. A few minutes came and went, and it dawned on me that Allison might not have said what she was actually doing. I checked upstairs and Allison was having a shower and needed a hair dryer that was at the rehab centre. We worked through that crisis, took in the Farmers Market and the Red Dot Cafe, and got home for the music therapy session.

The first phrases that Cheryl worked on with Allison were "The concert went well." and "I am very tired." Cheryl would put the words with a melody, have Allison sing them, and as she did, tap out the rhythm on Allison's left knee. My understanding from Cheryl was that Allison's "library was intact" and that this process assisted her in "getting books (words) out of the library." Gradually, when the melody was withdrawn, Allison would have fluency with the words. I will defer the rest of the discussion to Cheryl in Appendix 1; however, Allison became very engaged, and she also became increasingly fluent.

In the afternoon, we did some errands together to TD Bank, Billings Bridge and Home Depot. I was charged with constant supervision of Allison, but she fatigued easily and sometimes stayed in the car while I did errands that had to be done. I constantly worried about the wisdom of this, and when I emerged from Home Depot, Allison was getting out of the car in the parking lot. A few minutes later and who knows where she might have been. Even going to an Instant Teller was a challenge, as I would ask Allison to stay where she was, turn my back to do banking, and she'd be gone. It was a delicate balance.

Sunday September 23rd was a great day for Allison. Tyler and Marya both visited, and we all sat out on the deck at midday. Allison said goodbye to Joan and Ben and thanked them for coming. Besides Joan doing all the cooking, Ben worked non-stop the whole time he was in Ottawa, fixing things around the house and doing an humongous amount of yard work. Allison went back to the rehab centre at about 5:00 p.m. We'd had discussions about whether Allison should attend her own benefit concert that evening. We expected a big crowd, and with so many people potentially wanting to speak with Allison, our consensus was that it might be overwhelming. Dr. Lesiuk thought it would be okay if she was there for a little while, but we decided not to chance it. Allison didn't seem to disagree and still doesn't today.

Besides the CBC Radio spot referred to above, there was a massive amount of publicity for the concert, including television interviews, newspaper stories, and a Facebook site. Advance ticket sales were hot.

From: Marya Woyiwada
Sent: September 22, 2012 11:00 AM
To: Benefit Concert for Allison Woyiwada
Subject: Benefit Concert for Allison Woyiwada

IMPORTANT NOTE!!!! The Folklore Centre has run out of tickets AGAIN. I am doing my best to get them more, but please visit the blog for tickets http://woyiwada. blogspot.ca/ They are also available at the door. I will let you know if I am able to get more tickets to the Folklore Centre

I tried to do justice to the benefit concert in my Week Eighteen Update.

From: Robert McMechan
Sent: September 24, 2012 9:02 PM
To: Allison's Brain
Subject: Week Eighteen Update

Hi

The past week goes down as a most memorable one in Allison's ongoing story. Every weekday she had a few hours of therapy at the ABI rehab clinic, and came home in the late afternoon for dinner, returning around 7:00 P.M. ready for bed, so she would be well-rested for more therapy sessions the following day. Plus, for the first time, she had a weekend pass, subject to 24-hour supervision by family, and injections given at home by me. This went well, but it was not without its priceless moments, which I won't share here for fear of exhausting you all.

The Sunday evening benefit concert (which Allison did not attend, as we think it would have been overwhelming for her) was successful beyond belief. Marya, with the aid of an exceptionally talented and dedicated group of friends and performers, put on what was truly an extraordinary event. With almost 400 advance tickets sold and a walk-up attendance estimated at around another 200 (with people turned away at the door) the Southminster Church was packed (this is at least triple hearsay, but my understanding is that John Graham said he had never seen so many people in the church!). And people were treated to a gem of a concert. In the words of others:

Lauren Phillips: It was a really excellent concert, and for such an awesome cause — Mrs. Woyiwada is such an amazing music teacher, she's one of the main reasons I went into music. Congrats to all involved, and my very best to Allison and her family!

John Forster: Congratulations, Marya, for a job well done. Last evening's concert was a brilliant one and enjoyed greatly. We are all proud of you and all your efforts.

Andy Iotici: Marya, It was a pleasure to attend, the performances were absolutely superb, both Liz and I were moved throughout.

Allison's Brain • **207**

Shelly Calhoun: Hey Marya....it was a phenomenal event... congratulations on such a success....thoroughly enjoyed it.

These are just a few of the multitude of tributes. As a fundraiser, the event was a smashing success. Host Rob Clipperton announced at the concert that total donations and ticket sales reached $35,000. This is far beyond anyone's expectations and is a huge boost in funding for Allison's rehabilitation and related medical expenses!

While the performers all deserve enormous accolades for their wonderful contributions, I am compelled to mention Doug and Pat MacDonald for their splendid appearances as the Duke and Duchess, with eloquently re-written G&S lyrics featuring Allison and some tax lawyer guy — please see the attachment as evidence thereof.

This update could go on much longer, but in the interests of maintaining your future readership, I will sign off here, subject to this one further personal note — a big Thank You to my sister Joan and brother-in-law Ben for driving to Ottawa from Manitoba, putting in untold hours doing many things around the house that have been left undone for the past few months, and for adding much levity to the goings-on throughout the week (not to mention rescuing my Ottawa Race Weekend medal from the garbage after one of Allison's "clean-up" sprees!).

All for now and thanks again for your terrific support!

Bob

P.S. Looking around the church on Sunday evening and realizing that there were many people in attendance who I did not recognize, I had the sense that students and parents who met and worked with Allison over the years through the Hopewell School music program turned out to support her in absolutely amazing numbers.

DUET — DUKE and DUCHESS.
Recitative

DUKE. To help unhappy taxpayers and add to their enjoyment,
       Gives me the opportunity for prosperous employment;

DUCH. To all my skills with music scores, much time have I devoted;
       I love to lead a chorus tune, I'm sure you've duly noted.

VERSE I

DUKE. Deductions and rebates
       And minimum probates
       I get — and my clients are delighted –

DUCH. They're highly delighted!

DUKE.   I find in our tax code
          Loopholes by the armload,
          I'm sure they will soon get me knighted –

DUCH.   He soon will be knighted.

DUKE.   Mathematical playing
          I find very paying:
          It adds a large sum to my makings –

DUCH.   Large sum to his makings.

DUKE.   My professional skill set
          Ensures that I will get
          At least ten per cent on the takings.

DUCH.   One-tenth of the takings.

DUCH.   I'm known as a person
          Who waves a white baton
          That calls all musicians to follow –

DUKE.   Musicians to follow.

DUCH.   And whether they're voicing
          Their pain or rejoicing,
          I don't let their talents lie fallow –

DUKE.   They never lie fallow!

DUCH.   My talents, I got them
          At Hopewell I taught them
          My kids could all play a toccata –

DUKE.   All play a toccata.

DUCH.   For my erudition
          The school's new addition
          Should carry the name Woyiwada –

DUKE.   It certainly oughta!

VERSE II

DUKE.   gather great plaudits
        When from nasty audits
        I save all my clients the trouble –

DUCH.   He saves them the trouble.

DUKE.   They're pleased with the outcome
        On their final income
        And thank me by paying me double –

DUCH.   They do pay him double!

DUKE.   I go through my paces
        In Iron Man races
        Along the whole course I go prancing –

DUCH.   You should see him prancing!

DUKE.   On land and water
        I do what I oughter
        To hold back my old age advancing –

DUCH.   His age *is* advancing!

DUCH.   At Savoy, no fiction,
        I always stressed diction
        As singer or maestra, no matter –

DUKE.   Oh no, twas no matter.

DUCH.   Quartet or trio,
        I led them with brio –
        But needed a man to do patter –

DUKE.   A man to do patter!

DUCH.   My baton was swinging
        With all the cast singing –
        I knew I was reaching my mission –

Allison's Brain · 211

DUKE.   So close to her mission!

DUCH.   To light up all stages
With shows for the ages,
And so make a lasting impression –

DUKE.   An awesome impression!

VERSE III

DUKE.   We're ready, together,
To face heavy weather
Through hell and high water we're sailing –

DUCH.   Sometimes it's rough sailing.

DUCH.   Through lightning and thunder
We stand here in wonder
At those who our boat are a-bailing –

DUKE.   Yes, everyone's bailing!

BOTH.   In short, we're a twosome
But not really lonesome,
Because we are gently surrounded,
Yes, gently surrounded –
By friends and by family,
Who hold our hands firmly

DUCH.   And keep us in their arms a-bounded –

BOTH.   By love we're surrounded!

I can tell you that the whole evening was a very emotional time, and I can still feel the emotions just writing about it. I recall that when Justice Campbell Miller of the Tax Court of Canada stopped to ask how I was, it was all I could do to blurt out that it hadn't been much of a summer. As luck would have it, Ron and Jacquie Holowka were seated near the front of the church, and Ron took an excellent set of photographs. With Ron's permission, I am including

212   •   *Robert McMechan with Allison Woyiwada*

some of his photographs below. Ron also did a terrific job of preparing a set of thank-you notes to the performers, which included their photographs.

214 · *Robert McMechan with Allison Woyiwada*

There are a couple of things that I should add before leaving the benefit concert. Marya's organizational skills and tenacity were what made the event possible, but we are deeply indebted to Southminster

Church, its members, the performers, and all the people who helped Marya make the concert such a success. Allison's post-ABI Rehab Centre therapy has continued by reason of the money that was raised, and we realize that many people are not nearly as fortunate. The other thing is that apparently John Graham's statement that he had never seen so many people in Southminster Church was said by some people to be quite hilarious, as they didn't think John was in a good position to judge.

Allison called the following morning to say she needed to see Dr. Lesiuk because her left side vision was not very good and it was nauseating her. I passed along the message to a nurse, and an appointment was made for Allison with an ophthalmologist. Allison didn't mention this problem later in the day, and we went to one of Allison's favourite Italian restaurants with Tyler and Marya for a celebratory dinner. I recall Allison being indignant about slow service, as she was used to having dinner when she sat down.

On September 25th, Allison called me about 8:30 a.m. to say she was ready to come home as all of her classes had been cancelled. I checked with a nurse and found that only physio had been cancelled. Allison had coffee with Mike Hayes at the rehab centre, and he reported later on what he saw as her wonderful progress. Allison came home for dinner with Marya and did her music therapy homework. We also briefly visited Don and Pauline, watched an episode of "Mentalist," and then Allison went back to the rehab centre, where she had another short visit from her friend Janet Busche-Wisker before going to sleep.

I'm including the email update from Mike Hayes below as it is fairly precious.

> **From:** Mike Hayes
> **Sent:** September 25, 2012 10:42 AM
> **To:** Bob McMechan
> **Cc:** Janice Hayes
> **Subject:** Just had a fabulous visit with Allison
>
> *Bob,*

I was at the General for a follow up with my shoulder surgeon, so I took the opportunity to see if Allison had a minute to visit.

Was of course questioned by staff and met her nurse who told her Mike the bald guy was here to see her. She came down the hallway with the most incredible smile and hugged me and said so great to see you. The nurse said we could go for coffee, and Allison led the way to the elevator and to the main floor cafe. I was totally lost, but she sure knows her way around.

We had coffee and chatted for a good 30–40 minutes, Allison checking her watch and reminding me she had a 10 am meeting. Lots of questions about the concert, who was there, etc. We had a few good laughs. She is very excited to see it. We met a Doctor who Allison said "oh meet Cathy" (not her name) but a doctor who Allison taught, and she said oh I heard about you and the concert on the radio, you are a star here Allison.

I have not seen her in some time, and I am so excited about her incredible progress and how fantastic she looks. The smile, the gestures, the catching everything that is going on. Someone passed while we were having coffee, she leaned around to see who it was, she says "Hummmmm I had to do a double take."

I got a tour back to Ward C (I was totally lost and sort of doubting we would get back), security check from bracelet alarm at nurses desk. Allison stops, hold up her arm, "we're back," and turns to me and says "lots of rules here, but I'm being good." Then a chuckle!

I asked her if there was anything food wise she missed or would like as a treat that could bring her. She said, "the meat here is the best I've ever had, and good cookies too." So

*I said I would bring her some warm cookies one night after
dinner and I could walk from home. She said, "well I'm in
bed by 7 every night." Again she had me laughing, and her
too.*

Incredible progress.

Mike

Mike's reference to the doctor who Allison taught is to Dr.
Lauren Reid, the resident doctor who looked after Allison during
much of her stay on Ward C at the rehab centre. Allison taught
Lauren music in Grade 7 and Grade 8, and was her home room
teacher. The resident doctor is a member of the team of specialists
who work with patients on their rehabilitation. The team members
assess patients when they are admitted and set goals that are related
to being able to send the patient home safely. Most patients only
stay at the rehab centre for a matter of weeks, and their recoveries
continue after their discharge. Dr. Reid credits the nursing staff at
the rehab centre with being especially adept at working with patients
with brain injuries. She recalls that when Allison was admitted she
was having trouble understanding what people were saying and
expressing herself. She thinks Allison's perseverance was absolutely
helpful in her recovery and that her good mood was also a contributor.
Dr. Reid says that one of the reasons she has liked working at
the rehab centre is that she often sees patients making recoveries.

On the 27th, Ruth McEwen joined us at home for dinner.
Allison remembered the door code, which I thought was very
impressive. The next day, we ran into Marylen Milenkovic as we
were leaving the rehab centre and invited her to our house. Allison
was fatigued though, and they had a short visit. On Friday afternoon, when I picked up Allison, she was watching TV in a lounge
with a couple of fellows. She said goodbye to them but didn't get
a response. That evening Gordon and Pamela brought us another
Indian food dinner, and the next morning we set out on a road trip
to Lac Xavier to overnight with Dan and Sharon. My *Allison's Brain*
Week Nineteen Update describes some of the highlights of the trip.

218 • *Robert McMechan with Allison Woyiwada*

From: Allison Woyiwada
Sent: October 2, 2012 7:26 AM
To: Allison's Brain
Subject: Week Nineteen Update

Hi,

Allison has had another good week, coming home for a couple of hours for dinner on a daily basis, and also coming home for the weekend.

We travelled on the weekend to Lac Xavier near Tremblant to stay overnight with our friends Dan and Sharon. This was Allison's first trip anywhere since the spring, and she said she "adored it." Her only complaint was that she wanted to sleep in the car, but the fall foliage was so spectacular that she couldn't keep her eyes closed! The route was a familiar one, and Allison showed good improvement in her long term memory, suggesting we take a back road shortcut, pointing out where we had taken a wrong turn before, and asking whether we would have to walk down the long hill to Dan and Sharon's cottage.

Allison's short term memory, on the other hand, is not so good. However, short term memory is not a complete bust, e.g. Allison was able to say in the afternoon what she'd eaten in the morning for breakfast. On the subject of eating, we bought sandwiches at Tremblant for the ride home. Allison ate all of hers, and I ate half of mine. When I returned to the car after fetching some tea, Allison was eating the last half of my sandwich and asked if someone had eaten the other half. Eating has taken on a whole new importance for Allison, and she is now cleaning up her plate and looking for dessert, whereas pre-surgery she ate like a sparrow and almost never ate dessert. Her appetite is a good thing, as she's lost a ton of weight over the past few months.

Also in relation to Allison's memory, the interval of time pre-surgery through her hospital stay seems to be a blank. At one point, when I mentioned people visiting her in the hospital, she asked me why she had been there. She recalls, however, that there was a benefit concert for her, to which a great many people contributed and gave their support. She's been a little chagrined at times about people making such efforts on her behalf, but when she reads cards and letters from supporters explaining why they are helping, she is very rightly pleased.

Apart from memory, Allison's main difficulty is with speech, although we are noticing continuous improvements. She is making up fewer words these days, and she also now quite frequently tells us she knows that she isn't using the right words. Allison's speech-language pathologist Mary Pole at ABI tells us that Allison has made "quite a marked improvement" in her ability to comprehend single words and to find the right words, when given semantic cues (such as carrier phrases) or phonemic cues (such as "um" for "umbrella"). Mary says that although Allison is "much improved" on this front, she "fatigues quickly" and then has a tendency to perseverate on a word she has used previously. Mary adds that this is "quite normal" for someone with the type of head injury that Allison has, and for the level she is at now. Mary also says that Allison is "highly motivated" (this is a surprise) and that she managed to convey to her that she wants to work with a music therapist. Mary advises that she thinks this is a "great idea" and she has offered to collaborate in any way, and so I've put Mary in touch with Cheryl Jones. Music therapy re-commences this week.

All for now and thanks for your great support!

Bob/Grandpa, etc.

P.S. While we are noticing continuous improvements in Allison's bearing and speech, people who have seen her recently for the first time in a few weeks are generally quite amazed. Yesterday she showed off her croquignole ability, soundly trouncing Marya and Brian Hay. When I told her Brian Hay was dropping by, she asked "Brian Hay from Winnipeg?" Brian is in fact from Winnipeg and made the time to visit!

In the morning on Sunday September 30th at Lac Xavier, I told Allison that it had only been six weeks since I was there previously for the Mont Tremblant Ironman and that at that time I didn't know when she would get out of the hospital, since her condition had improved spectacularly over that period. This was one of the dozens of times afterwards that Allison told me, "It better keep going." — or words to that effect. She asked me again why she had been in the hospital, and when I explained about her brain aneurysm, she said she had forgotten. Allison asked Dan and Sharon's son αλέξανδρος how his "saskatoon" (saxophone) was going, and he helped Allison with her iPad speech therapy program.

The brain has a fantastic ability to re-boot, and here is another uplifting story from Allison's cousin Jill.

From: Robert Lee
Sent: October 2, 2012 8:01 PM
To: Robert McMechan
Subject: Update Week 19

Dear Bob:

Wow, I have actually been looking forward to the weekly updates and wondered why none had arrived this past Sunday!

Allison's progress is truly amazing, and because the body wants to constantly heal itself, she will keep progressing with therapy.

My mother in law, Toots Lee (75) has had MS since the late 50s (she wasn't diagnosed until 1962) and has lived in a nursing home for only the past few years.

She is wheelchair bound and requires 24/7 care.

Her most recent attack was a year ago when the left side of her face drooped and she lost the ability to swallow. This was devastating as life in a nursing home revolves around meals.

Now, along with a permanent feeding tube for hydration, she has regained the ability to swallow and speaks clearly once again.

All of this without therapy (nursing home is in Gainsborough so very limited specialty services).

Allison with a healthy brain and body before surgery will make great gains and already has been as described by your updates.

Wow! We think of her so much and are so thankful that she is doing better every week.

Thanks so much!

Jill Lee

On the 2nd, we had Cynthia Taylor for dinner, as I wanted to thank her for her insights and visits with Allison. Cynthia explained again what her own rehab had been like, which was directly relevant to the experience that Allison was having. Since Cynthia was back playing tennis, coaching Running Room clinics, and playing the piano, I thought it was good for Allison to hear about Cynthia's recovery.

The following morning, I met Julie Nishimura, Allison's rehab centre physiotherapist, and also attended a speech therapy session with Mary Pole. I reported back to the family later that morning.

From: Robert McMechan
Sent: October 3, 2012 11:31 AM
To: Tyler Woyiwada; Marya Woyiwada
Cc: Laurie Souchotte; Phil McMechan; Joan Veselovsky; Bette-Lou Paragg; Jim Rennie
Subject: Update re Today

I met Allison's physiotherapist Julie — she seems great and explained what she is doing with your mom, including work on balance, strength and her shoulder. I also went to the speech therapy class with Mary Pole. Your mom did quite well on most of the exercises except one that required her to name various objects.

Mary says that it often takes brain injury patients years of continuous work to recover their language. She mentioned one of her patients who has completed a Ph.D. and is still re-learning language.

Mary also mentioned the October 23rd discharge date that Susan Lindsay the social worker first told me about. The

Allison's Brain • **223**

reasons she mentioned for releasing her then are that your mom is physically able, not impulsive and doesn't need supervision. There is a chance she will get day-patient status for a few hours a couple of days a week if she still needs a couple of therapies. There is concern for all patients when discharged that they may suffer depression because of the withdrawal of so much stimulation. This means that optimal use needs to be made of community resources so that your mom remains continuously active.

We can discuss at dinner on Thursday.

Bob

I detected some testiness and stubbornness when Allison was attending to the speech therapy session, but Mary credited Allison with being "persistent." Allison resented being asked by Mary to walk in front of us to the speech therapy offices; Mary was trying to establish whether Allison knew where she was going. At the speech therapy session, Allison was able to identify all of the things that she was wearing, but insisted that her shoes were "t-shirts." Mary told me that fatigue was a huge factor in recovery, as the brain takes about 25% of the body's energy and that stamina would improve in time.

That evening, we enjoyed salmon dinners that Duff and Linda Friesen left for us, and Allison expressed disappointment that she couldn't stay home overnight. For the most part though she was a real trooper about going back to the rehab centre, as I think she knew there were good things happening there. It also didn't hurt a bit that the centre has a homey atmosphere, with a staff that is warm and friendly.

On Friday October 5th, Allison had her eyes checked by an ophthalmologist, who discovered that she had blind spots in the upper left quadrants of both eyes. He held out the possibility that this might improve with time — which later turned out to be the case. Marya took her mother to the Georgetown Pub on Bank Street, which was a favourite gathering spot for Hopewell teachers, and said that Allison "loved it." This wasn't much of a surprise, as Allison has a social gene that doesn't appear to have been much impacted.

On Saturday morning, Allison worked on trying to figure out her email. She said that it was really hard to draft an update to her *Allison's Brain* group, and she didn't complete it. In the afternoon we drove to a B&B in Cumberland, where we stayed overnight so I could run in a 10K in the morning. We met the Passmores as Cameron was running, and Shannon watched over Allison. We also ran into the MacPhee family from our street, which was a bit of a reunion, as Allison taught music to two of their daughters.

When we got home, we had one of innumerable chats over time about Allison's recovery. Allison was intent on talking to Dr. Lesiuk about "fixing some things," but agreed with my assessment that music, a good attitude, determination and family support were all big factors in her favour going forward. The subject of her recovery was always on Allison's mind and was the focus of virtually every one of our dinner conversations.

On Thanksgiving Monday, Allison was pleased to have nearly finished a Sudoku for the first time since her surgery. Pre-surgery she had been religious about this, and she still tackles Sudoku on a daily basis. As I'm not up to cooking turkeys, and always have a ton of other things to do, we went to Les Fougeres Restaurant near Wakefield, Quebec, with Marya for Thanksgiving dinner. This was quite enjoyable, and Allison brought home part of her dinner so she'd have room for pumpkin pie. Later she worked on her *Allison's Brain* group email, which she sent out the following morning, and got a flurry of responses.

From: Allison Woyiwada
Sent: October 9, 2012 9:22 AM
To: Allison's Brain
Subject: hello y'allere

Hi everyone. It's Allison here. Many thanks for your numerous gifts for Benefit's Concert. What a beautiful concert! People had to be turned away at the door.

I'm hoping this future won't carry again, but time will tell. The method book was my first book that actually succeeded (Grade 6) — very exciting, although I have plans to play in concert in near future — wish me luck :).

My recovery is slow, but it's there. Ain't that good news, and good news for future to come. Wish me luck with my good luck, high society.

Ciauu
Allison xo

From: Bette-Lou Paragg
Sent: October 09, 2012 11:08 PM
To: Allison Woyiwada
Subject: Re: hello y'allere

Hi Allison,

So glad your benefit concert was so successful and that you are well on your way to recovery. I hear from Bob that you are working hard on your therapy. Congrats! You have come through a lot, and I admire your stamina. Keep up the good work! We send love from all the Paraggs!!

From: Joe Hershfield
Sent: October 10, 2012 7:50 AM
To: Allison Woyiwada
Subject: RE: hello y'allere

Welcome back Allison; We are so very happy that you are recovering so well.

Love and good wishes, Joe and Fern

From: Tyler Woyiwada
Sent: October 10, 2012 7:37 PM
To: Allison Woyiwada
Subject: RE: hello y'allere

*Hi Mom! Nice to hear from you from your own email
again, you're back!*

Tyler

That day we had a raft of medical appointments, and while we
were killing time in the Civic Campus Hospital cafeteria we ran
into Catherine Chubey, who had been Allison's original speech
therapist. Catherine had seen Allison through her darkest days, and
was very impressed with her progress.

Mary Pole called the next morning with a report about the
success of Allison's speech therapy session.

From: Robert McMechan
Sent: October 10, 2012 12:24 PM
To: Marya Woyiwada; Tyler Woyiwada
Cc: Laurie Souchotte; Phil McMechan; Jim Rennie;
Bette-Lou Paragg; Joan Veselovsky
Subject: Mary Pole Called

*Allison's speech therapist called to say that Allison made
a "big breakthrough" today with "truly amazing" results.
She scored 34/39 on the first exercise, 44/50 on the second
exercise (on a totally new category — food instead of
clothing), and also scored 64% on the last object-naming
exercise although she was fatigued and started to perseverate a lot on words she'd used previously (e.g., watermelon,
watermelon, watermelon).*

*Mary was also impressed with how well your mom now
identifies that she is not using the right word and described
her as "incredibly dedicated" (acknowledging that the
support your mom is receiving is a contributing factor). She
says she'd like to continue working with your mom on an
out-patient basis after she is discharged, but doesn't think
that's possible because of workload, so is putting together a
list of therapists.*

Mary was very excited about the session today, and she doesn't strike me as a very excitable person!

Bob

P.S. The speech therapist at the Civic (Cathy) who we met with yesterday says she thinks your mom is doing so well because of her strong musical skills. Although I made a point with your mom of locating the iPad in a drawer last evening, she couldn't find it today.

Cheryl Jones also provided a report that evening about Allison's music therapy sessions.

From: Cheryl Jones
Sent: October 10, 2012 8:16 PM
To: Robert McMechan
Subject: update

Hi Robert,

I wanted to give you a brief update on Allison's NMT sessions. Also, a thanks to Marya for your practice with your mom between sessions.

Last week when I asked Allison how the concert went, she responded, "the concert went well" and then struggled a bit finding words to continue. The MIT response that Marya had practiced with her had transferred very well into a conversation context. It is normal that the following words may have been a bit more difficult, but the musical cue enabled Allison to answer the question fluently with the MIT response. At times in the session there was difficulty with word access, but sung phrases went well. I left 2 more phrases on manuscript with her today. I believe she put the page in her Clementi sonatina book.

During her session this afternoon, Allison asked me if I thought MIT would work. I have the impression that

*she may have been questioning this due to the simplicity
of the musical lines that accompany the MIT phrases. I
explained that the MIT phrases were kept simple to reflect
the speech shape and also to make them easier to remember
as we would be adding more each session. I also assured
her that I knew she was an accomplished musician and
that we would be including music of more complexity in
other aspects of her sessions. I believe she felt better once I
explained the above.*

*Allison is working very hard in her sessions. Thanks Marya
for your work reviewing the phrases.*

Please feel free to contact me with any questions,

Cheryl

On October 11th, Allison enjoyed a DVD recording of the
benefit concert before dinner, but seemed quite fatigued. The following day she was diagnosed with an infection, and had to stay in
the rehab centre on Friday overnight. This was a shame, as a group
of her friends had organized a birthday party for her. She was finally
released to come home on Saturday afternoon but was weak and
confused. A nurse had told me that the infection would exacerbate
Allison's aphasia, and that this reaction was typical. Allison was
weak in the night and couldn't get back to bed from the bathroom
without my help. Her speech was poor all day Sunday, and she wasn't
feeling energetic, but she rearranged the dining room furniture. This
was a sign that Allison was regaining her form, at least in some
respects. She has a long history of tackling things on her own. Once,
when I came home from a trip, a wall in the kitchen was missing.

Allison had been given permission to stay home on Sunday night
as Sunday was her birthday. We had an Indian food birthday dinner
from the Coconut Lagoon, followed by cake, birthday presents and
croquignole. It became evident during presents that Allison was
down to size 4 jeans. Allison's sister Linda came from Manitoba to
help celebrate Allison's birthday. They make quite a pair, and here's

Allison's Brain • **229**

the best way I can describe it: At Allison's retirement gala she introduced Linda as "more like me than I am." I was just a small-town Prairie boy, and I could never have stood up to the Cameron sisters.

The following morning, Allison called me a "pooper" for asking her to get dressed so we could go back to the rehab centre. Before doing that, I went over the events of the next few days a couple of times as Allison wasn't clear about them. I picked her up in the afternoon and went to a follow up appointment with Dr. Lesiuk. He seemed pleased with Allison's progress, and emphasized these were "early days" in her recovery. Dr. Lesiuk also confirmed to Allison that there was no additional surgical procedure which would improve her speaking ability and that her progress now depended on work with her therapists.

One other thing we discussed with Dr. Lesiuk was whether it was okay for Allison to fly. He said that it was, explained why this was the case, and gave her a note about the titanium alloy in her skull in case it was needed for airport screening. Allison and I had been discussing a trip to Calgary to celebrate Blake's arrival, but

Allison's concern about flying was omnipresent. We ended up discussing this with two more doctors. Dr. Marshall at the rehab centre gave his approval at the discharge meeting with Allison on October 25th. Next we got Dr. Blake's approval at his office. As we were getting into our car afterwards in the parking lot, Allison asked me if I was just going to take Dr. Blake's word for it. She then added that she was making a joke, but the subject came up again many times before we flew to Calgary.

On October 16th, a nurse called and told me that Allison was asking if she could have privileges to walk around the rehab centre and the hospital like some other patients she saw. We agreed that the nurses could work with Allison on this during the day, as Allison was never at the rehab centre in the evening. When Allison came home for dinner that afternoon she was still having lots of trouble with speech, but she took the initiative to rearrange the dining room furniture again, and went through her box of cards.

Mary Pole called again on October 17th with another good report about Allison's progress.

> **From:** Robert McMechan
> **Sent:** October 17, 2012 12:18 PM
> **To:** Marya Woyiwada; Tyler Woyiwada
> **Cc:** Jim Rennie; Laurie Souchotte; Phil McMechan;
> Bette-Lou Paragg; Joan Veselovsky
> **Subject:** Mary Pole Called
>
> *Mary (Allison's language speech pathologist) says Allison is "back on form" today "doing really well" and scored in the 70% range on the exercises she did. She is also "showing a lot more awareness" when she isn't speaking correctly and is asking for repetition when she doesn't understand. Her motivation is "high." Also, there are new employees seeing patients on an outpatient basis. Natalie Pincombe will be able to work with Allison on an out-patient basis on Tuesdays and Thursdays "for a couple of months." Mary*

Allison's Brain • 231

says this should be some help as private speech therapists are "horrendously expensive."

Bob/Dad

Marya and I met with Susan Lindsay on October 18th to discuss the plans for Allison's pending discharge. Susan told us that Allison was doing well because she is intelligent and motivated. I related this to Allison while she was at home reading the Mainstreeter, our community newspaper, and she asked me where it was in the paper. Susan also told us that a complete neuropsychological assessment couldn't be done because of Allison's aphasia / communications problems. I was told Allison shouldn't be left alone, and Susan asked whether I would consider installing the Lifeline service, which I did for several months. I was concerned about how I could manage with Allison full time, run my tax law practice, and keep my sanity. It turned out that with Allison back at home the next few months were very trying.

Allison had resumed using her email frequently but the topic wasn't always easy to decipher.

From: Allison Woyiwada
Sent: October 18, 2012 6:04 PM
To: Robert McMechan
Subject: mpac

dinner ware

702,000 and 380,000 – your class calendar both band

xoxoxo

Gordon and Pamela brought us Indian food again, and a pumpkin pie that their daughter Emma made, for dinner on October 19th. It was incredibly helpful to have friends do this for us, as I found that I was always scrambling to plan meals, buy groceries, prepare the meals, and clean up. Previously Allison and I had shared all these jobs, and now she wasn't up to it. When Allison did start putting things away after dinner, I had no idea where to find them afterwards, and she had no recollection of where she had put them. But the most exasperating daily chore of all was finding the iPad so Allison could do exercises.

We had taken to having walks together around the neighbourhood as it was a good way for Allison to continue building her strength. On Saturday the 20th, Allison asked me when she would be able to go for walks by herself. This came up again a few weeks later when she asked me if she could cross Main Street and walk along the Canal by herself. It was a scary thing to be completely responsible for Allison's welfare, and I weighed the risks of something happening to her against the likely boost to her from doing something on her own. She went for the walk and I was very relieved when she returned.

Although it was the weekend, Allison was very deliberate about what she did. First there was Sudoku, then we went for a walk, Allison played the piano, and we did some iPad exercises together. To this day Allison continues to have a structured approach to her day, doing some variety of self-improvement activities. She is absolutely convinced that there is payback in terms of gains on the cognitive front.

On Sunday, Marya had arranged for a hairdresser friend to come to the house to do Allison's hair for the first time since before her surgery. Once in a while in the hospital, Marya or a nurse had done Allison's hair for her although at one time a nurse said that it had become so badly matted that there was a chance it might have to come off. That didn't happen, and she was finally able to get it professionally done. Unfortunately in December, when Marya was brushing Allison's hair, she discovered a bare piece of the titanium which had been put in place in September to replace the missing piece of her skull. This necessitated yet another operation, during which the titanium was removed and replaced by Dr. Peters.[11]

---

11 Unfortunately, we were informed by Dr. Peters in August 2014 that two more operations may be required in the coming months to replace the titanium piece again.

Allison's Brain • 233

The next day, I sent out a Week Twenty-Three Update to the *Allison's Brain* email group.

From: Robert McMechan
Sent: October 21, 2012 4:11 PM
To: Allison's Brain
Subject: Week Twenty-Three Update

Hi,

Almost five months to the day since her brain surgery at the Heart Institute on May 28th, Allison is being discharged from the Acquired Brain Injury Rehabilitation Centre later this week!

She will be continuing as an outpatient at the rehab centre for two speech therapy sessions a week (we're alternately told for two or a few months); plus, she will also be having music therapy sessions at home twice a week. The rest of her weekly schedule is a work in progress. It will involve a few occupational therapy and recreational sessions, some of which may be arranged through the Aphasia Centre of Ottawa and/or the Champlain Community Care Access Centre. Both centres have been contacted and have asked for a referral, which we are now in the process of obtaining. My understanding is that once the referrals have been completed, case workers will be assigned to assess Allison's needs and to make recommendations.

We are told that a full neuropsychological assessment is not possible at this time, because of Allison's aphasia-related communication difficulties. These consist principally of difficulties expressing thoughts through speech and writing, and difficulty using the correct names for objects, people, places, etc. We are also still witnessing some confusion, but not nearly on the scale that existed a few weeks ago. In fact, as anyone will tell you who has seen Allison recently after an interval of a few weeks, she has made remarkable progress in a short time. This progress appears to be related to a variety of factors, not the least of which are the excellent therapy she has been receiving and Allison's marvellous dedication and her upbeat bearing.

While Allison has been very much looking forward to the day that she can remain at home full-time, she has also been a "real trooper" about going back to the rehab centre on weekday evenings. This is partly due to her own formidable constitution, but it is also greatly due I think to the very positive atmosphere that the staff at the centre manages to maintain. The daily social interactions that Allison has enjoyed at the centre appear to have been large contributors to her progress. Once that daily interaction is off the table it is a whole new ball game. Our plan is to try to build a weekly schedule for Allison, with her participation, that meets both her social and therapy needs, while being cautious to ensure she has lots of time for rest.

Allison's daily regimen while at home on weekends now includes going for a walk, various exercises on an iPad speech therapy program, and playing piano. She has also been trying her hand at a bit of Sudoku, reading the newspaper and a novel, and restoring some order to our house. This latter activity she carries on quite relentlessly, generally with the result that I never know where anything can be found. While being discharged from the rehabilitation centre is a very major milestone, it is only one step along the road in a long journey ahead.

All for now and thanks for your great support!

Bob

P.S. A big thanks to Allison's sister Linda for her recent visit and splendid contributions to our well-being. One of these was a terrific turkey dinner, that we are still enjoying

Allison's Brain • **235**

*the leftovers from, and that we are all (including Allison)
still talking about. Lynn Graham also made a magnificent
contribution to our larder this past week, for which we are
extremely grateful. Pamela and Gordon too have treated
us, for the second time recently, to a delicious dinner of
Indian food. All of this goes a long way to compensate for
my lack of culinary skills!*

*P.P.S. These "weekly updates" stopped once Allison re-
instituted her own e-mail communications; however, apart
from her hello y'allere e-mail to the group on October 9th
she hasn't been too active with e-mail, although she does
read her e-mail regularly. I am prompted to send out this
update because I've been told by some that they'd like to keep
abreast of what's happening. I will therefore try to ensure
that there are periodic (although not weekly) updates,
and hopefully Allison will be venturing again before long
into trying to write out her thoughts to you, as part of her
medium and long term road to recovery. She has mentioned
a few times that writing her hello y'allere e-mail to the
group was a very hard thing to do.*

Marya attended Allison's morning speech therapy session on
the 23rd. She reported that her mother scored 82% in identifying
images when she listened to the word, and 62% when she had to
orally identify items based on an image; however, she got 88% when
given the first letter. In the afternoon when Allison was back at
home, she spent a long time looking for a "library card," but when
she drew a picture Marya figured out that she was looking for a
nail file. This problem of selecting wrong words has diminished
with time, and Allison has gotten skillful at finding alternate ways
of describing things.

On the 24th, Allison asked me if I was feeling better about making
arrangements for her to be home full time, as I had been open with
her about my concerns. By then I had contacted Abbotsford House
in Ottawa about providing drivers to take Allison to appointments,

and I had begun to arrange for personal fitness sessions for Allison at the YMCA near us. In the evening Allison went to Jill Berry's place for a belated birthday party, and then she went back to the rehab centre for a final night as an inpatient.

October 25th was a watershed day, as Allison and I attended a discharge meeting with rehab centre personnel in the afternoon, and then Allison was released to go home, on the basis that she would remain as an outpatient for speech therapy sessions for the next couple of months. The decision was made that outpatient occupational therapy would not be offered, as Allison should concentrate on recovering her speech. I tried several times to obtain occupational therapy for Allison through various routes, but short of hiring a private occupational therapist there was nothing anyone would do for her.

At the discharge meeting, Allison was in great form and asked lots of good questions. Nurse Katie reported that Allison had "blossomed like a flower" while at the rehab centre and had "done amazing" since she arrived. Julie the physiotherapist described how when Allison arrived at the rehab centre she had trouble running into anything in her way on the right hand side. Mary Pole described Allison's large gains while at the rehab centre and reported that she would have two outpatient speech therapy sessions a week. Dr. Marshall outlined the recommendation that Allison be supervised at all times. There was much laughter when it was suggested that it is people "less like Allison" who are at low risk when they are left alone. In just a few weeks at the rehab centre Allison had left a definite impression.

Allison's Brain • **237**

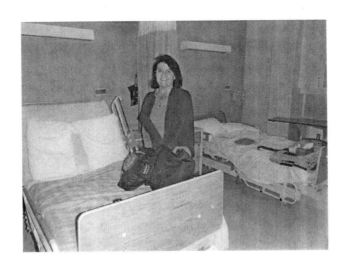

Mary Pole's FAMILY CONFERENCE NOTES shed a good deal of light on the state of Allison's recovery.

Issues Identified:
Severe Aphasia affecting comprehension of speech, reading, speaking and writing. Yes/no responses were unreliable. Speech was repetitive, with word jargon.

Lack of awareness of her communication breakdowns, with no monitoring her listener's reactions.

Loss of orientation to person, place and time, except for family members.

Inability to find her way around the Centre, without apparent concern or frustration.

Additional Comments and/or Recommendations:
Allison has excellent family support and has made good progress with her comprehension of words and phrases, both spoken and written.

Her use of the iPad has helped her work on comprehension and naming in categories. She has covered body parts, clothing, food and common objects. She still finds pen and paper tasks more difficult than using the iPad and has difficulty following directions or explanations.

She benefits from both written and spoken cues. Giving the first letter or sound of a word or giving the use of an object is now helpful for her.

Naming is improving more slowly than comprehension, which is normal for language recovery.

She will perseverate on a previous response, without self-awareness and needs cues to get the correct words.

She is more aware of communications breakdowns, recognizes some staff members and still gets lost in the Centre, without apparent anxiety.

Allison will be followed twice a week, on an outpatient basis, with Natalie Pincombe, S-LP at the Rehabilitation Centre for approximately six weeks.

A referral to the Aphasia Centre of Ottawa-Carlton has also been made, as she will need ongoing cognitive communication therapy on her return to the community.

Allison's Brain • **239**

The next while was an intense period at our house. To give you a picture of what it was like, I will mention a few of the highlights. Allison had forgotten her VISA pin number, and was adamant that there was something wrong with her card. We went to the bank and had her pin number reset. I found a photograph album with lots of good photos in the garbage. Allison often lobbied me about her driver's licence, which had expired earlier in October. Allison called the YMCA a few times asking for "Paul," who she said had been a yoga instructor, when I was promoting the idea that she have sessions with a personal fitness trainer. Allison needed dental work, but she was confused about what I wanted when I asked her for an old dental bill so I could find out who her dentist had been. There were a lot of medical appointments scheduled, which I had to take Allison to and explain to her why she was going. We also had a massive ongoing battle about whether Allison would take Vitamin B12. She had been diagnosed as anemic, and advised by Dr. Blake to take 1000 mg a day, but for reasons I could never understand, she was dead set against taking it. I had to get the iPad unlocked at the Rideau Centre, because the wrong password had been entered too many times. I had to hire a guy to take the stove apart, because somehow it too had gotten locked. The matter of flying to Calgary came up constantly.

From: Allison Woyiwada
Sent: November 2, 2012 12:23 PM
To: Robert McMechan
Subject: Mar

...got a call re worry re heavy re my worry during flight.

xoxoxo

I didn't understand this email, but I was certain that it related to our ongoing discussion of flying.

In early November, I sent out an *Allison's Brain* Week Twenty-Five Update.

From: Robert McMechan
Sent: November 4, 2012 10:23 PM
To: Allison's Brain
Subject: Week Twenty-Five Update

Hi,

Allison has spent her first full week at home after her discharge from the rehab centre! She had two outpatient speech therapy sessions at the rehab centre last week and one music therapy session at home. Her music therapy at home is being bumped up to twice a week, and so her regular weekly outpatient speech and home music therapy sessions will total four in number. Otherwise, her weekly calendar is still a work in progress, as we are waiting for a Home Visit from the Aphasia Centre of Ottawa to find out what programs it has that are recommended for Allison. Once we have the Aphasia Centre programs lined up, and add a couple of weekly personal trainer sessions at the YMCA, she will have a fairly full agenda.

In the meantime, Allison spends her time quite gainfully, playing the piano quite a lot (her favourite activity it seems and she is playing very well), working on her speech and music therapy exercises, trying some Sudoku, going for accompanied neighbourhood walks, reading (although her vision has been impacted, and she is going for an appointment with her optometrist soon to see if her prescription is part of the issue), and catching quite a few naps during the day. When she is well-rested, Allison's energy and sociability are reminiscent of the pre-surgery Allison, and if you met her casually to just exchange hellos, you would never know anything has been amiss. When working through the speech therapy exercises with her though, it is evident that the "word-processing" deficit is quite profound. The good news is that Allison is making continuing progress (her music therapist hadn't seen her for a couple of weeks and said she found Allison's progress "remarkable"). The other good news is that Allison is confident that she can recover her ability to speak coherently with the benefits of therapy and time.

This coming week we are travelling to Western Canada to visit family, including our new grandson, Blake. Allison has been very apprehensive about flying, as she is fearful about ending up back in a hospital. After three of her doctors (neurosurgeon, rehab doctor and GP) all gave their approvals for her to fly, Allison asked me if I was "just going to take their word for it" and then quickly added that she was making a joke. When Allison is back in Ottawa in mid-November, we are hoping that her full weekly agenda will soon be in place. Subject to needing time for lots of rest at various points during the day, and getting through her scheduled activities, it will be great if she can have the opportunity to benefit from social interactions with friends. I believe I mentioned last time that the night before her discharge from the rehab centre, several of her school teacher gang had an evening with her which she really enjoyed!

Allison checks her email often, and I think that corresponding by email is one of the ways that she can continue to progress with her language. This is a bit of a delicate point, as with such a large group of you there could also be a bombardment factor, but I think an occasional email will certainly be welcome. Just remember that Allison's responses can be quite puzzling!

All for now,

Bob

P.S. While it isn't a lie to say that Allison's favourite activity appears to be piano-playing, the post-surgery Allison has emerged as quite a fancier of desserts. When we were grocery shopping on Saturday, Allison's only contribution to the shopping cart was a giant container of cookies. I convinced her to downsize on the basis that we are going away soon, but by late afternoon on Sunday the cookies were entirely gone. This is so not like pre-surgery Allison...

Cheryl Jones gave us a report on Allison's music therapy session on November 7th.

From: Cheryl Jones
Sent: November 7, 2012 8:39 PM
To: Robert McMechan
Subject: Re: Allison's next session

Hi Robert,

Allison had a good session today. We are continuing to work on securing last week's phrases. I had brought some new phrases today but only added one. I wrote it at the bottom of a page she already had. ("The days are getting shorter.") Allison felt, and I agreed, that a total of 6 phrases for this week was enough. She worked really hard and I'm pleased with how the session went.

I wasn't able to speak with the speech therapist yesterday, but I did leave a message for her and hope we will be able to connect later this week.

Cheryl

Early on November 8th, we rose and went to the airport to catch our flight to Calgary. Allison got through check-in and security with no problem and was light-hearted at take off as she had taken an Ativan that Dr. Blake prescribed. This worked so well that she told me that she loved me, "in spite of what you are making me do." When she got on the plane, Allison paused to ask the flight attendant whether it was safe for her to fly, but it wasn't clear to the attendant what Allison was saying, and I hustled her away explaining that she had aphasia-related communication difficulties. Then,

Allison's Brain • **243**

in the vein of small miracles, Allison's hearing improved during takeoff. For days prior Allison had been raising hearing troubles as part of her defence against flying.

When we landed in Calgary, we were in the middle of a winter storm. I had rented a vehicle, and we were headed to my daughter's house, a long way from the airport, driving on major thoroughfares. The roads were covered with snow, the storm was continuing, there was a ton of traffic, and the wiper blades on the vehicle weren't working — I later came to believe they were frozen. With barely any visibility, and Allison giving wrong directions, we somehow made it to Laurie's house without dying.

We met our grandson, Blake, had lots of great meals and visits with Laurie and Joel, and Phil and Kristie, and stayed at Phil and Kristie's to sleep. After the first night, when we were sleeping in a guest room on a mattress on the floor, we had to switch beds with our hosts, as Allison found she wasn't strong enough to get up out of bed on her own. Kristie fortunately noted some of the vocabulary Allison was using — there are tons more of these that we can't remember, as we didn't write them down. When Allison wanted a hair dryer she called it "dishwashing liquid"; making coffee translated into "rustle up some dudes"; and, the Saddledome, which we could see from Phil and Kristie's, became a "ship." Popcorn came out as "blueberry coffee." Kristie also noted though that Allison had no problem reading music.

We visited Allison's former sister-in-law Diny in Okotoks, and Diny's daughter Kelsey, who had ceased having epileptic seizures after brain surgery. Kelsey is also a musician, and while Allison played the piano, Kelsey sang some Christmas songs.

Next we flew to Regina, where we visited with my mother at Qu'Appelle House, my sister Bette-Lou, her husband Ralph, and one of their daughters Karla. Everyone was impressed with Allison's progress, and Allison was in good spirits, as she is most of the time. The next day, however, she began to develop a cold. Any kind of illness brings with it a dip in Allison's cognitive state, and she continued having a lot of trouble with words for days until her cold symptoms abated after our return to Ottawa.

We enjoyed our visits with family, but we found that the wintry conditions in Calgary and Regina were appalling. Allison had gotten past her concern about flying, and so I promptly did some research on the Internet and came up with a January holiday in Antigua. We nearly didn't make it to Antigua, because of the need for Allison to have a second cranioplasty to replace her titanium skull piece in December, but we made it by the skin of our teeth. Allison was still suffering from some confusion the first time we came to Antigua, but things went well enough that we both knew we wanted to come back if we could.

When we returned to Ottawa, Allison ate all of the cookies my sister Bette-Lou had sent except two that I had eaten. She then made some chocolate chip cookies to atone for this, but then ate them all in the afternoon, except two that I had eaten. This was Allison's first foray back into the kitchen. At first I had our evening meals delivered by Red Apron, but as time passed Allison ventured more and more into the kitchen. Initially this led to some interesting meals. On one occasion I recall that I explained to Allison that I had picked up lasagna, and that we also had ingredients for a spaghetti dinner. Allison prepared our dinner, and the lasagna ended up as the spaghetti sauce. Allison had lost track of how things worked in the kitchen, and pretty much everything ended up in the frying pan.

Allison's Brain   ·   245

Once Allison became an outpatient at the rehab centre, I was able to use the Lotsa Helping Hands calendar to arrange some Sunday afternoon musical visits. Doug and Pat MacDonald, Carol Alette, Marylen Milenkovic, and Gloria and Matt Young came to our house at various times to sing and play with Allison. Some of these visits were more successful than others, in terms of getting Allison to participate, but she always enjoyed the company. But once in a while I had to explain to Allison who these people were, and why they were coming for visits.

Later in November, we attended JoAnne Sulzenko's *Welcome Winter* concert, and Allison received a bouquet of flowers when she was introduced to the audience at the end of the program. This was one of many musical outings we attended before Christmas. They included Metropolitan Opera broadcasts, the Orpheus show *Footloose*, Bach's Christmas Oratorio by the Ottawa Choral Society, and a stunning performance of the *Messiah* at the National Arts Centre. Inevitably, Allison knew audience members and performers at these events, and she remarkably rose to the occasion when speaking with them. We noticed too that when we went out for social occasions with friends Allison's language skills were often nearly impeccable. We discussed this, and Allison said she didn't know where that came from.

By late November the verdict had been rendered about the necessity for another cranioplasty.

From: Robert McMechan
Sent: November 29, 2012 11:10 AM
To: Tyler Woyiwada; Laurie Souchotte; Phil McMechan; Jim Rennie; Bette-Lou Paragg; Joan Veselovsky
Cc: Marya Woyiwada
Subject: FW: Allison Woyiwada

Hi everyone:

Not great news — Allison has a small bare spot on her head where the incision was made to install the titanium

piece. The plastic surgeon we met this a.m. (Dr. Peters) says
that he "sees this sort of thing all the time," but it usually
happens much closer to the date of the original surgery.
In any event, he says that the titanium piece has to be
removed and replaced because the exposed piece isn't sterile
any longer, and that this should be done within the next
few weeks. Before anything is scheduled, he needs to confer
with Dr. Lesiuk, who is back in Ottawa from Australia
next week. The extent of the operation will be determined
after consulting with Dr. Lesiuk, but we are told that it
will involve skin grafting this time.

Allison, as usual, is remarkably calm and composed about
this turn of events.

Bob/Dad

This led to an early round of Christmas shopping, at Marya's suggestion, as Allison would be hospitalized before Christmas. When I took Allison out shopping, she didn't recall the names of the places where she wanted to go, but she recalled the directions to the places. I sometimes drove dubiously, but we always ended up where Allison wanted to shop, and a couple of times at places where I had never been before.

Cheryl Jones provided another update about Allison's music therapy.

From: Cheryl Jones
Sent: December 3, 2012 12:00 PM
To: Robert McMechan
Subject: Re: Hi Cheryl

Thanks for the update Robert.

I wanted to also touch base on Allison's sessions. Allison
expressed a bit of concern a couple of times about her NMT
homework phrases… i.e. that sometimes key words were
not placed on the downbeat (main beat). This is because of

Allison's Brain • **247**

her music and especially her background in composing. I assured her it was ok and that the guidelines for preparing her phrases were different from those for composing vocal music. With the phrases, the musical guidelines are related to following the melodic shape and rhythmic pulse of speech for the specific phrases. Plus, there needs to be clear variations between the phrases. Allison understood and accepted this, but later expressed concern again. (That's no problem... I'm understand it...) I just wanted to let you know about this so that if she is concerned or questions her phrases when practicing, you can assure her that musically "it's ok."

Because of the above, and also because a week ago she mentioned feeling a bit discouraged about her pace of recovery, I decided to include Allison in the notation of recent homework phrases. It is my hope that this will give her a sense of empowerment in the rehab. She is working really hard and is very committed. I am seeing progress. I am hoping that notating her latest phrases and having everything organized in a binder will be an encouragement for her. If however, it is extra work and more of a burden, please let me know.

Please feel free to contact me with any questions or comments.

Allison will be in my thoughts and prayers this Friday regarding her surgery.

Cheryl

I attended an outpatient speech therapy session with Allison and Natalie Pincombe on December 4th, the highlights of which are recorded in my next *Allison's Brain* update.

From: Allison Woyiwada
Sent: December 4, 2012 7:32 PM

To: Allison's Brain
Subject: Week Twenty-Nine Update

Hi,

Allison has been home for five weeks since her discharge from the rehab centre and has gotten into a solid routine. She has been having two speech therapy outpatient sessions at the rehab centre, two music therapy sessions at home, and two fitness sessions with a personal trainer at the YMCA each week. Allison also plays piano, works at Sudoku, does speech and music therapy homework, goes for walks, and has been attending a number of musical performances (Welcome Winter, Bach Christmas Oratorio, Metropolitan Opera broadcasts, Orpheus, etc.). She has also enjoyed musical Sunday afternoons at home with Doug and Pat MacDonald, and Carol Alette. We are hoping for more of these musical Sunday afternoons, as Allison's music therapist says that music, music and music are all important to Allison's recovery!

Allison's speech therapist at the rehab centre says that Allison hasn't hit a plateau, and that she is now making particularly good progress at being deliberate with alternate word selection after recognizing that her initial word selection isn't correct. This is a big difference from when her outpatient speech therapy started a few weeks ago, as at that time Allison used a lot of jargon and her speech was confusing. This morning Allison aced a few speech therapy exercises that she had struggled with previously, to the extent that the speech therapist accused her of showing off for her husband. However, naming objects continues to be problematic for Allison at times. At one point when Allison identified a bookstore in a picture, the speech therapist said that Allison had argued with her on an earlier occasion that there is no such thing as a bookstore. Following this, and keeping in character, when Allison mistakenly

Allison's Brain • **249**

*identified a lamp as a bedside table, she insisted that
the lamp was really a bedside table. Regarding Allison's
continuing good humour, the speech therapist says that she's
told her own husband that if she had to have a brain injury
she "would want to be like Allison because her good humour
gives her about 50% more function." Unfortunately the
rehab centre outpatient speech therapy will not last much
longer, and we will begin the search for a private speech
therapist soon. However, Allison's speech therapist says she
has recommended that Allison begin receiving occupational
therapy at the rehab centre as an outpatient in the new
year, as her communications skills have improved enough
that she will now be able to benefit.*

*A representative from the Aphasia Centre attended for
an initial home visit with Allison last week, and set up a
follow-up meeting with Allison at the centre. Beginning
in the new year, Allison will also be able to attend a
weekly two hour session at the centre. The Aphasia Centre
representative explained that aphasia affects (1) word
processing; (2) reading; (3) writing; and (4) comprehension in varying degrees, and emphasized that often the
effects are not fully apparent in individual cases until well
after the brain injury occurred. The speech therapist at the
rehab centre is encouraging Allison to take advantage of the
Aphasia Centre's group sessions, as the group environment
will present new challenges.*

*The less-good-news is that a bare spot has appeared on
Allison's head, where the incision was made to insert the
titanium piece in place of her missing skull section. Dr.
Peters, the plastic surgeon we met last week, says that as
the titanium piece is no longer sterile it has to be removed
and replaced with a new titanium piece in an operation
which will involve skin grafting. Allison's neurosurgeon
Dr. Lesiuk and Dr. Peters have scheduled the surgery for*

250 • *Robert McMechan with Allison Woyiwada*

this Friday, and Allison is expected to be in the hospital for a few days afterwards. Allison's attitude towards this new development is that regardless of what has to be done, she will just keep dealing with any and all obstacles until they are overcome. Remarkably, over the past twelve or so months I've never heard any "Oh woe is me" comments or reactions from Allison.

Marya and Allison have jointly taken on the traditional Christmas treat-making that Allison has done over the years, so no worries about a treat deficit over the holidays. All for now and best of the season!

Bob

P.S. Allison enjoys hearing from you and depending on how busy she is / what's been happening she may well send you a response.

I received an interesting email from Allison on December 5th.

From: Allison Woyiwada
Sent: December 5, 2012 8:44 AM
To: Robert McMechan
Subject: worrying about me

Allison here. You are doing too much :) Seriously, this is going too far. This surgery will give me credit for more days than it's due, I'll be back home before you know it.

Having said this, having a new "bill" placed in your head is not rocket science again, but it's not a hard thing to have done.

Cheers
Allison

Xo

Allison's Brain • **251**

The same day I received an email from Evelyn Tan, who became Allison's speech therapist in 2013.

> **From:** Evelyn Tan
> **Sent:** December 5, 2012 9:11 AM
> **To:** Robert McMechan
> **Subject:** Re: Speech Therapy
>
> *Hi, Robert. Amidst preparation for the winter holidays, you are now busy planning for your wife's continued rehabilitation... a wonderful thing that she has your support. I will be abroad from December 28 to January 18, and will not be taking on new clients till the end of January. Please let me know if you would still be interested in contracting services from me; I am sure you and your wife will have some questions.*
>
> *This is my educational background:*
>
> *BSc. Occupational Therapy (1977)*
> *MA Speech-Language Pathology (1981)*
> *Certificate in University Studies in Theology (1997)*
>
> *My area of expertise is primarily in neurological cognitive and communication disorders and swallowing disorders (pediatric and adult) I work in hospital and community-based settings. I am also a trained facilitator in mindfulness and meditation.*
>
> *Thank you for contacting me.*
>
> *Evelyn Tan, MA SLP, reg. CASLPO*

Unknown to me at the time, Evelyn had done some group therapy sessions with Allison at the rehab centre, and so had some history with Allison that gave her a foundation for their sessions together.

I also brought the Terry Evanshen and Gabrielle Giffords stories to Allison's attention.

From: Robert McMechan
Sent: December 5, 2012 12:26 PM
To: Allison Woyiwada
Subject: Terry Evanshen

This is the fellow who lost his entire life's memories, ability to speak, and had multiple bodily injuries — who is now a motivational speaker. Xoxo

Terry Evanshen Official Home Page

terryevanshen.com/ Football Legend, Terry Evanshen inspires you to look at your own life in a way you have never done before. He shows you the never-ending power of the human spirit...

From: Robert McMechan
Sent: December 5, 2012 12:35 PM
To: Allison Woyiwada
Subject: Congresswoman Giffords/Music Therapy

This is the woman, who was shot in the left brain, lost her ability to speak, and has recovered it through music therapy / she is also using an iPad:

Gabby Giffords: Finding Voice Through Music Therapy — ABC News

abcnews.go.com › 14 Nov 2011 – Gabrielle Giffords, D-Ariz., underwent music therapy as part of her recovery. (ABC News)...

xoxo

Allison had her surgery on the 7th, which went "absolutely great" according to Dr. Peters, and remained in hospital for three days. Early after surgery, she was hallucinating, and later she was incoherent. I sent an update to the family in Western Canada on December 10th.

Allison's Brain • 253

From: Robert McMechan
Sent: December 10, 2012 4:19 PM
To: Laurie Souchotte; Phil McMechan; Jim Rennie;
Bette-Lou Paragg; Joan Veselovsky
Subject: Allison back home

Allison is back home today after only three days at the hospital. She's taken a bit of a cognitive hit, but we're told that this is to be expected and that she will rebound. I've cancelled all of her activities this week except for essential medical appointments.

Allison sent her own report to us on December 12th.

From: Allison Woyiwada
Sent: December 12, 2012 10:51 AM
To: Marya Woyiwada; Tyler Woyiwada; Robert McMechan
Subject: I think I've recovered!

OK, I opened what was not "brain" at 5:00 in the am and that hurt like a buggar. But I hate taking any pills, so I took a Halls pill and slept like a baby until 8am! Seriously! Brilliant! Ha! I still have no sleep disorder hanging around.

He will want to see my phyzician in the hospital arm . Hope he likes it.

cheers
aw

xoxo

Shortly afterwards, Allison rallied to celebrate Marya's birthday with her:

Allison also had Christmas on her mind.

From: Allison Woyiwada
Sent: December 12, 2012 6:38 PM
To: Tyler Woyiwada; Marya Woyiwada; Robert McMechan
Subject: the Tree

Monday the 20th is needed to enjoy the necessty day of festivitivities and mounce the Christmas tree. Need someone to help by dropping over on the other four would be ideal (Saturday or Sunday). If Monday is no good, pick another spot.

Thanks
Mom

x0x0

I had arranged for Abbotsford House to provide rides to Allison for her speech therapy sessions.

From: Robert McMechan
Sent: December 14, 2012 2:00 PM
To: Allison Woyiwada
Subject: Speech therapy rides next week

Monday December 17th 10am — Sheila Steeves — pick up at 9:30 a.m.
Tuesday December 18th 11am — Valerie Clement — pick

Allison's Brain • 255

up at 10:30 a.m.
Friday December 21st 10am — Marco Scaini — pick up
at 9:30 a.m.

xoxo

Allison was still confused about a lot of things and sent me this well-written response.

From: Allison Woyiwada
Sent: December 14, 2012 2:07 PM
To: Robert McMechan
Subject: Re: Speech therapy rides next week

Who are these people? Please don't invite them next week.
I'll be fine without them, and, quite frankly, embarrased if
they are here.

xoxoxo

Allison didn't like the idea of being "babysat," but she was OK with the speech therapy rides when she understood. It was crucial at this time to ensure that everything for Allison was clearly scheduled, and I wrote the day's activities for Allison on a whiteboard. Much later she resumed keeping her own diary.

From: Robert McMechan
Sent: December 15, 2012 9:17 AM
To: Allison Woyiwada
Cc: Tyler Woyiwada; Marya Woyiwada
Subject: Schedule for Week of December 17th

This is your last week of classes before the Christmas
holiday break, and it would be nice if you could have cards/
small gifts for Natalie, Cheryl and Debbie:

Monday December 17th

10:00 a.m. — speech therapy with Natalie at Rehab
Centre

1:00 p.m. — personal fitness with Debbie at YMCA
6:30 p.m. — JoAnne and Andrei bringing pizza dinner
for us all to have together

Tuesday December 18th

9:20 a.m. — dental appointment with Dr. Polonsky at
Alta Vista Dental Clinic
11:00 a.m. — speech therapy with Natalie at Rehab
Centre
2:30 p.m. — medical appointment with Dr. Blake at 1500
Bank Street

Wednesday December 19th

12:30 p.m. — music therapy with Cheryl Jones at home

Thursday December 20th

11:40 a.m. — appointment with Dr. Peters to have
sutures out at Civic Hospital
1:30 p.m. — personal fitness with Debbie at YMCA
[7:00 p.m. – 9:00 p.m. — Bob playing pool with David]

Friday December 21st

10:00 a.m. — speech therapy with Natalie at Rehab
Centre
11:30 a.m. — music therapy with Cheryl Jones at home

Saturday December 22nd

Nothing planned yet

Sunday December 23rd

2:00 p.m. — music afternoon with Gloria Young at home

If you would like Louise to come to our house any time during the week, let me know when.[12]

xoxo

The week before Christmas was very busy and complicated by horrible weather, and I went to Allison's last outpatient speech therapy class at the rehab centre.

From: Robert McMechan
Sent: December 21, 2012 10:59 AM
To: Tyler Woyiwada; Marya Woyiwada
Subject: Last Outpatient Speech Therapy Class Today

I went to this today as Abbotsford House cancelled its driver. Natalie says that Evelyn Tan — the private speech therapist who we are meeting on the 27th — is very good. Natalie has provided your mom with some exercises to do. She says the point is not memorizing things but to get the neurological processes stimulated.

If we hire Evelyn, there won't be any private speech therapy possible for your mom until around the end of January.

Cheryl Jones cancelled her music therapy class and the next one is in mid-January.

If either or both of you can spend some time with your mom doing iPad speech therapy / music therapy that's great. I have papers to write and client work to do before we leave for holidays.

Bob

The end of the year SPEECH-LANGUAGE PATHOLOGY DISCHARGE REPORT by Natalie was quite positive.

---

12   Louise is a wonderful lady who watched over Allison during the week after her second cranioplasty operation.

Overall, Mrs. Woyiwada exhibited significant progress in both auditory comprehension and verbal expression.

- *She can now participate in conversation with only mild to moderate difficulty with an attentive communication partner and can consistently follow 2-step instructions. Lengthy instructions continue to cause her difficulty. She benefits from repetitions, keeping information short and simple and verifying her comprehension.*

- *Verbal perseverations and jargon in conversation decreased significantly. She is usually able to make herself understood when the context is known and by describing difficult to name words. She benefits from semantic cues for word-finding and verifying that the communication partner has correctly understood her message. She is not always aware of paraphasias and communication breakdowns.*

- *Her reading and writing skills are functional at the simple level and reflect similar receptive and expressive difficulties as those described above. She could benefit from further speech-language therapy as she continues to show improvements.*

Thus ended Allison's time as a patient at the rehab centre. She had made tremendous strides since her May 28th brain surgery, and she would make many more in the year ahead. The last thing I'll say is aren't we lucky to have a health care facility like the Rehabilitation Centre at the Ottawa Hospital.

8.
After the Rehab Centre

Christmas came and went in 2012 in a much less stressful fashion than it had in the previous year. I was a little chagrined to find that, when Allison told me she wanted yellow Christmas lights, she didn't really mean yellow Christmas lights, especially since I had gone to so much trouble to find them. The sizes of some of Allison's gifts were out of whack, but she was getting back into the swing of things. We managed to have our traditional Christmas turkey dinner as Marya cooked the turkey, and the rest of us all contributed one way or another to preparation of the rest of the dinner and the cleanup afterwards.

Allison's Christmas Day telephone conversations with family in Western Canada were quite excellent, and I noted that she almost used no wrong words. Earlier in the day, when trying on a pair of boots that she'd gotten from Marya, she'd said they might fit better if she had her "Christmas trees" on. She was aware that I was diarizing a lot of the goings on and suggested that I write how smart she'd become.

After Christmas, we met Evelyn Tan together and spent quite a lot of time between Christmas and the New Year getting thank you cards ready to send to people who had donated to Allison's trust fund. Things got a little tense at times — I was sometimes impatient with my responses — but somehow we managed to muddle along together. We had a raucous time at Don and Pauline's on December

30th, having another scrumptious dinner with their family, and Allison wasn't bothered by the commotion.

Allison was keen to go to Antigua for a week, and she talked fondly about the week we'd spent in Sayulita, Mexico, a couple of years earlier. I'll leave the last words of 2012 to an email exchange between Allison and Carol Anderson.

From: Carol Anderson
Sent: December 31, 2012 3:06 AM
To: Bob McMechan; Allison Woyiwada; Marya Woyiwada
Cc: Gerald Oakham
Subject: Contemplation

I was just thinking about 2012 and all the many things that have happened. For me, a highlight was when Alastair flew up for a visit at the end of August. Got to hang out with my son for a couple of days — very rare! Best part was cycling down together to visit you Allison. We had an awesome visit; Marya was there too. Just a great day!

So looking forward to seeing you in Feb.

Happy, happy New Year to you all.

Love from Carol and Gerald

Oxoxoxoxoxo

Carol Anderson

From: Allison Woyiwada
Sent: December 31, 2012 11:14 AM
To: Carol Anderson; Bob McMechan; Marya Woyiwada
Cc: Gerald Oakham
Subject: Re: Contemplation

Me too. Still working on my mental improvement. I think it's coming along. I have had my 2nd head injury done — harsh and not easy to hear about the facts, but I'm trying to improve. Bob and I are off to Arrugua for an extended week as of Jan 2. Can't wait.

cheers all

aw

I won't give you a day-by-day account of 2013, as it would fill another book, without nearly as much drama. Instead, I've chosen to highlight a few notable things that occurred during the year. Most notably, Allison worked all year with Cheryl Jones and Evelyn Tan, and you can read their accounts of working with Allison in Appendices 1 and 2. Also, of course, the last word (before the Appendices) is from Allison in the Epilogue.

We had an enjoyable week in Antigua although Allison wasn't completely on her game. We realized though that we liked Antigua a lot because the people were friendly and out-of-their-way helpful, the scenery was very beautiful, the climate was warm without being stifling hot, and it was affordable. I looked at leases by the month in the Jolly Harbour area, as it has all the amenities you need and is a very secure environment. Allison was comfortable going for walks on her own, and that meant a lot.

Later in January, I sent out a Week Thirty-Six *Allison's Brain* update.

From: Robert McMechan
Sent: January 20, 2013 3:32 PM
To: Allison's Brain
Subject: Week Thirty-Six Update

Hi,

2013 got off to a great start, as we were able to take our first holiday together in about 1 ½ years! We spent 8 days in Antigua in early January and liked it a lot. Circumstances permitting, we will go back to Antigua for a longer period next winter. Allison has had a raft of medical appointments since we came home. Dr. Peters, the plastic surgeon who operated with Dr. Lesiuk to do the second cranioplasty on December 7th, says that the incision is healing very nicely and Allison will go back to see him in six months. Dr. Lesiuk's impression after meeting with Allison this past week is that she is continuing to improve. Allison says that she has good days and bad days, which Dr. Lesiuk says is completely normal for someone recovering from a brain injury. Dr. Lesiuk is arranging an angiogram in the next while, as since the May 28th operation there haven't been any pictures of what the aneurysm site now looks like. Dr. Lesiuk says this is because the four titanium clips used to block off the aneurysm are so large that they cast a shadow which prevents capturing an image of the area with any test other than an angiogram.

We also had a meeting at the Aphasia Centre of Ottawa last week, and Allison is interested in going to weekly sessions there once her overall health permits her attendance. Allison's outpatient speech therapy sessions at the rehab centre have ended, and she has a new private speech therapist (Evelyn Tan) coming to our house twice a week, beginning on January 23rd. Allison also continues to have twice weekly music therapy sessions with Cheryl Jones, which she enjoys a lot. My understanding is that, at times, there are issues as to whether the music element of the therapy meets Allison's rigorous standards; however, with the benefit of Cheryl's advice and guidance, sometimes Allison is able to be convinced, at least for a period, that it is the process of doing music therapy, and its hoped-for by-product of stimulating neurological pathways, that is the more important for present purposes. That said, Allison continues to also play the piano regularly, and also to enjoy musical visits from a number of friends. We also take in a fair number of musical productions and found Handel's Messiah absolutely enthralling in December.

Allison's most recent rehab centre speech therapist recommended that Allison commence occupational therapy, as her communication skills are now strong enough to benefit from it. However, we are being told that, because of limited resources, Allison would receive very little OT as an outpatient, and we've also been told that receiving much OT through the public health care / Community Care Access Centre is also unlikely. The upshot of this is that we have recently been in touch with a private occupational therapist who we will likely end up engaging also.

264 • *Robert McMechan with Allison Woyiwada*

On the physical front, Allison is herself noticing that she is getting stronger, and she resumes twice weekly sessions with a personal fitness trainer at the YMCA this week. Unfortunately, the crappy weather here makes Allison going outside for walks very often fairly problematic.

Our long-time friend Nick Newton, who has been in the news in Ottawa recently on account of his own health battle, and his longstanding philanthropic efforts, is organizing an event from 4:00 p.m. to 7:00 p.m. on Sunday February 10th in Ottawa. One half of the proceeds of the event is being donated to Allison's trust fund, and the other half is going to the Boys and Girls Club of Ottawa — which is hosting the event. In case anyone is interested in attending, I am copying a poster about the event below. Attendees are asked to RSVP to Nick.

All for now and thanks to everyone for your good wishes and support!

Bob

Nick passed away before February 10th, but the *Celebration of Life* went ahead, and there were tons of tributes to him. Nick was an active philanthropist, and one of a kind, and the world is a much poorer place without him. As Nick had promised, his *Celebration of Life* raised money for Allison's trust fund.

Allison hasn't made it back to the Aphasia Centre although we were impressed with the staff and the facility. Allison's spring surgery precluded her from attending right away, and when she recovered, she found that her days were quite full with her work on recovery. The centre is a 30 to 40 minute drive from our house, and when you double that you are taking quite a chunk out of your day. Allison had always worked in Ottawa no more than a few minutes away from home, and she even recalls a time when she didn't like to leave her neighbourhood. The Old Ottawa East community where we live is very well located, and we are reluctant to spend a lot of time commuting.

Allison announced in early February that she was very pleased about having read her first book post-surgery — Ken Follett's *Code to Zero*. She was especially pleased because she didn't have to go back and re-read parts of it in order to understand it. Allison's reading is still a work-in-progress today, and she is very diligent about reading every day, for she is confident that this is the ticket to reading improvement.

We flew to Toronto in early February because I was speaking on taxation law at the annual Ontario Bar Association mid-winter conference. We arrived at the Island Airport, and Allison's luggage hadn't made it. The next day featured the beginning of a serious snowstorm, and I left Allison at the Cambridge Suites Hotel on King Street while I was speaking at the conference. I had an understanding that Allison wouldn't venture out. Instead Allison took a cab to the airport, checked for her missing bag, and then caught another cab. She didn't know the name of the hotel, but she and the cab driver figured it out. When Allison was at the airport, a Porter Airlines employee asked her if she was the person who'd had the brain surgery and, when she responded that she was, told her that she was doing really well. We had apparently made an impression after we landed while there was a hunt for Allison's missing iPad.

In February we also attended the annual Can-Go Afar fundraiser banquet put on by Warren Creates and Joan Duguid in aid of the Afar people in Ethiopia. Allison knew a ton of people at the banquet and spoke with most of them during the evening. We had taken Allison's speech therapist Evelyn Tan with us as our guest, and Evelyn commented on how confidently Allison approached people and talked with them. I think this is one of the propellers of Allison's success: she just keeps on going despite any difficulties.

In March, we went to our Harris Lodge weekend near Mont Ste. Marie, which we had missed in 2012 because Allison was at risk and waiting for surgery. Harris Lodge is a wonderful place owned by Chris and Wendy Harris that we take over with twenty to thirty people for one weekend every year. The Saturday night dinner is always a highlight, mostly thanks to Joan Duguid and Warren Creates. Allison stood up after dinner and made quite a moving thank-you speech about her recovery and the way ahead.

In mid-March Allison began sessions at the YMCA with Brian Lloyd, a fellow she'd met through the Savoy Society. Sometime later, Brian asked Allison for a voice lesson. I happened to notice that during Brian's voice lesson Allison sounded exactly like she sounded when giving voice lessons before her surgery.

I'm including an email from Allison in March, for it shows how dramatically her writing had improved.

> **From:** Allison Woyiwada
> **Sent:** March 18, 2013 11:39 AM
> **To:** Marya Woyiwada; Robert McMechan
> **Subject:** Re: Happy st patty's day!!!
>
> *Dinner is fine today. I have a physio appt at 3:30 at YWCA. I then intend to walk home after the appt. I'll have my phone. Likely home by 5:00 - 5:30.*
>
> *I found out today that my surgery is scheduled for April 10th. This is good news, especially that I'm hoping to go to*

Allison's Brain • 267

*California 2 weeks later. Have to wait and see how my
recovery is going. Fingers crossed.*

Mar 18 3:30 physio appt, Marya for dinner

Mar 19 9:30 Allison appt with Dr. Blake

Mar 22 out with Carol and Gerald for dinner

Mar 30 Bob and Allison's 17th anniversary in Wakefield

*Mar 31 Mariposa Farm Easter dinner with Tyler, Mar
and Alian, ready to leave by 11:00am*

April 10th Allison's surgery

April 17th release from hospital (maybe earlier)

*April 25th Bob and Allison to California (if surgery
recovery is taking a long time, I'll stay here)*

*May 7 return from California — better be summery here
by then*

One other email from March tells an important part of the
Allison's Brain story.

From: Robert McMechan
Sent: March 27, 2013 7:59 PM
To: Evelyn Tan; Cheryl Jones
Cc: Marya Woyiwada; Tyler Woyiwada
Subject: Today

*Thought I should mention that this evening Allison said
words to the effect of "the two ladies I work with (the two
of you) are really awesome."*

*I am doubting there is higher praise anyone could earn
from Allison's point-of-view, and we want to thank you
both for your stellar efforts!*

Robert

268 • *Robert McMechan with Allison Woyiwada*

We had Easter brunch at Mariposa Farm outside Ottawa with Tyler, Marya and Alain. In one of very many funny moments, which are too numerous to fully recount, Allison returned to our table after having seen a frozen partridge for sale in a freezer. The word "partridge" eluded her, but Allison managed to describe it as "a very small bird that sits on a tree," adding that it was "quite dead."

That evening, we had a terrific Easter dinner at Joan and Warren's with their family, and Mike and Janice Hayes. The next day, Allison got a delightful email from Janice, but it may have been an April Fools joke.

From: Janice Hayes
Sent: April 1, 2013 4:01 PM
To: Allison Woyiwada
Cc: Robert McMechan
Subject: Good to see you

Dearest Allison. So nice to see you last evening... Bob too! Just needed to say that you have made spectacular progress and should be so so proud of your accomplishments. Your wit, charm and good humour have remained fully intact! I will miss you in California but am looking forward to our next adventure. Love, your friend!

Janice

Allison had surgery in April to remove the malignant tumour from her liver after a series of tests had come up with the diagnosis of neuroendocrine cancer. We were both very impressed with Dr. Fairfull-Smith, who we met with a few times and did the surgery. Our understanding is that neuroendocrine cancer is often a slow growing cancer that isn't detected for years, and so the accidental finding of the tumour in Allison's liver was, in a sense, fortunate. This surgery affected Allison cognitively for quite a period. Because I was running the Big Sur Marathon near the end of April in California with Phil and Kristie and a bunch of great friends, Allison's sister Linda came and looked after her while I was away.

I felt that Allison's sister Linda was the best possible person to stay with Allison while I was away for a few reasons. Besides the family connection, Linda is basically a no-nonsense person, and she had spent her entire career working with adults with mental disabilities. Allison had made it clear that after her surgery she did not want me to recruit people to babysit her, but she was delighted to see her sister.

From: Allison Woyiwada
Sent: May 2, 2013 11:25 AM
To: Jim Rennie
Subject: my help line

Dear Jim and Linda:

Thanks for letting Linda come to stay with me for a week. It's a big deal, and it means a lot to me.

My little "devil" system that is there for me when needed came in again. Tis true, Linda was a welcome assistant to fall back on, but for the most part, I survived. Every once in a while, a word escaped me, but she helped me find the culprit and carry on. I will persist until this problem disappears, by gum! However, rest assured that the culprits are few and far between. No need to worry. I am more stubborn than they are.

*It was good to talk to you once in a while, Jim. Taking
Linda out to meet my neighbourhood friends and to attend
concerts etc was fun from this end.*

Thanks to you both for being such good friends.

Love you
Allison xo

Allison and I had been planning the trip to California for quite
some time, and she always loved to be amongst my running friends
(and any friends for that matter), so it was quite disappointing that
she wasn't able to go. I had lost track of Allison's ring after her last
surgery and, after hunting high and low, concluded that I must have
lost it. So when I went to San Francisco, I bought another ring.
Within a few minutes of having given it to Allison, after my return
to Ottawa, she promptly found her missing ring.

Around the middle of May, Allison went for her first post-surgery
bike ride, and she was thrilled that she could ride her bike again. She
had also stopped relying on me for doling out her daily medication.
One thing that was still confusing her, however, was the respective
roles of all of her various medical doctors. This wasn't too surprising,
considering that in less than a year she'd had appointments with
Drs. Lesiuk and Kassam (neurosurgeons). Dr. Masters (cardiologist), Dr. Dupuis (anaesthetist), Dr. Marshall (Rehab Centre), Dr.
Blake (personal physician), Dr. Peters (plastic surgeon who did the
second cranioplasty), Dr. Fairfull-Smith (Liver and Pancreas Unit),
Dr. Polonsky (dentist), and Dr. Eric DesGrosiellers (optometrist).

On the one year anniversary of Allison's surgery, we took the
train to Toronto and drove to Niagara-on-the-Lake so I could serve
as a faculty member at an annual Canadian Bar Association tax law
course for lawyers as I have done for the past twenty years. At a
breakfast one morning, we were seated at a table with a group of
people that we'd never met before. We began telling the *Allison's
Brain* story, and the people at the table seemed to be completely fascinated. The experience solidified our intention to write this book,

so if you don't find reading it has been time well spent, you have tax lawyers to blame.

We next proceeded to have a one year anniversary celebration at home for people in Ottawa who had been part of the Allison and Bob support group, and while for space reasons we weren't able to invite everyone who had lent their support, we hosted quite a large gathering with Marya and her boyfriend Alain's help. People were very excited to see how well Allison was doing. Allison was pooped afterwards, but said she had a very good time.

RAISING OUR GLASSES TO YOU!

Hosted by:
Marya and Bob

When:
Saturday, June 1, 2013
4:00 PM - 7:00 PM

We also jointly sent out a Week Fifty-Two *Allison's Brain* update to mark the one year anniversary.

From: Allison Woyiwada
Sent: May 19, 2013 8:30 PM
To: Allison's Brain
Subject: Week Fifty-Two Update

Hi,

Here is a message from both Bob and I. My message is at the bottom and Bob is written up top.

–AW

It's been a while — here is the one year update! Allison has made truly remarkable progress in the past year. After having essentially no motor skills for a considerable time following her May 28th brain aneurysm clipping operation, Allison gradually re-learned how to walk, has had personal fitness sessions at the YMCA for several months, and last week resumed bicycling for the first time! After having essentially no command of language for a considerable period after the surgery, Allison passed through a time of great difficulty with language and has at times this year spoken with such precision that you couldn't have guessed that she'd had a brain injury. However, Allison's prowess with language ebbs and flows, and this is a source of frustration for her, as we all know that Allison likes to be perfect! And, not remembering the time when she couldn't speak at all, less than perfect seems like quite a handicap to Allison, although the progress she has made is actually ginormous. Memory too has improved by leaps and bounds, as has Allison's writing. While these improvements may be partly attributable to the natural healing powers of the brain, there is no doubt that Allison's dedication and persistence in working at her speech and music therapy exercises, and her positive attitude and humour, have contributed a great deal to her recovery. Having outstanding speech and music therapists hasn't hurt either. Allison's music therapist, Cheryl Jones, who is about to embark on a PhD program in the music therapy field at the University of Toronto this fall, was the subject of a feature article in the Ottawa Citizen on Saturday May 18, 2013: (reproduced on the website of The Palm Beach Music Therapy Institute) http://

Allison's Brain • **273**

pbmti.com/singing-in-the-brain-therapist-uses-musics-patterns-to-help-patients/.

Given Allison's own excellent musicianship and the extent of her recovery, she may be nearing the end of what Cheryl thinks music therapy can accomplish; however, Cheryl is consulting with leading experts in Australia and the United States for any ideas they have about continuing music therapy with Allison.

On the surgery front in 2012, besides the brain clipping operation, Allison had two shunt operations (the first shunt was infected) and two cranioplasty operations (the first cranioplasty was unsuccessful). As if that wasn't enough surgery, she has also had a liver resection operation this year in early April to remove a neuroendocrine tumour. Allison has been on the mend / rebounding for several weeks since this last (successful) operation, and she is now consulting with a medical specialist regarding any possible further courses of treatment.

If I may be permitted a personal note, besides bearing witness to Allison's remarkable resilience and recovery, this past year has also brought home what I take to be a valuable life lesson. Small (and not so small) acts of kindness go an incredible distance in buoying up people when they are having difficult times. But for the amazing generosity and support of family and friends, who are nearby and in far-flung places, this experience would have been immensely more difficult. So a huge thanks to everyone who has helped out along the way.

All for now and have a great summer!

Bob

P.S. Allison is proudly becoming an honorary lifetime member of the Savoy Society in early June. She is also itching to put her musical talents back to use in the next while — so stay tuned.

****

Hi Y'all

This is Allison here. Thanks for reading and taking such an active part in helping me get back to "normal." The Medical Doctors I came in part with, were not aware that I was likely to end up being so normal when all was dealt with. I had to work hard on that from time to time, but I continued to argue that I should be normal, regardless of how long it might take me. And so I persisted.

My Medical Team was imperative and outstanding! Evelyn, Cheryl and Brian helped me on all sorts of fronts for several months. Bob, Linda, Marya and Tyler are people who loved me immensely. I received so many messages of support from you. I can't begin to share my feelings with some of you who have stood by me in the hospital and pretended I'm getting better. Whatever plan you chose, thanks for the help. I may not have noticed it at the time, but it seems to have worked for me.

And so, I say thanks. You helped me and I'm grateful. I'll do the same for you when I can.

Love
Allison

xoxo

This, of course, yielded an avalanche of responses, of which I will share a couple.

From: Victoria Henry
Sent: May 20, 2013 10:34 AM

To: Allison Woyiwada
Subject: Re: Week Fifty-Two Update

Dear Allison and Bob. Sharing the experience with all of us makes us better people and more aware of how to meet life's many challenges with courage and humour. You both deserve all the love and support you have been shown. I am so glad to hear the good news.

Vicki

From: JoAnne Sulzenko
Sent: May 20, 2013 7:03 AM
To: Allison Woyiwada; Robert McMechan
Subject: Re: Week Fifty-Two Update — a salute right back at you from the Sulzenkos

Allison and Bob:

A remarkable Update from two remarkable people on behalf of everyone on their team. We thank you for these wonderful and inspirational and loving words.

JoAnne and Andrei (Looking forward to seeing you at Reach this week, with real pleasure.)

By early June, Allison was back to keeping her own calendar in her usual fashion.

From: Allison Woyiwada
Sent: June 2, 2013 4:40 PM
To: Robert McMechan
Subject: this week

June 2

June 3: 10:00 workout YMCA (walk)

June 4: 10:00 Dr. Blake

June 5: 12:30 music

June 6: take in blood test (I can walk it in — not far)

June 7: 11:30 Music

June 8

Xoxoxo

Carol Alette had been coming to our house regularly to play piano duets with Allison, and in June they played together at our annual block party. This was especially memorable, as I went to the 2012 block party alone, while Allison was still in the Neurosciences Acute Care Unit.

In June we also attended a memorial service in Prince Edward County for David Shilton, who had been a good friend of Allison's for a long time. Allison and David's wife Tricia Davies had performed in a few Gilbert and Sullivan shows together as leading ladies, and David was also one of the Savoy Society's performers, as well as its President. Allison proceeded to write a letter to David to read at his memorial service. She worked hard on this for days and got it into good shape. However, when she started to read it at the memorial service, she realized that reading wasn't her forte. She still did quite a good job, but was sorry afterwards that she hadn't just spoken with bullet points. I had often seen and heard Allison speak publicly at concerts, and she never had a note, but was always clear and well-spoken. In any event, Allison was very glad she'd seen David at his nursing home when she visited with Tricia in early May. Despite his own health problems, he had been very concerned about Allison's well-being.

Another email in June from Allison to Dan Hermosa helps to illustrate the level of her recovery.

> **From:** Allison Woyiwada
> **Sent:** June 10, 2013 4:59 PM
> **To:** Dan Hermosa
> **Cc:** Robert McMechan
> **Subject:** have a great time
>
> *Hi Dan*
>
> *I hope you all have great time while you're away on that fantastic vacation.*
>
> *I needed to talk to you about my current situation. I really feel good and look forward to my future. We enjoy lots of laughs all the time. However, there are times when I have a bad memory. It doesn't seem to be long lasting, but it seems to be an issue for me. There are times when I speak in error and don't notice it until someone else mentions it to me. There are times when I will have several days of smooth sailing, followed by a day that has a few gaps. I have been told that my bad days may become more and more rare. That's good.*
>
> *I have been discussing my situation with both of my teachers/educators, and each came out to the same solution for me. Bob agrees. All of them seem to be concerned that this won't recover itself immediately, so they should all stop worrying. They enjoy working with me and they enjoy watching me get stronger. They do, however, recognize that I will have a drop once in a while. We'll have more discussion when you guys get back so forget about me and enjoy yourselves.*

278 · *Robert McMechan with Allison Woyiwada*

Feel free to share this with Sharon. See you when you return.

Cheers
Allison

xo

At the beginning of July we had a relaxing one week holiday at Lac Xavier courtesy of Dan and Sharon. While there after reading *The China Study*,[13] and some other books, and watching the film documentary *Forks over Knives*,[14] I concluded that a whole food plant-based diet was one of the best things we could do as a defence against cancer, amongst other ailments. Allison agreed with this, and we have happily been vegetarians ever since. Also while on this holiday, Allison did some difficult and lengthy bicycle rides, and although she found them challenging, she characteristically never gave up.

The summer passed quickly, as it always does, but Allison managed to get in a week of holidays with Marya and Alain at

---

13 T. Colin Campbell and Thomas M. Campbell, *The China Study*, BenBella Books, Dallas, 2005.

14 Lee Fulkerson, *Forks over Knives*, 2011.

Jim and Linda's cottage on Lake Manitoba. This has always been a favourite spot of Allison's, and she was very pleased to see that it had survived the massive flooding from the spring of 2011.

In August, Allison had a breakthrough in regaining an understanding of neuroplasticity thanks to Cheryl Jones. When they were discussing whether Allison would have lifelong aphasia, Cheryl explained that she could think of the matter as analogous to what would happen if the fourth finger on her hand was injured. The adjacent little finger and middle finger could take over what the fourth finger used to do. This explanation buoyed Allison up considerably, and she gave it as an example to many of her friends.

At the end of August, Allison was doing projects in the back yard. One day I looked out and saw that the shed in the back yard had been emptied. Allison wasn't feeling well, and I asked her what was going on.

> **From:** Robert McMechan
> **Sent:** September 15, 2013 3:05 PM
> **To:** Laurie Souchotte; Phil McMechan; Bette-Lou Paragg; Joan and Ben; Jim Rennie; Marya Woyiwada; Tyler Woyiwada
> **Cc:** Allison Woyiwada
> **Subject:** Allison is Back in Form
>
> *On Sept. 15th last year Allison had just begun her 6 weeks in residence at the ABI Rehab Centre. This year, although she didn't get a full night's sleep, as we were out late watching Carmen at the NAC last evening, and she has a head cold, I found her cleaning out our storage shed this a.m. — see the attachment. When I remarked on this she told me "There's stuff to do."*
>
> *I may have mentioned that the CEO at the Ottawa Hospital has put us in touch with the VP Communications, who will assist us making contact with people we want to interview for "Allison's Brain," which we are hoping to get written this winter. The first written contribution from*

280 · *Robert McMechan with Allison Woyiwada*

someone who visited Allison a lot while she was in hospital last summer arrived this week, and it is very moving to read.

Dad/Bob

P.S. Ben, look at how excellent your back yard work has turned out!

In September we were off to Lake Tahoe to stay with Laurie, Joel and Blake at a great cabin for a few days, courtesy of our running friends Meredith Mills and George Dies. One day Allison and I climbed up the Cascades Trail, which isn't exactly Mount Everest, but it was a spectacular comeback for Allison. I didn't buy Allison another ring in California this time, but we did manage to see a Kokanee salmon run.

Allison also joined the Brahms Choir in September. She says she enjoyed the experience, partly because she was not known by the other Choir members, and she didn't tell them her story. She worked very hard on the music the choir was singing, and participated in an early December Christmas concert. The concert was about 90 minutes in length, and the songs were sung in English, French, and German. Mary Pole, Allison's first rehab centre speech therapist, happened to be in the audience, and she told us afterwards that when she saw Allison singing with the choir it blew her away and made her want to cry.

In October we began making strides on the *Allison's Brain* book project.

From: Robert McMechan
Sent: October 18, 2013 5:33 PM
To: Lotsa Helping Hands
Cc: Allison Woyiwada
Subject: "Allison's Brain" Update

Some exciting news today! Following our letter to Dr. Jack Kitts, CEO of The Ottawa Hospital, concerning our plan to write a book on Allison's experience through the brain aneurysm journey she's had, we met today with Allison Neill, Senior VP, Communications and Outreach, Ottawa Hospital. Allison Neill is enthusiastically supporting our project, and is putting us in touch with many Hospital personnel who have been involved in the story. Our plan is to interview as many of these people as possible this year, and then proceed to putting together our manuscript early next year. Allison Neill is also offering to support us on the publicity end of things, including with the book launch when that comes to pass. We've already received a couple of splendid contributions from friends, and we are hoping for many more by the end of the year.

While Allison's story is an inspirational one, we also want to portray the difficulties and uncertainties along the way, and we invite you to share any doubts / dark thoughts, etc. you may have encountered. That said, we also welcome your recounting of any humorous moments.

We sincerely appreciate your assistance, and also want to say that while we think our project is important, we know you have many things to do. That may mean, in some cases, you are unable to send a written contribution, but you have all been part of an amazing journey!

Thanks for your support,
Allison and Bob

*P.S. The Nature of Things recently documented the work
of a therapist in Montreal using music to help people with
brain injuries rebuild neural pathways. This is a fascinating area, in which Allison's music therapist Cheryl Jones
has just embarked at U. of T. on her Ph.D.*

*P.P.S. In the "it's a small world" realm of things, it
turns out that Allison Neill co-presented Allison with
a "Community Builder" award thirteen years ago at
Hopewell School on behalf of the United Way — they
realized this during the course of our meeting today.*

An email from Allison in November displays what a tireless worker she has been. Allison had sent the story of Jill Bolte Taylor's recovery, as told in *Stroke of Insight*, to her kids and they were discussing it.

From: Allison Woyiwada
Sent: November 24, 2013 11:42 AM
To: Tyler Woyiwada; Marya Woyiwada
Cc: Robert McMechan
Subject: Re: Jill Bolte Taylor

*I can feel how she does. The initial time does not allow so
much memory time loss for me, other than the initial 2/4
months. The interesting points for me are that recovery will
take far less than 8 years due to the fact that there was less
injured initially.*

*My work continues, and improvement continues at a faster
pace than usual. The improvement pace is interesting to
watch —more interesting than in the older days. But there
are times when a down slump comes on with no warning.
And there it is. A down period is there. I watch more
carefully. I study more rigorously to overcome. There are
times when I miss the down time until it has become more
evident to myself. I wait and watch my down sides. I add
some mental exercises. I add some physical exercises. I read.*

Allison's Brain • **285**

*I write. I sleep when I need some. I practise piano. I also
sing with choir three hours each week.*

*The up-side for my recovery from down side is that up-side
goes higher each time. I continue to notice the difference.
The changes for the previous periods are noticeable and
quite thrilling. I will work to stay here. I can't predict what
may cause a down slide next time, but I will deal with it
when it comes.*

Allison wrote a thank-you note in December to the music director of the Brahms Choir.

From: *Allison Woyiwada*
Sent: *December 03, 2013 5:57 PM*
To: *Denise Hawkins* ET AL
Subject: Re: Christmas concert kudos

*Denise, you are such a pleasant force to deal with, and we
appreciate to have been involved with you and the fine lead
cast. Great thanks to all of you for all you've done.*

*My husband and I will be going to Antigua from January
— April and, regrettably, I will miss singing with you
in the new year. I am recovering from a Brain Aneurysm
that occurred last May 2012. The recovery is remarkably
quick — to the point whereby my Doctors will wish us well
on our time away. My husband, Robert McMechan, will
be writing a book called Allison's Brain during this period.
You may be asked if you saw any remnants of one :)*

*It was a great time to be there with all of you. The feature
cast is remarkable and need to be thanked and applauded.
I so enjoyed making new friends throughout the rehearsal
time. I already miss you. Perhaps we can do this again next
fall.*

Denise, "she who knows all," you are remarkable. Thanks for getting your points across to us. We needed you, and you delivered.

Have a happy new year to you all.

Cheers and best wishes
Allison Woyiwada xo

Late in December, Allison shared her thoughts with my sisters about her latest visit with Dr. Lesiuk.

From: Allison Woyiwada
Sent: December 28, 2013 11:13 AM
To: Bette-Lou Paragg; Joan Veselovsky
Cc: Robert McMechan
Subject: Re: Photos

*Ah! I love to look at the photos but I also love to look at the normal photos of myself. Good to be normal again... sort of.
:) This is my next project, and my surgeon thinks I'll begin to lose weight once I cut back on some potent drugs. I can't believe he said this to me, but he did! He actually let me give him a big hug and kiss, and he hugged and kissed me right back. We're both happy guys!*

Love
Allison

Then came the last *Allison's Brain* update of 2013.

From: Allison Woyiwada
Sent: December 30, 2013 9:44 PM
To: Allison's Brain
Subject: Happy New Year and thanks for all you've done for me

Hello my friends:

Allison's Brain • **287**

Hope you're all having a wonderful down time during the season. Bob and I are enjoying that in Ottawa at the present, but we are leaving for Antigua on January 4th. We will make a short return in middle March, but returning to Antigua until April 23rd. We have both decided not to tolerate cold weather. I know a number of people who have made this choice and it makes them happy.

Regarding my current situation, all is going pretty well. The people who performed the surgical "miracle" are in awe. The surgeons understand that I need to practise to get back to my normal status, but they are very pleased with my rate. I told them at one point what I expected of recovery. They felt I was setting too high a goal, but they have since agreed that I am keeping up after all. (I intended to keep working and end up being smarter than them, but decided that sounded like too much work. :)

I have been working to improve my brain. I lost a portion during surgery, (rats!) but the miracles of the brain to recover are staggering! I study and watch my goal go upward. Following that, I take a day to allow the brain to rest. This is not fun for the brain (nor for me!) but following the resting period, the brain gets back in action. Last summer, I met the woman who was staying with her family next door to us. She went back inside after we chatted and told Meagan that I wasn't the person they had described with a brain injury. Meagan set the record straight. We all had a chat after the fact, but basically, this is where I am. And so, you see, you don't need to worry about me any more.

Early days in the hospital when I couldn't walk or talk, I was wheeled up to the piano. My daughter, Marya, placed my wheelchair in front of the piano. She placed the Beethoven Pathétique in front of me, and I played it, almost flawlessly. I have played it at one point in my life, but it hasn't disappeared.

And so I discovered that the brain can recover! Knowing that, I have begun to apply my new skills. Once I have returned home, Bob and I have hired two new therapists. One is a Music Therapist and one is a Speech Therapist. Their assistance has been extremely valuable.

I know this is lengthy. I apologize, but you need to know. I believe I can recover from this and I am "over the moon," so to speak. Bob has become quite "over the moon" as well and, he has begun preparing a book called Allison's Brain.

We have spoken with several surgeons and professionals who have helped by reporting on their roles. It is lovely to reacquaint ourselves with them. They can't stop smiling! And neither can we!

Cheers and love
Allison xoxoxo

Throughout the year, whenever we talked with people about going back to Antigua, Allison told them we were going for four months. At first, I thought four months was an impossibility, but here we are in Antigua for about four months. Allison bicycles every day, takes swimming lessons, does Sudoku, plays the piano, reads, and loves to ride the local bus to St. John's.

One of the keys to Allison's recovery is that she doesn't give up on things. During the month of March in Antigua, she didn't feel up to climbing to a viewpoint above the Wallings Dam. However, about three weeks later, she climbed Mount Obama, which is the highest point in the country.

Allison hasn't yet made a 100% recovery from her brain surgery, but with her enthusiasm and dedication to the project, I wouldn't bet against it. While here in Antigua, Allison has met a woman who says she'd had a similar experience, and that it had taken her eight years to fully recover from her surgery. Remarkably, we also met a fellow on a beach here who had Dr. Lesiuk as his neurosurgeon in the fall of 2012. Allison and John Tobias are two of the most devoted members of Dr. Lesiuk's fan club. John had a tumour removed from his brain and says he asked Dr. Lesiuk to fix his golf swing while he was in there. Now John says he wants a refund.

It's been quite an odyssey, and as it becomes less so, a few things come to mind. While no two brain injuries are identical, it looks to me as if having a more-or-less constantly positive attitude can have a great deal to do with what lies ahead. Good humour and a tireless work ethic are also obvious assets, and having a brain saturated with music might actually be a huge advantage. But above all else, as a caregiver, I think of support from family and friends. It's fair to say that without it I'd have been toast.

Allison has benefited a great deal from the music and speech therapy sessions she has had beginning in September 2012 until the end of December 2013 when we left for Antigua. We have fortunately been able to recruit all four of her speech therapists to give us their recollections and views. In the case of Evelyn Tan, who has worked extensively with Allison, we have also luckily gotten her expert input in writing — see the *Say No More and It's A Fact Jack* appendix.

It is a testament to the work of Allison's music therapist Cheryl Jones that speech therapists at the rehab centre credit music therapy, and Allison's musicianship, for a considerable contribution to Allison's recovery. At first Allison didn't understand the reason for her sessions with Cheryl, and kept "correcting" her as if she was giving music lessons. But in time Allison understood that the

Allison's Brain • 291

sessions weren't music lessons, and that her speech was improving. I think Cheryl's account of the neuroscience behind music therapy and the methodology she employed with Allison is absolutely fascinating. You will find this set out in the *Power of Music Therapy* appendix.

Finally, over the years, we've heard a lot of complaints about shortcomings in the Canadian medical system. But you have to wonder how many countries in the world have the health care resources to pull this sort of thing off. There's also the point that we haven't had to exhaust all of our savings or sell our house. Once Allison's medical journey got underway, there were a lot of caring and talented people doing their utmost for her, and the health care benefits she received far exceeded our expectations.

Epilogue —
From Where I Sit — May 2014[15]

This is Allison writing to you at last. I'm back, I'm ecstatic, and I've almost completely recovered. This is indeed good news! Dr. Lesiuk, Dr. Kassam and their staff are to be credited for bringing their extraordinary talent my way! Bravo to both of the surgeons! They have put me back in action. My humble thanks also need to be offered to all of the people who assisted with my rehabilitation including the therapists and nurses at the Civic and all of the staff at the Rehab Centre.

It is still much more difficult for me to write clearly than it is to speak. Writing this chapter has been very challenging. However, doing challenging things is unavoidable if you hope to recover from a brain injury. And that is what I have hoped for from the moment I decided to go ahead with surgery.

Reading the earlier chapters in this book, you are aware that I had been told of some frightening possibilities before surgery. Medical responsibility demanded that these things needed to be stated by the surgeons. Understood. However, having listened to the risks, I contemplated my own situation. I did not smoke. I drank a minimal amount of alcohol and was engaged in regular exercise. I didn't like the doctors telling me that life risk was a possibility. I got a little spooked, but I just ignored it. They liked my low heart rate.

---

15 This Epilogue has benefitted from the lightest of touches by an editor who was nonetheless incredibly impressed by Allison's prose.

They liked my positive attitude. There were no signs of Alzheimer's in my brain. I felt my body could handle this, so I asked Dr. Lesiuk to go ahead.

You have already read about the time I spent waiting for my brain surgery to occur. Post-surgery placed me in another space altogether. Big difference! Given my difficulty remembering this, I was reluctant to launch into this chapter. But Bob was adamant (I would curse silently, even though I love the guy), and so I began. My writing skills were terrible! I had practiced reading, playing the piano, singing, physical exercise and many more activities, but I had not written long notes or explanations. Oddly enough, I couldn't present an accurate account of my life recovering from brain surgery. I would write a passage but when I re-read it, it seemed to make no sense. So I would start again and again, several times over, until it seemed to make sense. I stuck to this with my typical dogged determination, hoping I have reached a point where I am making sense to you.

Recovery from Surgery: May 2012

I began taking Dilantin before surgery to prevent my brain from having seizures. I have continued taking Dilantin during and after surgery, up to today's date. I don't always like the side effects. It seems to create a doziness I'd rather not have to put up with. However, in the coming months, I will be discussing with Dr. Lesiuk whether it can be reduced or eliminated.

Starting on the morning of May 28th, 2012, I slept through a full day of surgery, followed by ten days of coma, followed by more than two months of no memory. This is quite a phenomenon! I was not prepared for this to happen. I remember nothing of this period. I am told that I spoke to people — sometimes at random. I did not know the people who were there. My brain was not co-operating. There was nothing I could do for myself. I was helpless. Apparently, I had chats with the nurses and friends and family that made sense

— or not, humorous at times. But nothing stuck with me. It seemed that my brain had not liked to be maneuvered.

I have seen a list and photos of people who came to visit during my time with no memory. This was astonishing to see after the fact. This was a system Bob had set up for people to assist me in my recovery. Not only did people come over, they came over often. The list is amazing, and I owe a deep debt of gratitude to these people not only for helping me, but for assisting my family. Donna Walsh came over to show me several photos. Jill Berry, Louise Hall and Susan Smith came to visit as well. I know that because I have seen photos and diary entries by them. I have no recollection of that happening. Jill has reminded me that she taught me how to eat by using my utensils. I still used my fingers and laughed at myself. (I'm better now.) I've seen photos of Micheal, Marianna and Stephanie Burch when they came over with a card and pyjamas for me. Nice gesture, but I don't remember seeing them. Once Gord Bourgard walked into my room, and I said, "Hello Gord." I guess I sounded friendly. I think I was, but I don't remember he was there.

When memory finally started to appear in late August, I knew not what to expect. I intended to say something, but I stopped part way through. I couldn't remember what to say. In fact, memory skills often seemed useless. Bob would come to visit me often. However, I found it hard for him to leave. Whenever he said he was going, I would find something to talk with him about that was often quite incomprehensible to him. He came up with a plan. He would plan to leave just as the other people would arrive. I would ask him to stay anyway, but he'd leave. Poor guy. Gets no break! Peggy Elliot brought games for us to play. I knew immediately that this was going to be too hard for me to learn. Couldn't be helped. What I can do in the morning, often means it's too hard to do in the evening. The brain needs a break. I might be able to do it now, Peggy!

I recall Sharon Neill visiting me. We chatted a few times. She once asked me a question, and I answered. She responded with, "That's a good idea." Then she said goodbye and left. I was proud of my answer, but had no recollection of what I'd said to her. Carol

Allison's Brain   •   **295**

Anderson and her son Alistair biked over on a Sunday afternoon. I said hello and called them by name. We talked for a short time, and it was obvious that I knew who they were. In Alistair's case, I told him a joke, and he laughed. It's the little things that keep people happy! Carol was excited. She had seen me previously, but this was the first time I knew who she was. Deidre Garcia and Lynda Rivington both came to visit me while I was having a nap. In both cases, I awoke, looked at them and asked what they wanted. They both claimed to be there for a visit. I rolled over and went back to sleep. I had a visit from JoAnne Sulzenko as well, but I couldn't remember why. I guess I was sleepy, or I would have had a chat. Seems to be rude. I needed to relearn everything, even my good manners.

However, worse than this would be my ability to guide my thought pattern. I was frightened. I was ashamed. I had gone to great lengths to assure family and friends that I could recover quickly. This thinking proved to be wrong. As time went on, it became more frightening. Efforts were made by the people at the hospital to help my recovery, but the corrections were slow going. I was still in a fog. And so, more efforts had to start coming from me.

Time spent in the hospital was quite telling. Looking from person to person and observing their state caused me to be anxious. So many of these people looked helpless with no one coming by to help them out. Many people looked sad and alone. Forgive me, but I never wanted to look like that. I never wanted to be brain damaged. I was not looking for pity. I had so many things I needed to do. I had so many people I needed to see. I needed to become healthy again.

I needed a long nap, and I did this often. Seems incredible, but there were several sleeps during the day. My body needed to learn to do so many things, including walking. I had been lying about for months! This was going to be long and harsh.

I have read articles about and watched videos of Jill Bolte Taylor who has recovered from a serious brain injury such as mine. She says it took eight years to recover from her brain injury. Eight years!

I refused to believe that I would take that long. My surgeons acted on a potential injury, not an accident. Eight years sounded over the top to me. However, as I watched myself recover, or not recover fast enough, I worried.

Treatment for the Body: August 2012

This was the easiest part to fix.

I had a somewhat fast recovery for the physical body once I was coming out of memory loss. Being in a wheelchair was a big moment! Getting out of bed into my wheelchair made me feel like a new woman. I was no longer held captive in my room. Moving from my bed to my wheelchair was somewhat difficult, but it meant the world to me. Now, I could see the ward in my pyjamas. However, shortly thereafter, I was taken to the area where I was going to be taught to walk again.

My first treatments were by my physiotherapist, Christine. While suffering through memory loss, my effort was minimal and my initiative was poor. But once I understood what I was trying to do, my strength and drive increased. I learned to walk. I got up and got dressed one day. Bob took me to walk in the community near the hospital. It was scary to walk on an uneven surface, but I managed. I was exhausted, so I sat on the grass. I felt like a lump. Getting up by myself wasn't possible. This needed to be entered on my "to do" list. I went back to my bed, and I slept.

After the first surgery, my head remained "skull-less" until there were no further signs of swelling. During that time, I wore a helmet for protection. It was the ugliest, most expensive contraption I have ever seen. I chose not to look at myself in the mirror. My eyes didn't match. One was swollen. I did not want to go through the rest of my life without one side of my face matching the other. On top of this, surgeons had removed some of my hair during surgery. I was not what you might call "pretty."

One day I awoke and got up from my bed. I've been told this was early September. I don't think this was the first time I did this. As

Allison's Brain • 297

I was standing there, Dr. Lesiuk walked towards me. I said, "Hello, Dr. Lesiuk. I think this is the first time I've seen you." This turned out not to be true. He had come to see me countless times, and I had remained unaware of his presence. He did, however, smile when I spoke. I continued to ask if he could consider replacing my skull helmet. He agreed and would make an appointment. I thanked him and said goodbye. I believe this became a good day for Dr. Lesiuk. For me, I was having a lucid moment. For Dr. Lesiuk, I believe he witnessed me as the 'coming back' of a normal person, and he was pleased to catch even a brief moment.

I don't know what I did to deserve this, but I was sent to the General Hospital for my next step. Christine felt I was focused on my needs and had been showing improvement. Bob agreed with my move. And so, we had a new place for me to live — even though I wanted to go home. There were more physical improvements at the Ottawa General Hospital, but the biggest challenge at the time was help for the brain. I still needed that. However, once the memory started coming back even more, one might expect the brain to recover to a natural state. This seemed not to be the case. I initially felt that the brain would help me out. In fact, I discovered later that the brain needed my help, not the other way around. This eventually became my goal.

The Rehab Centre: September 2012

The new facility I was travelling to was the Rehab Centre at the Ottawa General. This ward was in a hospital that was much closer to my own home. Sharon Chartier was visiting me at the Civic Hospital at the time. She was informed that, if I didn't physically take occupation of the other room immediately, the room would be passed on to someone else. Bob and Marya had both agreed that I be transferred, but they had not signed the procedure. Sharon became quite anxious about this situation. I was content to have a new "job." I said goodbye and thank you and was moved to the Ottawa General Hospital.

This facility was different from any other ward I had been on. The room was nicely decorated with a wall map at the end of every bed. The list of activities would be itemized with their time for the day. This made me look like I was a big deal. I felt that I was being treated like royalty. Having said that, I had one or two activities to complete. That's not much, but I often needed a nap to follow. This planner always had my nurse's name. I would never have remembered that name for the day. I could have tried to write things down, but I couldn't write very well yet. There were so many things to learn all over again. One step at a time.

Patients rose and dressed each day. They would then go to the dining room area for a meal. We would all eat together and hope to have sensible conversations with each other. However, there were often awkward moments. Some of the brains still needed recovery. I required assistance more than many others without being fully aware of my limitations. That started to become clearer to me as time went on.

I had people who could definitely help me. My first therapist who came to find me was Julie. She was very accommodating and friendly. She smiled and laughed a lot. We went to the gym, and she took me through a number of body strengthening exercises. What a great way to start the day. I had made some progress on this at the Civic Hospital. This was helping me get even physically stronger. The fact that I was walking independently after a period of a few weeks was very encouraging. Julie always escorted me to and from the gym because there was too big a risk that I would lose my way. There was a second session mid-afternoon that I did with my group in the gym. Some of the actions were a little bit of a challenge, but I succeeded. Improvement for the body over the course of a short time was fast and rewarding.

This treatment indicated to me that my physical abilities were showing recovery. What was not progressing at the same rate was my mind. There were times when I was fully aware and had ability to perform tasks. However, there were other times that this area

Allison's Brain · 299

needed stimulation. I wanted this to improve. I needed someone to give me advice. Fortunately, this ward had people there to help.

For the time I was in the General Hospital, Marya had arranged that I would be home for dinner every day. I was over the moon! I began to get ready to be picked up at 4:30 p.m. and delivered back to the hospital at 7:00 p.m. It was not a perfect situation, but it made me happy!

Benefit Concert: September 2012

Marya organized a concert featuring some of my favourite friends and musicians to perform. This was to raise money to help support my recovery. It was a beautiful concert featuring opera singers and pianists, many friends from the Savoy Society, and local musicians from Southminster United Church. Other good friends were present, acting as hosts. The concert was so well attended that people were eventually asked to go home as there was no room. I was not in attendance at the concert, but I saw the video sometime later. I was extremely honoured for the attention that I was being given. It made me feel very proud of what you did for me! Marya can do a lot for me when I need her. This concert, on top of all the times she visited me, was astounding.

Treatment for The Brain: September 2012

However, good news was followed by less good news. The brain turned out to be the most difficult thing to fix, and at the time we had no promise that this would work. This was frightening. In my former situation, I had been cared for by hospital staff, family and friends. I was well looked after. Now that I was placed in the rehab centre, my existence had started to include other patients. These were people who had suffered brain damage and were in the process of recovering.

We looked for ways to retrieve my brain skills. It proved to be somewhat more of a challenge. Initially, I didn't think that was the case. I assumed my brain might take a little longer to recover than my body functions, but things turned out quite differently. My body learned quickly to adapt from instructions. However, my brain did not accept new instructions as readily. I was not even aware that I was misunderstanding my instructions. This was the most challenging thing I had ever met with.

I had a session with Mary, a speech therapist, in her office. I visited Mary in the morning. As she came to pick me up at my room, she asked me to walk to her office ahead of her to determine that I knew where her office was. I was embarrassed. I felt silly. I didn't think it was necessary. But I did it. This was a challenging session. I was to identify items in a drawing. Anything that was not supposed to be there was to be identified and removed. As Mary explained this to me, I found her instructions to be unclear. She invited Bob to a later session and explained to him that I could not follow her instructions. However, as I heard her instructions to him, it did become quite clear. As a result, I followed the instructions correctly from then on and made her extremely happy. I asked myself if this was beginning to look like positive steps for me. This seemed like it. However, my pattern was ebbing and flowing. I had no sense of which was advancing and why.

I attended some sessions which included my "classmates" and other therapists. Evelyn, the leader of the group would ask for opinions, and each person would be expected to give his/her opinion. I gave mine, and it made no sense to anyone but me. I had had surgery close to four months ago, and I was still missing my logic and my common sense. Two other classmates started to laugh at what I said. I thought they were being silly. To me, it made perfect sense. This occurred more than once, and it became clear to my instructor that I needed individual attention. Evelyn spoke to my other class members and asked them not to make fun of me. I did not know I was being teased or laughed at. I didn't even know that what I had said was not sensible. I worked with people who recognized that I didn't know what I was talking about. My classmates

Allison's Brain • 301

could write their answers. I could not do that. I could not even sign my own name.

As time passed during my sessions, I listened to discussions, but I commonly misunderstood what was being said. And I didn't even know that I was missing the point. My recovery was taking far too long. Perhaps I never would recover. I had thoughts such as this when I was alone in my room. I was scared. Was I as good as I would ever get? This may have been my darkest period. As I had gained some of my cognitive abilities, I had also been made aware that my brain was not recovering as it should have been. I was frightened. There were times I remembered and times I did not. I was puzzled. I tried to remain optimistic in front of my family and friends, but I was scared. Being moved to the new hospital and the new care facility was a positive thing. However, the new position provided me with a new challenge. Once I knew I had to make more progress, I ensured that my work level continued to increase.

I was attempting to remain optimistic. I had motivation for doing this. I had promised friends and family that I would overcome this surgery and get back to normal in a short period of time. This was not happening as quickly as I thought and there was some embarrassment. I had lost my fine tuned skills. My friends kept our conversations at a simplified level. This made me sad. I feared that my brain had been seriously damaged and recovery was impossible. When one's brain needs repair, there is a fear that it won't happen. I liked my brain the way it was. I wanted it back, but there was no guarantee that this would happen. This made me even sadder.

Sign Out: October 2012

Yes! I was called to a meeting with various therapists to discuss my readiness to be released. I was so excited, I could barely contain my excitement! This is the first time in my life I was kept in a hospital for this length of time. I had a chance to thank people for what they had done for me. I also made some lighthearted comments which roused a few rounds of laughter.... I hope.

Though my state of health was not perfect, I loved being at home. This was my place to recover after hospital life that lasted for five months. It was hard for my husband to cook meals on top of everything else he was doing, but he made it work. Now, I could stay home and go to bed whenever I was tired. I napped several times throughout the day, but I would sit in the living room and turn on the fireplace. This was like a dream come true. There was one exception. I had stopped studying and needed to increase that to aid my brain.

When I came home, I couldn't remember the names of most things in the house. One of the ways I dealt with this was by putting labels on things. Marya helped me to do this. Even though I knew what the things in our kitchen were for, I couldn't remember what they were called.

I was called back to the hospital a few times each week for testing and evaluation. In addition, I had therapists visit me at home to help me work through my brain challenges. Parts of my brain were starting to understand. I was pleased to see how clear and concise I could be at times.

After I was released from the hospital, I walked a great deal throughout the neighbourhood. I even walked to and back from the General Hospital for blood testing. There were routes in the community where I could find a shortcut. I could shop for groceries. I could walk in unusual places, but have no problem finding my way home.

I had friends, Pat and Doug MacDonald, who had been waiting to come and visit me at home so we could play and sing music. One thing I may not have been able to express to them was that music had stayed with me, regardless of what other things had slipped from my memory. When we got together and sang and played, I was able to sing and play whatever I had done before surgery. I'm told that this was demonstrated earlier when Marya pushed my wheelchair up to play the music on the piano in the Civic Hospital. It was much later explained to me by Catherine, my speech therapist at the Civic Hospital, that music was stored by my right brain

Allison's Brain • 303

and, as a result, never forgotten. Music has always meant a lot to me. It was always a big relief that it stayed status quo, and it has always remained important as a regular part of my life.

Another time, Eileen and Geoff Wilson drove us to Kingston to see a curling game. Wow! This was a big deal for me. We even ate in a restaurant before the game. I loved this event because it had nothing to do with music. I love music, but the rest of the world is fun as well.

I was being picked up and dropped off at the hospital twice a week. In both cases, I was meeting with Natalie, a speech therapist. She was a very nice person, and we liked spending time together. We had good times. We would work to solve problems. We laughed when we could. Working with Natalie was quite encouraging. She was able to find alterations in her approach to improve my success rate. This appeared to me immensely due to her ability to adjust. It was much appreciated to experience alternative learning styles. However, I was only allowed to report for these sessions with Natalie for a limited period. Beyond that, we needed to look for other new teachers. We found two eager teachers named Evelyn and Cheryl, twice a week for each one.

Evelyn was a treat for me. She explained things to me. She offered advice. Evelyn was good at this. We did things together. We would go for long walks and have discussions along the way. She came to the Afar Fundraising Banquet. She was happy to see me reuniting with people I hadn't seen for some time. Evelyn would often come to our session with a different agenda each time. I have never had extensive discussions with her about this approach, but I felt these types of assignments would offer room for improvement. For someone like me, who has gone through life dealing with learning things through repetition, working with Evelyn was presenting a new challenge for me. Each time she came for a lesson, we often tried a new activity. Sometimes it was a brand new skill area. Other times it was a revision on something we had already attempted. Between each session I practiced what we had already discussed. Some days I spent time working on a diary to enhance my writing skills. At other times I would read the newspaper and write a brief synopsis of any particular story

This has never been a typical learning style for me, but with each new therapist I had, I followed their advice. The pattern that was chosen was seen by them as being the most useful strategy. The one down side I experienced was when Evelyn noticed that my speaking ability had taken a serious decline as I was struggling with aphasia. This had occurred shortly after my surgery for the removal of a malignant tumour. This was the first time that I was facing this subject. I was warned before my brain surgery that this could happen, but I had ignored the possibility that it would happen to me. I was overwhelmed. I began to believe that this condition would never go away. This was the most frightening period I had ever experienced so far. Evelyn continued to work with me to help me overcome my current situation. My fear caused me to increase my daily work to catch up to where I had been before surgery. One never knows if this will truly happen, but the work is worth the risk. And so, we worked harder than ever. Many thanks to Evelyn for all the periods she helped me get through.

Cheryl was also a treat for me. I have been one of her oldest students. I have also possibly been one of the most experienced musicians she has worked with. Our lessons were simply extensions of the one we had completed and preparation for the next one. For a mind and a memory such as mine, this was a pattern that worked for me.

I began to put the pieces together. Most verses would include peoples' names, street names or nouns. Beyond that, I would have created the rhythm that fit with the music. One that was introduced most recently for me was "Bob and I are getting ready for Antigua. We need to pack our passports, flashlights and reflector vests." I would then create a rhythm and melody and assign it to the collection of words. When Cheryl came for the next lesson, she played the melody on the piano, and, without looking at the score, I would sing the song that I had created with the correct rhythm and melody. This may not seem difficult, but I had written a total

Allison's Brain • 305

of more than 75 pieces by the end of the time we spent together. I required the melody to bring the collection of words to mind. (Many of my songs are about some of you, but that will remain a secret. :)) I would put some of the pieces together bit by bit — perhaps the last phrase or the characters' names. The words would be assembled like a crossword puzzle before it began to make sense. Sometimes even after lengthy practice, I could not recognize these tunes during my lesson. If I was having difficulty, there was nothing I could do to help myself. My brain was struggling in a downward pattern at the time. I would nap and try again later. Once my brain switched to upward movement, everything seemed bright and clear. You've all had that feeling. You know what it's like, and you love it. I know the two opposite feelings, and I've learned to wait to see which direction I'm going each day. I'd like to keep going up. Much more fun!

Cheryl understood what my brain could do, and she gave me encouragement. She made me believe I could recover. She explained to me that, although part of my brain could no longer do its job because it had been injured, other parts of my brain could take over. This made me very happy and made me feel optimistic about my chances of recovering. I felt we were making satisfactory progress to help the challenges of the mind to have caught up with challenges for the body. Once again, however, I found that more things needed to be dealt with.

My skull had to be repaired in December 2012 as there seemed to be a small "leak." The downside of recovering from surgery is taking strong Tylenol. I seldom take this drug, and so I forget its side-effects. One night a group of school teachers all piled into a bus in the middle of the night. When I mentioned this to the doctors the next morning, they explained this did not happen. I was shocked but soon discovered that Tylenol was the culprit and stopped taking it. Another time, I had several thoughts, awake or asleep, that the 2nd and 3rd floors in my home had been converted to a medical area. I made myself stop thinking about it. I knew Bob would find a cure and this was not for me to solve the problem. However, this might have been a similar reaction to a drug.

Cancer: April 2013

Cancer did not seem to be threatening to me. I returned to the Civic Hospital in April 2013 to have cancer cells removed from my liver. To be cautious, surgeons had felt it necessary to explore internally, but found nothing more than what they had already expected. Further tests would be taken, but everything looked fine after the surgery. What happened following the surgery was staying in the hospital for several days with a fluid diet. That was hurtful and it took a while to come back. However, I moved home and restarted my lessons with Evelyn and Cheryl.

Aphasia: May 2013

During my lessons with Evelyn, she indicated that my memory was poor and I was getting worse. This was likely the result of a step down after surgery. This was typical. However, this was also frightening. I always got scared when I was getting worse rather than better. When I asked what was wrong, Evelyn indicated that I was suffering from aphasia. Dr. Lesiuk told us that this might happen and I thought, "No way. Not gonna happen." Well guess what, it happened! Evelyn also recorded my response to a question she had asked of me. When she played it back I was astounded! I was mortified! I was ashamed. Evelyn looked worried, which caused me to be even more frightened.

Many months after the surgery was completed, I was struggling, and I was getting ticked off. Words, names, descriptions, understanding were all areas that presented a challenge that wouldn't go away. Bob, my loving husband who explained every word or phrase that had slipped from me, was extraordinarily patient with me. I went through my existence with people pretending I knew what they were talking about. Extremely frustrating!

I remembered hearing the risks of struggling with aphasia. My husband and my family knew it was there, but I had ignored it. I knew this would be something I would need to work against, but

Allison's Brain • 307

I didn't know this was already applying to me. I felt I had enough things to fight against. I was angry. I slipped into a funk. This was tough! This was not what I wanted to recover from. I knew that once in a while, I could not revive a memory. However, it came and went, and at this moment, the memory needed to be rebuilt.

Time to Build Again: June 2013

A portion of my brain had taken a hit during my brain surgery. The left side of my brain lost some of its ability to do its jobs. However, given time and teaching, other brain sections have begun to adapt and take over what was once done in the injured area. I finally understood the process. My niece Kelsey (daughter of Diny Woyiwada and Kevin Knibbs) had some brain areas removed that were causing seizures, and removing them cured her. She no longer has petit-mal or grand-mal seizures. Removing parts of her brain didn't impact what she could do because other parts of her brain took over for the affected area. Lucky Kelsey. I was thrilled when I heard of the success of her brain surgery. Now I needed to train parts of my brain to learn new roles.

The damage to part of my brain means other brain portions need to join in and help with the work of the part of the brain that's been injured. My music therapist, Cheryl, quite calmly explained this process to me. We don't know exactly how long it will take it for my brain to adapt, but it will happen, and I will continue to work until all is done. I was afraid I wouldn't get better, but once I knew I had a focus, I had a new challenge. Yet again! One of these days, I would be a free woman. And I would work as hard as necessary, but the sooner the better.

And so I go back to the drawing board. I increase all the routines of brain and physical exercise. I work harder than before and as often as possible. Each time I increased my efforts, but there was still the next battle to fight. I refused to give up!

My Homework

I know you may feel that, at my age, you no longer need to do your homework. Perhaps under normal circumstances, this may be somewhat truthful. In my case, it's not. I had been doing homework on a regular basis, but once I understood the necessity, I did even more. I escalated my homework from four to six hours each day. I read the paper from cover to cover, and do a crossword puzzle and Sudoku puzzles. I read a novel for at least an hour each day. I download games and challenges to solve problems. I do exercises on my iPad to help my brain. In addition to these brain exercises, I attempt to exercise my body for one hour each day — Yoga, outdoor walking, outdoor cycling, swimming, tennis etc. And I play music, whenever I want to do something that is easy.

Back to My Normal Life

September 2013: I started teaching piano lessons as soon as I'd made myself available. Quite a comfortable thing for me to do. I also signed up to sing with the Brahms Choir. This group rehearsed at Southminster Church in my neighbourhood. I thought I would be with a neighbourhood group and they would all know me and my health. They actually didn't know who I was, so I just sang. Bonus! This choir sang in English, French and German, and it was hard, but I practised every day. My speech therapist Mary at the General Hospital attended our Christmas concert in December 2013, and she was overwhelmed that I had been able to sing successfully.

November 2013: I began to get adults to play together in a band at Abbotsford House. This required a little effort, but a few people began to play. They began to play in January and have continued to do so since then.

January — April 2014: Bob and I moved to Antigua for four months. Splendid place to enjoy your life! Many of our kids came and spent a week with us together. We'll work on getting more of them next year. The upside of this climate is bike riding, walking

Allison's Brain • **309**

and outdoor swimming. The climate is very pleasant for 24 hours a day. While we were in Antigua, I became associated with the Jennings Primary School to help out with music. We then became associated with the Ministry of Education and with the help of its Music Education Officer Marion Byron began to get organized to do a musical. We got students from several schools and prepared one of my musicals — *The Magic Book* — in two and one half weeks. One and a half weeks was part of their vacation, but most of them came to the rehearsals and learned their parts. It was a fine evening.

The Music Department of the Ministry of Education in collaboration with

The Education Officer, Principal, Staff and Students of the

Zone 1 Primary Schools

Cordially invite you to the premiere presentation of

"The Magic Book", a Children's Musical Theatre

Written and produced by Allison Woyiwada of Ottawa, Canada

on

Tuesday 15th April, 2014

5:00 p.m.

at

The Jennings Primary School Auditorium

Come and Be entertained!

This past winter, I climbed to the top of Mount Obama in Antigua. It's the highest mountain peak on the island. Breathtaking! I'll set this up as an annual event. I also intend to learn how to sail and golf next winter, and to present another school musical.

Some Thoughts About my Recovery

When you read my writing, sometimes it might sound like I'm making rules. This was always a big deal when I was a teacher. I kept setting my standards higher so my students would be the best ever. I've also been doing this all along since my brain injury, but I'm the student.

I think some of the worst experience of the past two years was fear. Thinking I might not recover was the most frightening feeling I had ever had. I knew there was a chance that I might not be cured. I woke in the middle of the night and thought about this constantly. It remained with me for a good portion of the day. I wanted my fear to increase my effort to get better faster. The recovery may be long and tedious, but one must keep working hard at doing this.

Recovering from my brain injury won't take forever. I can now feel that I am improving almost every day. Some days I'm as sharp as a tack. That is a very good feeling, especially when Bob starts laughing at my vocabulary. Also, remember that there are up and down days. I never know until after I've gotten up in the morning whether I am going to have a good day. If you're working on recovering from a brain injury, stay positive and don't give up.

Last summer, my friend and next door neighbour Meagan explained to her mother that I was recovering from a brain injury. Meagan's mother and I met on the sidewalk at the front of the house and spoke for some time. At the end of our conversation, Meagan's mother went inside and told her there was nothing wrong with me. There must be someone else who was "afflicted." We all had a good laugh. This is what I like to hear people say. I'm going for broke!

I made a phone call recently to speak to my 88-year-old uncle Murray Cameron. He answered the phone and I asked him if I could speak to Murray Cameron. He said, "You're talking to him." I was thunderstruck! We spoke to each other for quite some time. He knows everything! He knows more than me! We talked about all our families. He knew all the names and where they lived. He knows who own which farms and what they're growing. He told me about things I did when I was little that he remembered. Uncle

Allison's Brain • 313

Murray, I've decided to become as smart as you! Aunt Glenna Cobbe and I have been communicating via mail and Aunt Doreen Cobbe gets updates from her sons. They don't have access to email, but I know they're paying attention. By the way, I want to be as smart as them as well!

I will not take eight years to recover from this surgery. I have not accomplished all that I wanted to accomplish in two years, but what I have accomplished in the two year period since my surgery is something to be proud of. I will continue to work until I have reached my goal. September 2012 was when my memory began to come back. I am aiming for September 2014 for a two year period for measuring my recovery. Bob and I have been invited to speak at the Brain Injury Association of Canada Annual Conference in Gatineau, Quebec, in September 2014. I will be asked to share my story. I want people to feel positive about recovering from brain injuries!

The People I Love

My son Tyler managed to be strongly supportive when his mother was at risk. He's a brave man who knows he'll see me get through. My daughter Marya spent so much time with me. I'm never sure how she fit me in. But she did. She always does. My sister Linda came to look after me when I needed her. No questions asked. The rest of my family and friends were watching closely. There's a lot of love and care in this world.

My husband Bob will never stop until all of this is over successfully. He is my dream come true! Writing this book was valuable for Bob. He finds what to do, and he does it. Writing a book about our experience was the perfect solution for us. He has also been my editor. Many of you have watched him work, and you know he's good at this. I have actually allowed Bob to be my editor. This is a first experience for me, but I put absolute faith in what he says and does.

This book has been good for me. My hard work on writing this chapter has taught me to write again, to some extent. Getting through the harsh descriptions of what I've experienced was not always fun. Reliving them by writing all the details reminded me of some sad, harsh, nervous, scary times. However, I knew this had to be done. It made me cry, but it made me stop and get back to work. I am hopeful that our efforts in telling my story will encourage others to stay positive and be determined in dealing with a brain injury.

Many, many thanks to all of the people who knew enough to help me, and did. For those who thought I might never have gotten better, you were wrong. I am better and you get to benefit from my recovery. We're still friends! I know many of you have been thinking about me and helping me with your thoughts. Let's keep that up for each other, my friends!

Allison

xoxo

Appendix 1 –
The Power of Music Therapy

Meeting Allison
con deciso

I met Allison in September 2012, four months after her aneurysm clipping. I had been informed by her husband, Robert, of the importance of music in her life, how recorded music had been available to her during the early stages of her recovery, and that the first sign of life following her induced coma was her left hand conducting along to music. I was keen to meet Allison and to determine how music therapy might be used to help support her recovery and in particular her speech goals.

Allison was resting in bed when I arrived. Although she appeared tired, I was aware that she was actively listening to the conversation between her family members and myself. She verbally responded to all questions or comments directed towards her; however, words appeared to be random in choice and in order. None of Allison's sentences made sense to the listener.

I noted that, during our meeting, Allison held up a juice glass. Her daughter explained twice that the glass was empty. Although Allison acknowledged this, she attempted to drink from it. I was unsure at the time whether this indicated a cognitive deficit, a demonstration that she was thirsty, or difficulty processing verbal input.

After initial conversation about Allison's situation, I proceeded to describe to the family the potential interventions I might use in the upcoming music therapy sessions. I turned to Allison and told her that I would be giving her homework. She responded with a jargon-sentence, with seemingly random word choices. However, her sentence contained the word "student." Although I cannot be certain, I felt that the word "student" was in response to my comment about "homework." I told her that I realized she was a teacher and that she knew students needed to work on homework. Although Allison did not verbally respond, her facial expression seemed to indicate she was satisfied with that response.

I pointed to the cup on her tray and asked Allison to name it for me. She replied: "raindrop." Two other items I pointed to were also identified as "raindrop." Allison was experiencing both word retrieval challenges and *perseveration*, being "stuck" on a word.

At the close of our meeting, Robert looked at Allison and asked: "What do you think about music therapy, would you like to give this a try?" Much to my surprise, Allison looked at him directly and said: "let's do it!" I knew in that moment that Allison was a determined woman, hard working, and ready to fight towards recovery. She had two important things in her favour: the strong support of her family and her desire for recovery. She was a woman *con deciso*.

Language Impairment

straccicalando

A brief description of language impairment will provide context for the music therapy interventions used to address Allison's language challenges. *Aphasia* is the general term for language impairment following a brain lesion. This impairment may be noted in a range of language areas including speaking, reading, writing, or comprehension of spoken word. An individual may experience challenges in one or more of these language areas. Aphasic symptoms are largely dependent on the brain area that has been affected.

Two common forms of aphasia are Broca's Aphasia and Wernicke's Aphasia. Broca's Aphasia, identified by the French surgeon Paul Broca in 1861, results in non-fluent aphasia. With

Allison's Brain • 317

Broca's aphasia, the individual knows what they want to say but have great difficulty "getting the words out." In some cases they are only able to speak partial words or sentence fragments. In Wernicke's aphasia, identified in 1874 by German neurologist Carl Wernicke, the individual has fluent aphasia. That is, the individual can readily produce words, but the words are not related to each other, the sentences do not make sense, and the individual has challenges understanding what is spoken to him or her. Both Broca's and Wernicke's areas, named after the above doctors, are found in the left hemisphere of the brain.

Early hospital assessments of Allison's language indicated she had transcortical sensory aphasia. In this type of aphasia, speech is fluent, but meaningless or jargon-like. There is typically impairment in the comprehension of oral and written language, naming, reading and writing (Potagas, Kasselimis, & Evdokimidis, 2013).

It should be noted that the classifications of aphasia serve as a guideline, but due to the neural complexity of speech and the individuality of patients, there can be a range of symptoms, including some that are unexplained, in which case the patient's aphasia may be deemed "unclassified." In addition to these broad classifications of aphasia, there is a range of aphasia types. As a result, when preparing a treatment plan for speech rehabilitation, specific symptoms are addressed, not necessarily a general classification of aphasia.

Allison demonstrated anomia, which is having difficulty naming objects or people, and word-finding problems, sometimes inserting a random word, or at other times substituting a related word for the "lost" one. Word retrieval became a primary goal area for Allison's music therapy sessions.

Why Use Music to Address Language Impairment?

parlando

Although initially one might question the use of music to address difficulties with speech, clinical evidence, research, and neuroimaging studies have provided a strong case for music's role in speech rehabilitation. This includes the similarities between singing and speech, music's recruitment of the right hemisphere and its speech supporting potential, shared neural networks between music and speech, the distribution of music processing networks and the multi-site stimulus it provides, and music's influence for neuroplasticity. It is beyond the scope of this Appendix to discuss any of these aspects in detail; however, a brief discussion follows to provide a context for Allison's music therapy sessions.

SIMILARITIES BETWEEN SINGING AND SPEECH

The similarities between singing and speech have led to a great deal of research on the neural processing of music, of speech, and the possible correlations between the two. These similarities include the musical elements of melody, rhythm, and tempo. Both singing and speech use melodic shape. In music, this is literally the shape of the musical line, the "ups and downs" of the melody. In speech this melodic shape is referred to as prosody of speech and is key to expressiveness. Singing and speech share rhythm, the pattern of musical beats or of words, and tempo or rate of speed.

In addition, both singing and speech are emotionally expressive and engage the same oral-motor mechanisms for production.

Clinical evidence has revealed that, following an injury in the left hemisphere, some individuals retained the ability to sing although they had lost the ability to speak or had non-fluent aphasia. This ability to sing, yet not speak, indicates a distinction in brain areas for each function, while at the same time the similarities between singing and speech naturally leads to the question as to whether singing can be used to treat speech impairment. Sparks and Holland (1976) published a paper describing an intervention they had developed: Melodic Intonation Therapy (MIT), to treat individuals with Broca's aphasia. MIT has been foundational in using music to help support speech rehabilitation, and several studies have demonstrated its efficacy (Norton et al., 2009; Zipse et al., 2012; Wilson, 2006). MIT uses two key elements in supporting speech. First is the use of melody or tones, mimicking the prosody of a phrase, to accompany the phrase to be spoken. For example, the phrase "I

Allison's Brain • **319**

am thirsty" would use a higher note for "thirs" followed by a lower note for "ty," reflecting speech's natural rise and fall in that word. The second aspect of MIT is that it uses tapping on the left hand/arm, matching the rhythm of the words, while singing the phrase. Although the efficacy and added value of the left-hand tapping has been proven in research studies, it is not certain as to its exact influence. It is suggested that the left-hand tapping both arouses the right-hemisphere and provides a motor-timing cue for the oral motor mechanisms.

RECRUITING THE RIGHT HEMISPHERE

The success of melody to cue and support speech is supported by clinical evidence and study results. However, the mechanisms as to *why* it is effective remains unclear. Early explanations suggest a shift of encoding of speech from the left hemisphere to the right (Berlin, 1976). This shift or re-routing has been confirmed by other studies (Thulborn, Carpenter & Just, 1999; Hebert, Racette, Gagnon, et al., 2003; Overy et al., 2004). This would help explain the efficacy of MIT. Because the left hemisphere supports speech and the right hemisphere singing, MIT allows for word retrieval and fluency by recruiting the right hemisphere.

Schlaug, Marchina & Norton (2008) state that speech recovery can take two routes. Recovery from small left-hemisphere lesions can be a due to activation of peri-lesion cortex and some right hemisphere area. Larger lesions result in increased recruitment of the right hemisphere. They propose that a key component of the success of MIT, the combining of words and melody and rhythm, is that it arouses both hemispheres to support speech.

DISTINCT AND SHARED NEURAL NETWORKS
BETWEEN MUSIC AND SPEECH

Thaut (2005) proposes that the efficacy of musical stimuli for speech is due in part to neurologically distinct and neurologically overlapping networks for speech and music. He states: "shared and parallel processes may allow for flexibility to facilitate neuroanatomical reorganization or accessing alternative pathways of function in case of focal brain lesions" (p. 72). Patel (2012) also suggests distinct and shared processing of music and language. While acknowledging the independence of some aspects of music and language, he also describes a relationship between them as "resource sharing." Based on neuroimaging studies, Patel suggests that music and language have overlap in the cognitive processing of each. When discussing music therapy treatments for aphasia, Tomaino (2012) also acknowledges that neuroimaging studies have validated shared neural pathways for speech and music.

Clinical observations have shown that singing pre-learned lyrics or predictable lyrics could aid in word retrieval (Tomaino, 2012). As the ability to accurately sing lyrics increases, word retrieval and naming also improves. This relationship of success may further indicate shared neural networks or, as Patel described, shared resources in the cognitive processing of each.

MUSIC PROCESSING IS WIDELY DISTRIBUTED

Music cognition studies have revealed that music processing is widely distributed throughout the brain (Altenmuller, 2001; Peretz & Coltheart, 2003; Parsons, L., 2009). The various aspects of music — melody, rhythm, and harmony — arouse different brain areas.

There would be variations in brain activation sites depending on whether one was listening to music, what aspects of music that attention was directed to, whether the individual was actively participating in music making, and whether they were a musician or not. It is beyond the scope of this Appendix to explore the neurology of music cognition in any depth. However, the following provides a general description of brain activation to demonstrate the distribution of music processing.

Pitch discrimination activates the superior temporal areas: right hemisphere in non-musicians and left hemisphere in musicians. Middle and inferior temporal areas are activated by pitch in both groups (Parsons, 2009). Rhythm activates the basal ganglia and the cingulate cortex in both musicians and non-musicians (Thaut, 2008). Familiar rhythms activate the left frontal and parietal cortex and the right anterior cerebellum while unfamiliar rhythms activate the right pre-frontal and parietal areas, plus the posterior cerebellum

Allison's Brain • 321

(Parsons, 2009). When performing music, melody comprehension activates both hemispheres equally, while harmony and rhythm arouse more activation in the left hemisphere. Of note, reading music activates the right fusiform gyrus. This is comparable to the arousal of the left fusiform when reading words, demonstrating a structural parallel between music and language (Parsons, 2009).

This distribution of music processing allows music to be a multi-site stimulus following brain trauma, and this scope of distribution may also make it harder to disrupt musical processing in general, following an injury. When language has been impaired due to brain lesion, depending on the size and location of the lesion, the wide distribution of music processing may allow for music to serve as a stimulus for aspects of language.

MUSIC STIMULATES A NEUROPLASTIC RESPONSE

Music's influence on the brain has been noted in numerous music cognition studies. Of particular interest to music therapy is the evidence that music stimulates a neuroplastic response, that is, the brain can undergo structural change as a result of being engaged with music. This neuroplasticity is noted in neuroimaging studies regarding the impact of music education on the brain. Studies reveal structural differences in the brains of musicians compared to non-musicians as a result of engagement in music (Hyde et al., 2009; Pantev, 2009).

Studies have not only shown the influence of music education on the brain, but also the influence of music used therapeutically. Schlaug, Marchina, & Norton (2009) completed a study in which, following MIT treatment, six aphasic patients demonstrated an increased number of fibres in the right hemisphere arcuate fasciculus (AF).

It is important to note that neuroplasticity and brain reorganization is a result of experience, not simply a recovery process. Neuroplasticity is said to be a result of "experience-driven change." Stimulus strengthens neural connections. Hebb (1949) theorized that "neurons that fire together wire together." Just as learning causes change, so can structured experience following brain injury. This stimulus needs to be repeated in order to stimulate neural change, and according to Mateer and Kerns (2000), this stimulus needs to be varied and of increasing difficulty. Music therapy provides opportunity for repetitive rehearsal. In addition, by changing the music, it can be a varied and an increasingly more complex stimulus.

FROM MUSIC TO MUSIC THERAPY

The brain's response to music suggests the therapeutic potential of music as a rehabilitation intervention. Schlaug (2010) states:

"New insights from brain research using music listening and music making experiments have changed our understanding of how music can be used in rehabilitation and how to incorporate music into therapies that are geared towards retraining and rewiring an injured brain. Neurologically based approaches to music therapy techniques are now emerging and are being implemented in well-designed studies. Music makes rehabilitation not only more enjoyable, but also can provide an alternative entry point into a "broken" brain system, and can remediate impaired neural processes or neural connections by engaging and linking brain centers that might otherwise not be linked together" (p. 249).

Thaut (2008) draws the same conclusion stating that:

"The study of the neurobiological basis of music is inherently linked to music's influence on brain function. In other words, the brain that engages in music is changed by this engagement…these (new findings) suggest that music can stimulate complex cognitive, affective, and sensorimotor processes in the brain that can then be generalized and transferred to nonmusical therapeutic applications" (p. 62).

There is ongoing research regarding music's potential as a rehabilitation tool in a range of goal areas. In many ways, it seems as though we are only at the tip of the iceberg in understanding the potential of music's neurological stimulus and rehabilitation potential. As studies continue to add to the knowledge base, music therapy interventions can continue to be developed. At this point there is strong evidence, both in research studies and in clinical evidence, of the efficacy of music based interventions to cue and

Allison's Brain • 323

support language rehabilitation. Based on the evidence outlined above, and on Allison's symptoms, I planned the interventions I would use in her music therapy sessions.

Music Therapy and Allison
a poco a poco, cantabile

THE PLAN

Following my initial meeting with Allison, I set word retrieval as the primary goal to work towards in our music therapy sessions. I had the sense that, although I had witnessed her primarily speaking in jargon, she did have intention when she spoke. I could not be certain of this but would use Allison's responses in the early music therapy sessions as a baseline and assessment tool.

In rehabilitation there are two possible routes to take in supporting an individual to be as independent as possible and to support their success in activities of daily living. These two approaches are remediation and compensation. Remediation seeks to address the brain area affected, using specific strategies, striving to stimulate neuroplasticity. A compensatory approach seeks to provide resources that the individual can use to help compensate for an impairment. An example would be using a notebook to keep track of medication or appointments if the individual is experiencing memory problems. Both remediation and compensatory approaches are valid and effective.

Based on the evidence described in the above section, the goal in my work with Allison was remediation, using music's stimulus on the brain to encourage a neuroplastic response for speech. In order to achieve this, I used three approaches: linking target word(s) to melodic cue, sight-reading piano music, and the use of vocal music. Each of these approaches served a different role.

1. LINKING TARGET WORD(S) TO MELODIC CUE.

Although Allison's aphasia did not classify as Broca's aphasia, my approach with her was based on the neuroscience of MIT. In addition to stimulating the left hemisphere, I wanted to recruit the right hemisphere through its engagement with melody and singing and to stimulate its potential to support speech. This was targeted by the use of melody associated with specific words to help retrieve and access those words. Because Allison did not experience the traditional classification of Broca's aphasia with which MIT is typically used, I modified MIT to better address Allison's situation.

When a word was "lost," rather than encourage Allison to describe the word or its context (which in all practical senses is acceptable), I wanted to stimulate the *process* of retrieval. Thus, I created specific phrases with target words for her to practice between sessions. Because pre-learned lyrics, such as familiar songs, have been shown to support word retrieval in aphasia, using melody to cue target words may help to stimulate this retrieval process. Situating target words in melodies could stimulate the shared neural networks between singing and speech and is supported by Patel's proposal of shared resources for the cognitive processing of each. Because music and its elements stimulate both hemispheres, using music in combination with words could help to not only recruit the right hemisphere, but also stimulate peri-lesion areas in the left-hemisphere.

As Allison progressed, the assigned phrases shifted from short, simple functional phrases such as "I am tired," to longer phrases containing target words that were challenging for Allison, in particular, proper nouns. Rather than using two or three tones (or notes) to reflect the prosody of the phrase as in MIT, I created specific melodies using several notes for each phrase. This placed more cognitive demand on Allison as each melody needed to be remembered in addition to the words. It also gave Allison a cue to support word retrieval. Remembering the melody could help to retrieve the words that were associated with it. By continually adding new phrases and increasing their level of difficulty, Allison was able to consistently drive the process of word retrieval. This is important, for neuroplasticity is dependent on repetitive experience with variations and increasing complexity.

Allison's Brain • **325**

2. SIGHT-READING PIANO MUSIC

Sight-reading of piano music was used to take advantage of the multi-site stimulus that results from the cognitive processing of music and the fact that active music making stimulates neuroplasticity. This has been evidenced in numerous music cognition and music education studies. The combination of perception and motor action is a strong neural stimulus and integrates a number of systems (Yan et al., 2010). In recovering from an insult to the brain, I wanted to provide as much stimulus to as much of the brain as possible.

Because in the beginning I was uncertain as to the degree of impact the aneurysm might have had on cognition, I wanted to provide Allison with an increased cognitive load as a result of the cognitive processing that is required in reading and executing music performance. Sight-reading provided this opportunity.

I was also interested in Parson's (2009) study results that found that "cortical areas distinct from, but adjacent to, those underlying language operations were activated during sight-reading" (p.248). I recognized that these areas are distinct and that there is no evidence at this time that sight reading would arouse language sites; however, questions regarding distinct and shared neural networks for singing and speech had roused my curiosity, and I was drawn to the fact that sight-reading aroused cortical areas so close to language.

Earlier assessments indicated that Allison's reading comprehension skills were moderately to severely impaired. Allison's level of accuracy in reading music would enable me to observe her ability to read and interpret written information (as opposed to aural) and to note any progress in this language area. I also hoped that playing the piano would affirm and encourage Allison as a musician while she was adjusting to changes in her life following the surgery.

3. THE USE OF VOCAL MUSIC

As noted earlier, pre-learned and predictable lyrics aid in word retrieval. For this reason, and also because of the shared neural networks between singing and speech, Allison was assigned vocal music as part of her homework between sessions.

The Journey

IN THE BEGINNING...

From the very first session at the hospital, Allison was keen and ready to work in music therapy. As soon as I arrived at her room, she was up and heading down the hall to the cafeteria where we had access to a piano.

The first sessions allowed for me to assess the efficacy of a modified MIT approach for Allison and observe in greater detail the challenges Allison had with speech. Allison was now speaking with fewer "jargon sentences" and was able to communicate reasonably effectively. Her ability to repeat words was strong; however, her naming was poor, as noted in earlier assessments. For example, when shown a pen, Allison identified it as a lion, a briefcase as a single book, and a set of keys as a bridge key. When reading, not singing, the lyrics of a song, Allison had a 50% success rate. However, when singing, Allison sang the majority of lyrics accurately with a small number of word substitutions. The combination of melody and words increased the success of Allison's word retrieval. Naming notes, but not playing them, also had a 50% success rate. Playing a page and half of a song resulted in only 10 wrong notes. A music context for language, whether for reading information or producing words, increased Allison's accuracy.

In these early sessions Allison still perseverated occasionally on a word. For example, in one session when naming the notes in a song, she identified all the notes as "A" or "F", but when she played the piece, she performed with a high level of accuracy. This further demonstrated that Allison did, in fact, know the notes but could not name them. It was a question of retrieval, not a lack of recognition or understanding. At times Allison gave an approximation of a word, an improvement over substituting a completely unrelated word or feeling the intended word was "lost."

There were times during these early sessions when Allison identified having speech difficulties. She once told me how the word "production" was bothering her that day and how on the previous

Allison's Brain • 327

day "the word Waldo bugged me." Although I cannot be certain, I believe Allison was struggling with perseverating on a word and was aware of the dominance of that word in her language output. When exploring Allison's comments further, she was able to describe how words "feel ok when they come out" but then "are do not feel ok" (the wrong word was used). She explained, at other times "when it's time for them to come out, there is no word." She said: "sometimes some words come out but do not feel ok, but no sequence." I inquired: "Do you mean... some words do not feel ok, but substituted?" She replied: "Yes."

As Allison's speech improved and she spoke with less jargon sentences, she continued to demonstrate difficulty with confrontational naming. That is, when asked directly to name an object, the word often could not be retrieved. Retrieval of target words would later become the focus of sessions, but in the beginning, the goal was to provide short, simple functional phrases.

The first two phrases set to music were: "I am tired" and "the concert went well." The purpose of these was to give Allison functional phrases that she could use to communicate with those around her. She had a busy therapy schedule at the hospital and "I am tired" would enable her to express fatigue if need be. "The concert went well" was created to respond to inquires about the fund-raising concert held in her support. After introducing these phrases in the music therapy session, Allison was immediately successful in singing the correct response to the questions "how are you feeling?" or "how did the concert go?"

In the following session, when asked how the concert had gone, Allison immediately spoke "the concert went well" but struggled to express more. This was good evidence that the combination of melody and words could cue Allison's word retrieval and also that, with rehearsal, the phrase could transfer beyond singing into speech. Although Allison's success in this session was indeed a hopeful sign, she was not always able to do this. There were also times when Allison could not retrieve the words of the rehearsed phrases but would play or hum the melody that belonged to the phrase in response to the cue question. This demonstrated that she was successfully associating the melody to the phrase, she knew the "right answer" but could not always sing the words. Other times she would recall the words only after the melody had been played for her. The melody was the first step towards the word retrieval, and her playing of melodies to substitute for the correct words and the melody cueing words demonstrated the process was beginning to unfold. With continued hard work and practice, Allison began to increase the number of successful responses.

SEEING PROGRESS

Due to her recovery process and the support of family and therapies, by the end of October, Allison was speaking with increased success. She began to recognize more often when she misused a word or played errors in her piano piece. Her music therapy homework now contained several phrases including some of increased length.

At this time Allison also began to question music therapy. She appeared to enjoy the fact that it was music based, but expressed concern about her homework phrases. She pointed out that the main words did not always line up with the strong beats in a bar of music. In response I explained music therapy, MIT, and the goals that we were working towards, using music as the cue and support. She readily accepted this and I felt she was reassured and the issue was resolved. However, the question arose several more times in the following sessions as Allison had difficulty remembering previous conversations we'd had on this topic. Upon my arrival to one session, Allison explained that she had made some changes to one of the phrases to "fix it" (musically). I assured her that I respected the fact that she was a composer and pointed out that I too had written music. I explained that, because we were working on speech goals, the melodic shape of the phrases was following the prosody of speech and was not written to reflect musical creativity or to match the pulse of the music. The guidelines for MIT differ from those for writing vocal music. I also explained that the phrases were simplistic so that they could be easily memorized, as we would be continuing to create numerous phrases. I brought in a book on the

Allison's Brain • 329

cognitive processing of music and showed her MRI images of brain site activation during MIT. This seemed to reassure Allison. She occasionally inquired about her phrases in following weeks, seemingly not remembering our previous discussions. In approximately four months, this was no longer an issue, and I viewed this as a sign of progress.

Shortly afterwards, I decided that, for a number of reasons, it would be good to include Allison in the phrase creation from that point. I think I will always remember Allison with fondness regarding the journey of progress we shared in music therapy, and I chuckle to think she will probably be the only client who jumped in and wanted to fix her homework.

As Allison progressed, a shift was made from short functional phrases to those of increased length and containing proper nouns as this word group proved to be of particular challenge for her to retrieve. Initially the target word was placed at the end of the phrase, the easiest placement for word retrieval and memory. For example, "I walked with *Paul.*"

Allison and I generated the phrase theme together, I created the phrase in order to intentionally place words in a specific sequence, and Allison created the melody to go with it. This turned out to be a great solution to the question of the phrase homework. Sentences were constructed with words and word placement according to the appropriate level of difficulty, and Allison was able to create melodies that felt right for her.

Interestingly, there was a parallel improvement in speech and piano performance. During these sessions, as Allison's speech improved, so did her piano playing. She had a high level accuracy in both note naming and playing. But of particular interest, she sight-read and played with increasing attention to interpretive details and expression.

Although Allison was becoming increasingly successful in singing back the words of the rehearsed phrases, she still struggled in conversation. Music was increasing successful word retrieval, but it would take more time for this to transfer to consistent improvement in conversation. I noted, particularly towards the end of the sessions, that her conversation had more misused words. I suspect this was related to fatigue.

TEMPORARY SETBACK

In late January 2013, Allison experienced a setback in her music therapy sessions. Allison was aware of her struggles and told me at the beginning of her session on January 18th that she was "not doing well."

Her struggle was noted in both her speech and in piano playing. In the next few sessions, Allison had increased word substitution and "lost words." In some cases she was able to identify the first letter of the intended word, other times she could write an approximation of the word. She was so close to speaking the target word, but not able to.

During these sessions, Allison's piano playing also had a setback. Allison asked for clarification for several basic music elements. She was aware of information on the page that she did not know. My concern was that the details that she inquired about were basic music theory information. She had trouble playing the piece she had chosen.

It is common for clients to experience setbacks. I have witnessed individuals progress for a period of time, even have significant breakthroughs, and then inexplicably be challenged in areas that had improved. Therapists in other professions have said they have witnessed the same in their clinical work. When this occurs, I tell the client that we will continue for six more sessions to determine if there is any change or improvement before we decide if we should terminate music therapy. In all cases to date, progress resumed.

I was concerned about Allison's setback in numerous areas, yet I recognized that Allison had an important medical appointment in the midst of this. Stress of various forms may have been contributing to the speech and memory problems. Two weeks following her biopsy, Allison was experiencing increased success in her music therapy sessions and began a course of steady progress.

Allison's Brain • 331

IMPROVEMENT

Allison began accurately producing homework phrases in a reduced practice period. Typically phrases required practice over three or four sessions before they were consistently successful. She was now securing phrases in one or two sessions. I must highlight that Allison was working very hard at her practice.

Because of her improvement, sight-reading and vocal music were no longer assigned as homework, only encouraged as an activity to include in her schedule. Instead, music therapy sessions focused on phrases of increased difficulty.

Sentences now included two phrases, two or three proper nouns, and lists of objects in specific order to retrieve. The proper nouns were names of individuals Allison indicated she wanted to be sure to remember. She created a list of names that were important to her and wrote sentences about the person, including their name. Allison continued to learn these phrases in one or two sessions. I realized that Allison was using a mental picture of the person to help her remember their name and that remembering one name of a couple may help her to retrieve the second name. In some ways, this was triggering an "auto response." But I felt that this auto response was, in fact, accurate word retrieval and that I would use this as a first step. My goal was always to stimulate the *process* of word retrieval. Once Allison was consistently retrieving the names of familiar people, I shifted to using "random" names. Because of Allison's many years of teaching, it was challenging to come up with names that did not remind her of a student, and thus a visual cue.

Allison's improvement continued. With less practice time required, she had a high rate of success producing phrases of increased length, containing multiple proper nouns, and lists of objects. Proper nouns were now moved from the end of the phrase, to the middle or beginning, placements that are typically more challenging. This did prove to be more difficult for Allison, but with consistent practice, she eventually improved and progressed in this area as well.

In an assessment session, she successfully produced all but one of sixteen phrases. Ten of these were perfect on the first attempt;

in three she sang most of the phrase, completing it with melody only. Twice when singing the wrong word, Allison was aware of it and self-corrected.

I recognized that Allison might have progressed to the point where the music therapy interventions would no longer benefit her. Perhaps at this time her word retrieval had improved enough so that the melodic and rhythmic cues were not necessary or significant. I emailed Robert and described Allison's recent progress and suggested we consider terminating music therapy sessions in the near future.

He responded that, because of Allison's upcoming surgery and the potential for a setback following it, that we continue for six to eight weeks following her surgery and re-visit the idea then.

A SECOND SETBACK

Following her surgery, Allison did in fact experience a setback that lasted for a number of weeks. Allison struggled more than usual with speech both when trying to remember her homework and in conversation. Sentences contained several misused words, and at times it was difficult to understand what she was trying to express. I assigned previously secured phrases for review in order to take advantage of an auto response (due to previous rehearsal) to support the process of word retrieval. During this time, only one or two phrases at most were assigned.

In time, and with effort by Allison, she began to retrieve phrases with greater ease. As we gradually increased the length and complexity of text, Allison continued to maintain her progress. Although, in general, from session to session, there may be "good days" or "off days," these recent weeks were a second period of time in which there was a definite, although temporary, season of increased struggle and setback. As mentioned previously, at times these ebbs and flows of recovery are inexplicable, other times they are a result of stress, fatigue, or distraction. It is important during these times of challenge to provide encouragement and support to the individual, helping them to stay on course in their journey towards rehabilitation.

Allison's Brain · 333

Continued progress

a gioioso

Over the course of the summer, music therapy sessions were reduced due to schedules and holidays. Once September arrived, music therapy resumed with regular sessions. Throughout the fall and until the break to prepare this book, Allison continued to tackle phrases containing multiple proper nouns and lists of objects. Eventually she was also requiring less rehearsal time and on numerous occasions learned a phrase in only one week. Allison was able to achieve a high success rate in producing target words and at times described a phrase prior to hearing the melodic cue. For example, she would state: "there is a phrase about driving down Elgin Street." This was an important step as she was now retrieving target words, including those of particular challenge to her, without music to cue or support the retrieval. The retrieval process was happening without external stimulus. She was again making steady progress and improvement.

The neural stimulus of music and its elements, combined with words, successfully cued and supported word retrieval for Allison. Over the course of fifteen months, Allison progressed from short functional phrases to phrases of greater difficulty with a higher rate of successful target-word retrieval; from struggles in reading music to accuracy and increasingly expressive playing; and from using a melody to substitute for words to describing a phrase and its targets without a music cue being required.

BRAVO ALLISON

There are several contributing factors to consider in Allison's journey of recovery. One, of course, is the natural healing process of the brain. Secondly, as this healing process began, it is significant that her family provided cognitive stimulus for Allison from the very beginning. They played recorded music for her, provided opportunity to go to the piano (Allison's "other voice" and also a source of cognitive stimulation), and engaged therapists early on to support her speech rehabilitation. Music therapy served to complement other therapies and also provided a unique neural stimulus specific to language areas of the brain. Because music therapy was a structured intervention and could be presented in such a way as to be varied and to gradually increase in difficulty, it also could help to stimulate neuroplasticity.

Last, but not least, is the fact that Allison was motivated and willing to put in effort and hours of practice in working towards her rehabilitation goals. There were ups and downs from session to session, and times of unquestionable setback, but throughout it all, was Allison's determination to continue to press forward and her family's commitment and support for her.

Cheryl Jones, MMT, NMT-F, MTA

http://www.conbriomusictherapy.com

MUSIC TERMS

a gioioso	joyful, cheerful
a poco a poco	gradually
cantabile	in a singing style, song-like
con deciso	with determination
Fine	the end of a piece of music
parlando	sing in a style suggesting speech, in a speaking style
straccicalando	babbling

References

Altenmuller, E. (2001) How many music centers are in the brain? *The biological foundations of music. Annals of the New York Academy of Sciences: 930,* 273-280.

Berlin, C.I. (1976). On: Melodic intonation therapy for aphasia, by R.W. Sparks and A.L. Holland, *Journal of Speech and Hearing Disorders, 41,* 298-300.

Hebb, D.O. (1949). The organization of behaviour: A neuropsycological theory. New York: Wiley.

Hebert, S. Racette, A., Gagnon, L., et al. (2003). Revisiting the dissociation between singing and speaking in expressive aphasia. *Journal of Neurology, 126(8),* 1838-1851.

Hyde, K., Lerch, J., Norton, A., Forgeard, M., Winner, E., Evans, A., & Schlaug, G. (2009). The effects of musical training on structural brain development: A longitudinal study. *The Neurosciences and Music III: Disorders and plasticity. Annals of New York Academy of Sciences 1169:* 182-186.

Mateer, C., & Kerns, K. (2000). Capitalizing on neuroplasticity. *Brain and cognition, 42,* 106-109.

Norton, A., Zipse, L., Marchina, S. & Schlaug, G. (2009). Melodic Intonation Therapy: Shared insights on how it is done and why it might help. *The Neurosciences and music III: Disorders and plasticity, Annals of the New York Academy of Sciences,* 1169, 431-436.

Overy, K., Norton, A.C., Ozdemir, E, et al. (2004). Activation of the left anterior inferior frontal gyrus after melodic intonation therapy in a Broca's aphasia patient. *Proceedings of the Society for Neuroscience, 597, 7.*

Pantev, C. (2009). Musical Training and induced cortical plasticity. *The neurosciences and music III: Disorders and plasticity. Annals of New York Academy y of Sciences 1169,* 131-132.

Parsons, L. (2009). Exploring the functional neuroanatomy of music performance, perception, and comprehension. In Peretz, I., & Zatorre, R. (Eds.), *The cognitive neuroscience of music.* Oxford University Press.

Patel, A. (2012). Language, music, and the brain: A resource-sharing framework. *In Language and music as cognitive systems.* Rebuschat, P., Rohrmeier, M., Hawkins, J., 7 Cross, I. (Eds.), Oxford University Press, 204-223.

Peretz, I., & Coltheart, M. (2003). Modularity of music processing. *Nature Neuroscience, 6 (7),* 688-691.

Potagas, C., Kasselimis, D., & Evokimidis, I. (2013). *In Aphasia and Related Neurogenic Communication Disorders.* Papathanasiou, I., Coppens, P., & Potagas, C. (Eds.), MA: Jones & Bartlett Learning.

Schlaug, G., Marchina, S., & Norton, A. (2008). From singing to speaking: Why singing may lead to recovery of expressive language function in patients with Broca's aphasia. *Music Perception, 25(4),* 315-323.

Schlaug, G., Marchina, S., & Norton, A. (2009). Evidence for plasticity in white-matter tracts of patients with chronic Broca's aphasia undergoing intense intonation-based speech therapy.

*The Neurosciences and music III: disorders and plasticity: Annals of the New York Academy of Science, 1169:*385-394.

Schlaug, G. (2010). Music listening and music making in the treatment of neurological disorders and impairments. *Music Perception 27 (4),* 249-250.

Sparks, R. & Holland, A. (1976). Method: melodic intonation therapy for aphasia. *Journal of Speech and Hearing Disorders, 41,* 287-297.

Tomaino, C. (2012). Effective music therapy techniques in the treatment of nonfluent aphasia. *Annals of the New York Academy of Science, 1252,* 312-317.

Thaut, M. (2005). *Rhythm, music, and the brain: scientific foundations and clinical applications.* N.Y. Routledge Press.

Thulborn, M.H., Carpenter, P.A., & Just, M.A. (1999). Plasticity of language-related timing cues as external rate control to enhance verbal intelligibility in mixed brain function during recovery from stroke. *Stroke, 30 (4),* 749-754.

Wilson, S., Parsons, K., & Reutens, R. (2006). Preserved singing in aphasia: A case study of the efficacy of Melodic Intonation Therapy. *Music Perception, 24,(1),* 23-36.

Yan, C., Ruber, R., Hohmann, A., & Schlaug, G. (2010). The therapeutic effects of singing in neurological disorders. *Music Perception, 27 (4),* 287-295.

Zipse, L., Norton, A., Marchina, S., & Schlaug, G. (2012). When right is all that is left: Plasticity of right-hemisphere tracts in a young aphasic patient. New York Academy of Sciences, 1252, 237-245.

Appendix 2 –
Say No More and It's a Fact Jack

There isn't any doubt about the fact that the four speech language pathologists who have worked with Allison post-surgery have had a huge role in her recovery. This appendix contains the accounts of all four therapists and includes an in-depth report written by Evelyn Tan based on her experience with Allison.

The title of this appendix is based on the fact that, early on in Allison's speech recovery, she often resorted to colloquialisms to express herself. She did this to such an extent that Marya gave her a t-shirt that was emblazoned with her two favourites: "Say no more." and "It's a fact Jack." Allison's first speech therapist, Catherine Chubey, explained to us that this is not uncommon amongst patients she works with. This is because "rote things" in Allison's right brain such as colloquialisms were not adversely impacted.

Catherine works in the acute care area at the Civic Campus of the Ottawa Hospital, and she assesses patients after their surgery with a view to determining whether they could benefit from rehabilitation. Catherine says she tried several times to assess Allison informally, but Allison was unable to tolerate the testing. Catherine recalls Allison as having fluent aphasia, in that she was able to speak complete sentences, but the sentences did not make sense. Allison used lots of jargon and her responses were perseverative. "Confrontation naming" was severely impaired, and she was initially unable to follow any commands. Catherine noted that Allison's ability to concentrate and attend to tasks improved at the end of August, and that Allison began to be able to recall some events that had occurred earlier in the day.

Allison's first speech therapist at the Rehab Centre in September 2012 was Mary Pole. Mary has worked as a Speech Language Pathologist from 1966 to 2014 in a variety of locations and settings, eventually concentrating on adult rehabilitation with an emphasis on neurological rehabilitation. She evaluated Allison when she arrived at the Rehab Centre at the General Hospital Campus in Ottawa in September 2012 and found that she suffered from severe aphasia affecting her ability to read, write, speak and understand language. Mary's assessment of Allison in September 2012 is located in chapter 6.

Mary's recollection of her sessions with Allison is that they were "interesting times," for Allison had no idea she was not making any sense, and she would not always do what she was asked to do. At the outset of therapy, Allison's basic communications functioning was at the level of about a one year old. Mary says that there was a big gap between what Allison was doing and what she *thought* she was doing and that part of her job was to educate Allison to this fact without making her distraught.

When Allison was discharged from the rehab centre in late October 2012, she had more awareness that she was not getting out what she wanted to say. She had made good progress with her comprehension of words and phrases, both spoken and written. Allison's use of an iPad helped her in comprehension and naming in categories, and she had covered body parts, clothing, foods and common objects before her discharge. Mary says that at the time of discharge, Allison still had difficulty following instructions and explanations, and she still got lost at the rehab centre — although without any apparent anxiety.

After her October 2012 discharge, Allison began twice weekly therapy outpatient sessions with Natalie Pincombe, also an Ottawa Hospital speech language pathologist. Natalie focused at the outset on improving Allison's comprehension and recollects some of the

Allison's Brain • 341

issues she dealt with in working with Allison. When selecting words, Allison's brain would accidentally choose words of the same category, or same sounding words. This phenomena occurs when neurological pathways have become destroyed or tangled through a brain injury and is known as *paraphasia*.

The continuous inappropriate repetition of words, known as *perseveration*, also occurred frequently. Allison's brain would become stuck using the same word repeatedly. For example, after having learned to correctly identify and use the word "photocopier," Allison's brain would loop back to the word "photocopier" to describe the object in all of the successive images she was shown.

Inflexible thinking was another phenomenon that affected Allison. For example, Natalie recalls that, when Allison was asked to show her the bookstore in a picture they were examining, Allison was adamant that there was no such thing as a bookstore, and that books are not sold in stores. When given the example of Chapters as a bookstore, Allison told Natalie that they could "agree to disagree."

When Allison was discharged from outpatient therapy at the end of December 2012, having had eleven sixty-minute sessions, her severe receptive and expressive fluent aphasia had been downgraded to moderate. The SLP Discharge Report from this time shows that cognitive-communication difficulties with attention, impulsivity, verbal memory and planning skills were suspected, but not addressed directly in therapy due to the severity of Allison's aphasia.

When asked to comment on the evolution and practice of speech language therapy from a global perspective, Mary and Natalie say that there is substantial emphasis these days on obtaining cognitive gains by working towards enhancing functional communications, as opposed to learning through memorization by rote. When a new patient is evaluated, their weaknesses and strengths are assessed relative to their personal goals, and attempts are made to choose therapy methodologies which will assist the patient in regaining functionality in their daily lives.

Mary and Natalie say that every brain is different and that not everyone can make great gains in recovering from a brain injury.

Indeed, two patients with essentially the same type and extent of brain injury can obtain quite different results in their recoveries. Although there is no "magic wand" SLP therapists can use in recovery, the attributes which appear to contribute most to success are those you would suspect. Perseverance, a positive rather than defeatist attitude, and the confidence to plough ahead despite flawed communications abilities are all factors which predict higher levels of success with recovery.

In Allison's case, her SLP Discharge Report indicates that "she was always good humoured and participated eagerly." Natalie describes Allison's recovery as of December 2013 as "amazing" in light of the severity of her initial impairment, and she suspects that her musicianship may have been one of the important factors in her recovery. Mary adds that it was fascinating to see what Cheryl Jones could achieve with Allison through music therapy sessions. As mentioned previously, Mary was in the audience at a Brahms Choir Christmas Concert in Ottawa in December 2013, in which Allison performed with others in a ninety minute concert, singing in English, French, and German. Mary says she was "blown away" seeing Allison on stage singing in the choir.

When I asked whether being a speech language pathologist is a rewarding vocation, Natalie said that although when she started out she was frustrated by not being able to do more with patients to speed their recoveries, she came to realize that speech language therapists are often the only people who are able to spend the time with patients to find out what they are really feeling. This in turn helps with overcoming obstacles and assists with a patient's rehabilitation.

Part of the bright side of Allison's story, which has a wider application than to her case alone, is that the belief, which was at one time more or less cast in stone, that there are limits to the extent one can recover from a brain injury, which are tied to specific time frames, has now been widely abandoned. Mary recalls a case where a patient of hers earned a Ph.D., developing research and writing skills over many years. There is also the famous case of Jill Bolte Taylor, the Harvard-trained brain scientist who suffered a massive

Allison's Brain • 343

stroke in 1996, and had an eight year recovery. She subsequently wrote the bestseller *My Stroke of Insight: A Brain Scientist's Personal Journey*, which was published in 2008.

Evelyn Tan has provided her own written account of the year spent with Allison in therapy.

Evelyn's Account

When Bob said he was writing a book called *Allison's Brain*, he said he hoped that clinicians who had treated and worked with Allison would contribute to it. My first concern was for Allison's strong need for privacy and of presenting herself in the best light at all times. Perhaps this comes from a lifetime of successful musical performance, teaching, stage direction and production. Bob said that the book was for readers to learn about Allison's particular brain injury and what she and he went through at the time of diagnosis, treatment and rehabilitation. I asked him to tell me what he thought a reader would be interested in when reading my entry. He thought the reader would want to know what a Speech-Language Pathologist does and what Allison was like at various stages of therapy.

Anyone who wishes to know what the preferred practice guidelines are for cognitive communication disorders and aphasia can get valuable information from:

www.caslpo.com/PracticeStandards/
PracticeStandardsandGuidelines/
CognitiveCommunicationDisorders

http://www.asha.org/public/speech/disorders/Aphasia.htm

I first met Allison when I was doing a locum at the Rehabilitation Centre of the Ottawa Hospital, running weekly one-hour cognitive-communication sessions. These sessions were attended by inpatients whose abilities ranged from profoundly impaired to mildly impaired. Allison was the most profoundly impaired in the group; she responded to her name and cursory verbal phrases such as greetings but not much else. Her brain injury had resulted in a language impairment called Wernicke's Aphasia which is characterized by deficits in understanding spoken and written language and the severe lack of coherent spoken and written language. Because of the severity of her impairment, she did not understand her own language output, nor could she recognize that people did not understand what she was saying. She did not even pick up on a patient laughing at her when she produced a string of unrelated words, a word salad to answer a simple question. Allison received 1:1 therapy with the Speech-Language Pathologist who first assessed her abilities in order to plan treatment. After her in-patient stay, Allison received out-patient therapy from another Speech-Language Pathologist, and at the end of that treatment period, her husband contacted me for her to continue with therapy in the community setting.

When I first visited Allison in her home on a January evening, she participated in a three-way conversation with me and Bob. The conversation lasted just short of an hour, during which time the generalities were discussed: what she hoped to achieve in therapy, what other therapies and activities she was involved with, the frequency of visits and what my approach to therapy would be. She spoke in full sentences and required clarification only about 20% of the time. She was having a good day. As is true for everyone who has had a brain injury, there are times when one's cognitive communication abilities absolutely shine and other times when they don't. When the latter happens, it could be due to any number of reasons such as: fatigue; an infection such as a urinary tract infection; a cold; stress; overwhelming emotion such as anxiety or fear, etc. Often, the reasons may not be sufficiently clear. As good as her speaking and listening abilities were that day, her worst was at a time when she was dealing with a diagnosis of cancerous cells in her abdomen. That week, not even videotaping her totally incoherent verbal output was effective; we replayed the clip of her describing a simple picture sequence segment by segment, and she saw no problems at all.

A few days after our first meeting, we had our first therapy session. I first asked Allison to show me the work she was doing on her iPad. There are all kinds of apps which one can purchase

Allison's Brain • **345**

to work on reading, listening, spelling, math, etc. She showed me a reading task which required her to read with comprehension four sentences and to choose the sentence that best described a given photograph. While she scored 70%, she worked slowly, sometimes using the process of elimination to arrive at an answer. In this case, the goal would not just be to improve her score — since these sentences were, after all, relatively simple and concrete — but to improve her rate of reading. After using the iPad, we worked on her pointing to objects in her kitchen as I named them and, later, on her naming the objects as I pointed to them. If she could not name them, she was asked to describe or demonstrate its use. Still using the kitchen context, she was asked to describe the location of objects, for example, "in the top drawer" or "next to the fridge." As a listening comprehension and writing exercise, she had to spell (write) the names of objects as I described them. These written words were later used for her to label the objects after the spelling task ended. At the end of the session, we sat at a table, and I asked her to describe simple recipes. I modelled what I wanted her to do by describing my own simple recipes.

Ideally, a therapy session uses all modalities of language — speaking, listening, reading, writing. It has a rhythm and a flow that starts with one step leading to another and is punctuated with natural communication tasks. The naming that occurred early in the session was a simple naming of objects (i.e. nouns), of actions (i.e. verbs); prepositional phrases (e.g. "on top of the fridge") and adjectival phrases (e.g. "the bottom drawer"). By the end of the session, these simple words and phrases extended to full sentences and paragraphs which required correct sequencing as compared to the previous rather random naming of words. For example: "Wash the lettuce. Dry the lettuce in a spinner. Tear the lettuce up. Put them in a salad bowl. etc." What is termed "procedural discourse" requires more than just vocabulary and syntax; it also requires the cognitive ability to organize ideas in a coherent manner.

Therapy is always designed to provide some successes, but also to challenge the client. For example, after that initial session, instead of having her name objects within sight, Allison was asked to name as many objects as she could which met two (or more) criteria: "Name as many objects as you can which are small enough to put in your pants pocket and are *not* round." or "Name as many objects as you can which people hang on walls but are *not* paintings." A task such as this requires a certain amount of memory not only in recalling names of objects but in retaining the given criteria while searching for words. It is not necessarily functional or useful in daily life, unless, in the latter example, one is looking to decorate one's walls and has an aversion to paintings. Nevertheless, it is still a therapeutic activity.

A functional communication task would be something like storytelling. Allison is asked to stick to the facts, and to answer the who, when, what, where, why or how questions whose answers are the meat and potatoes of any narrative. Because of the kind of language impairment she has, Allison tends to be wordy, and a goal in therapy is to develop the ability to express herself succinctly. She is encouraged to pause before starting in order to think about what she wants to say. Having clear beginnings, middles and endings is another goal to avoid tangential speech. This requires more than good vocabulary and grammar, it also requires organization of ideas and the ability to filter unimportant details.

It can be challenging for Allison to listen to or read a story and then retell it. This requires not just expressive ability, but the comprehension and retention of language. She is encouraged to use strategies such as taking notes and asking for repetition (if listening to a story), and highlighting, underlining, numbering (if reading a story). Note-taking requires adequate spelling ability and the ability to use abbreviations or acronyms which she can make sense of when referring to her notes. Sometimes, Allison used abbreviations and could not remember what they stood for and would confabulate, or in the retelling of a story, she would use the words in her notes but produce a different story from the one she heard, making errors similar to those seen in the parlour game "telephone."

Allison's Brain • **347**

These experiences show how strategies have to be fine-tuned. Their usefulness depends on factors such as her familiarity with the topic, her level of fatigue, the length and complexity of the story, her attention and concentration, and her memory. Insight is extremely important for a client to choose appropriate strategies.

Early on, Allison was asked to keep a journal and, as a separate activity, to copy written passages which she found thought-provoking, inspiring and/or entertaining. The copying assignment was done when initially she had very poor ability in writing coherent sentences which were longer than three or four word sentences. In journal writing, she was instructed to first write spontaneously, and then to proofread only after giving herself a reasonably long break to rest her brain and her eyes. She had to complete these written exercises and other kinds of homework between sessions. Examples of homework included: reading classified ads and answering questions about them; and reading menus, movie schedules, recipes and making appropriate choices given specific parameters. Assignments which involve mathematical problems (numerical and word problems) gave Allison immense pleasure because she quickly learned that she was skillful in this area.

Functional tasks have included writing of simple email messages, keeping a directory of names of people with brief descriptions of them, using organizational and memory aids such as a paper calendar/daytimer as well as the iPad. As with most people who have sustained a brain injury affecting cognitive-communication, Allison needs more time and rehearsal to learn new tasks. She also benefits from error-less learning, meaning from tasks taught to her step by step with no room for her to make any errors. After a brain injury, some people find it extremely difficult to learn from their mistakes, and they are bound to repeat their mistakes over and over again, hence the error-less learning method.

Another aspect of therapy involves counselling of family and friends. I often suggested to Allison that Bob or her daughter Marya attend a session or two so that they can adjust their communication styles to suit her needs especially when she is tired or when the communication task is more daunting. What has happened thus far is that Allison gives my suggestions to her family members. For example, she has found the following strategies to be useful: when giving her important or complex information, the speaker has to first make sure that he/she has her full attention, that distractions are minimized, that the topic is clearly identified as is the purpose of what is about to be said (i.e. what is required of Allison — is she supposed to write down an appointment, call someone, purchase something, etc.). Having an important conversation while in the car is not a good idea whether or not it is Allison who is driving. In a moving vehicle, there are too many distractions, and she and the speaker cannot share good eye contact. Lengthy and grammatically complex sentences are to be avoided; pauses between sentences are necessary to allow her time to process information. She is to be asked "Could you tell me what I just said?" after sections of the narrative are given instead of the speaker launching into the entire length of the narrative. The latter is bound to create problems because if Allison misunderstands one important detail in the first part of the narrative, then the rest of the narrative can take a totally different (i.e. wrong) slant. My preference is for people to practice with the client and me how to slow one's rate of speech down, how to shorten and how to simplify sentences because people often *think* they are speaking more slowly or simply, but old speaking habits are not easily changed. Allison now has the ability to look at her communication partner and determine if there is a breakdown occurring. Many times, she has said to either Bob or me (or us both), "You are looking at me funny."

Allison has made significant gains in the year of community-based therapy. She is better able to use strategies such as self-monitoring — this entails listening to herself and correcting herself or asking for help as necessary. When writing an email message, she asks herself: *What is the point I am trying to make? Most details that do not contribute to the point can be considered superfluous and can be deleted. Tiny details that add personal warmth stay.* Her memory is improving so that she does not repeat stories as often as she used to, or she prefaces a story with, "Have I told you about....?" Allison has never lost her sense of humour. One activity we did involved reading and commenting on letters to the editor of a health/self-improvement magazine. One letter she read gave this tip: As a nighttime routine, slather lotion on both hands and wear cotton gloves to bed to have youthful looking hands. Allison quipped, "So you'll have wrinkles up to your wrist."

There are still areas that could use improvement. Email writing is one. When it comes to important email which consists of dates, times, names of events, names of tests and test results, etc., it has been recommended to Allison that Bob review the message before Allison hits the send button. This is because Allison does not always recognize her errors; interestingly, when the errors are pointed out to her, she is generally successful at self-correcting. Another area is household bookkeeping. Her math is fine, but Allison is challenged in her ability to visually scan rows and columns of text and figures, and in her ability to shift back and forth from one document to another looking for specific information or integrating informa-tion. It has been suggested to her that perhaps bookkeeping the old-fashioned way (manually filling in ledgers) might be a way to start, but this has not yet been trialled. A third area is reading. She used to enjoy reading newspapers — news, op-ed articles, etc. but the effort required in processing complex information, and the mistakes made in comprehension, can take away from the pleasure of reading. Allison still enjoys reading novels, and as a clinician, I respect her freedom to choose what she wishes to read without testing her comprehension of her chosen Grisham nail-biter and without insisting that she read shorter and easier text such as *The Reader's Digest*. Forms of the latter are used in cognitive-commu-nication therapy; reading novels is recreational as far as it affords her pleasure. Also, sometimes, the sense of autonomy in making a choice, without being questioned by someone else, can be more important than getting high scores in a reading test.

Not all therapy is done at the dining table. We have gone for long walks in the neighbourhood, conversing about a variety of topics and meeting various people with whom Allison converses. That she can talk and walk safely on various terrains at the same time, and listen and navigate taking the lead (because it is her neighbourhood and not mine) is always invigorating.

A year of community-based therapy can be tiring. Before her brain injury, Allison was always successful in the tasks she undertook. Being reminded of her losses can be draining, and so tasks which are extremely challenging naturally elicit an approach-avoidance reaction in her. On the one hand, she wants to get better at them, but at the same time, she prefers doing things she succeeds in. Allison feels quite confident in her ability to give music lessons because much of her adult life was spent doing this. In the fall of 2013, she went ahead and contacted a community centre to form an adult jazz band. As I have not witnessed her in action — nor have I read her email messages to the participants of the band — I have no way of evaluating how she is doing, yet I make the conscious decision to give her the space she needs to initiate something personally meaningful without a clinician's scrutiny. If an email message is unclear, then hopefully, the recipient will respond to her to tell her so, and she will do what she needs to to address this.

Far more can be written, but these pages should be enough to say to the reader that Allison within her circle of family and friends (and in the outermost circle, her therapists) is living proof of how life goes on and can go on despite seemingly insurmountable challenges. People often talk about how unbearable life would be without sight or sound or the ability to walk or feed one's self. Rarely do people imagine the possibility of not being able to understand simple words or to say one's name. Most readers of this book are likely never to have heard of Wernicke's aphasia and cognitive-communication impairments before. Neither did Allison; she simply woke up one day and experienced them first-hand long before she understood what those words meant. Since then, she has been picking up the pieces of her life and she seems to be able to choose to have a great time of it!

Evelyn Tan, MA SLP, reg. CASLPO

Allison's Brain • 351

Appendix 3 –
Lotsa Helping Hands

What you will find in this appendix are recollections by Allison's family members and friends who were with her throughout her aneurysm journey. These folks all had some — or a lot — of history with Allison before her surgery. They witnessed her before and at the beginning of her aneurysm diagnosis, through her wait for brain surgery, and then began interacting with her again post-surgery. Although Allison began recognizing some friends as early as June, she doesn't recall their visits before the end of August.

No one was asked to write a piece of any specific length, and all were encouraged to share any concerns they had along the way. Everyone was also asked to give their accounts of any humorous moments they remember. Allison can't contradict any of this stuff, so it is a rare opportunity to take liberties.

The pieces are arranged alphabetically by the authors' surnames, and Allison's daughter Marya has the last word. Marya's contribution is very different from the others, as she has taken the time to pen a very thoughtful piece about how to cope, going through a brain injury experience — from a caregiver's point-of-view.

Carol Anderson

As will be described elsewhere in this book, the surgery was long and complicated, and Allison was kept in a coma for much longer than anyone had anticipated. I first visited her while she was still in the induced coma in intensive care and connected to many machines. Marya was there that day, and this was my first opportunity to witness Marya's remarkable and, subsequently, unwavering positivity with regard to her mum's recovery. During the next three months, before Gerald and I left Ottawa for a sabbatical year, my hospital visits coincided occasionally with Marya's, and I was constantly humbled by her optimism, can-do attitude, and warm, bubbly, bedside manner, even during some really low points in Allison's recovery.

From mid-June to mid-July I visited Allison a number of times, sometimes with other people, and occasionally alone. For me, this was the most difficult time, and I rarely felt that I was adding any value. Generally I felt that Allison had no idea who I was, and I often felt that she was dealing with so much cognitive and physical turmoil that she didn't need someone there whom she didn't know. Others would write in the journal that she responded well to newspapers, books or verbal stories, but I rarely experienced any positive response and often just didn't know what to do to engage with her. In the early stages, I'd show her some photos, but was saddened when I didn't see any response or recognition, even with photos of Bob, Marya and Tyler. Sometimes she would just close her eyes, and I wouldn't know what to do. Later, when she had difficulties with phlegm, I just wanted to ease her discomfort and couldn't stand to see her in pain or yanking at tubes to try to remove them. For a while she was strapped down so that she couldn't pull tubes out, and I hated having to tell her not to touch the tubes, especially since she still didn't seem to know who I was. I felt quite helpless at times, especially on my own. It was incomprehensible to me how she could advance her recovery in an environment with so many machines beeping and buzzing in a fairly constant manner. On more than one occasion, I wept all the way home and felt pretty desperate about her ability to get through all of this, get out of hospital and live life again.

Allison's Brain • 353

In mid-July I visited one evening with Gerald. On this occasion, we took in some Gilbert and Sullivan scores to sing Allison some songs. We started off with *Pirates of Penzance* and "When a Felon's not engaged in his employment." Allison immediately responded with the chorus "his employment" — and I simply beamed. We had a jolly evening; she was free from many of her previous tubes and connections and seemed to really enjoy the sing-song. Gerald showed her some photos of his recent trip to Israel, and she handled the photos on his phone and asked him whether he had needed permission to take them. Wow! I noted in the journal that evening that I saw "big, big, big changes" since the previous time I had seen her — "lots of speech, lots more cognitive thinking."

We returned a few nights later and Gerald brought his iPod along. We had previously left a player — music was already a significant part of Allison's recovery process. We played Beatles tunes all evening and she conducted along perfectly. After "Maxwell's Silver Hammer," she remarked, "Oh, that's so good!"

Over the next few weeks, I think Allison was dealing with new physical issues, and my notes are scant on my observations during this time. In mid-August, Gerald and I visited and showed her my son's recent wedding salsa dance video, which she loved watching. She was talking quite a lot on this occasion, although it wasn't easy to grasp her train of thought. It was almost school time, and I'm pretty sure that she was talking about Hopewell School. At this stage she had a feeding tube, which she hated with passion. With her dogged determination, she waited until our backs were turned for two seconds and yanked the thing out. It was painful witnessing the sounds of her obvious discomfort as it had to be reinserted and then watching her frustration at being restrained again.

A few days later my son, Alastair, was visiting from DC and wanted to visit Allison. We cycled over on a beautiful Sunday afternoon. Marya was there. Allison was in fine form, and we had a great visit, with lots of laughs and conversation, in which Allison was very engaged, displaying some witty comments and lots of lucid commentary. I was completely astonished by the huge change in her linguistic and conversational abilities in just five days. On a lesser but equally impressive note, Marya offered Allison a lipstick since she had a new visitor, and Allison proceeded to apply the lipstick perfectly without a mirror — something I've never been able to do! For the first time in three months, I started to believe in the possibility of huge levels of recovery to her pre-op persona. I'm not entirely sure that she knew who Alastair was, but she enjoyed his company and thanked him for visiting and bringing his hair (dark auburn and quite impressive).

Five days later on August 30th, Allison called me Carol for the first time. She was finally devoid of tubes and wires, and we had a lovely, peaceful evening, with some gentle conversation. We looked at some photos from a skiing trip to the Alps that the four of us had made about seven years previously. The hospital was quiet that evening. Allison remarked that it was nice and peaceful in the suite — and indeed it was. This was the last time I would see Allison in hospital, as I was leaving the following week until the end of February.

Over the next six months, we followed Allison's progress via Bob's email updates and her personal return to the wonderful world of emails. When we next saw her at a fundraiser at the end of February 2013, the difference seemed nothing short of a miracle. I was overjoyed and incredulous by her progress on every front. There she was engaging in conversation with everyone, making introductions, telling stories, offering thoughts and opinions, asking about adventures — right back in the middle of the social arena she loves so well.

Gerald and I left for another few months over the summer and then caught up with her again during August and September 2013, marvelling anew at the continued positive changes. It feels a bit like watching our grandchildren grow. We don't see them enough, so the changes are always remarkable and delightful each time we get together. And so it continues to be with Allison.

It seems fairly evident that Allison's renaissance was aided and abetted by a huge group of loving family and friends, led by Bob and

Allison's Brain • 355

Marya, but I've known Allison for a long time and firmly believe that her own inner strength, fighting spirit and love of life is a huge reason for her remarkable and continued recovery. As anecdotal evidence, when I was speaking with Allison about her cancer and the plan to stay on top of it, her response was along the lines of, "Well, it's only cancer; I've had brain surgery, so we can beat this."

On a final note, we were at a dinner a few weeks ago, and I wore the dress that I wore to my son's wedding in May 2012, a wedding that Allison was invited to, but was unable to attend as she was awaiting surgery. She admired the dress and remarked that it was the wedding dress. The only time Allison saw that dress was in a few photos of the wedding which I showed her during the early stages of her recovery, when there was no evidence that she remembered me, my son, the wedding or the fact that she should have been there. Now, that's Allison's brain!

Jill Berry

What More Can One Endure?

This was my thought at every dip along Allison's journey. What more can one endure? It was a blind roller coaster with many scary and unexpected rides down and slow, laborious climbs up. No one ever knew if the ride would ever end, to return to level ground.

Throughout, Allison was positive, motivated, determined, persistent, and stubborn, but I wondered if also she was conveniently oblivious of the actual circumstances.

From the beginning, awaiting the surgery date all winter and most of springtime, it was hard for all concerned. With the frustration of delays, Allison was no push-over. Instead she was active in phone calls and emails to the hospital and to the doctors. Once May 28th was announced as the target date, we observed Allison as an organizer. She was proactive and ensured that Bob's 60th birthday and his convocation in June would not go amiss during her recovery in June. She was upbeat four days prior to surgery when we enjoyed a brew in the sunshine on a pub patio deck. Her impression of the procedures consisted of a ten hour intensive surgery, a seven to ten day post-op hospital stay, and then home for a six to eight week recovery period. I wanted to ask "what if you just keep on without the surgery?" but didn't want to rock her boat. With scant knowledge of the severity of the aneurysm, I was worried about possible risks of the operation. Allison was so confident about the necessity of this procedure. An email from Allison the day before surgery glossed over Dr L "giving all possible negative results" and instead exuded her positive approach to this necessary procedure.

None of us were ready for what ensued.

That was the last we heard from Allison for an excruciatingly long time.

Instead, Bob's voice was heard by email updates, conveying many dire details post-op. The first major dip in the roller coaster ride: seizures and a medically induced coma. The wait was unbearable. Twelve days seemed like a lifetime. Bob reports "she's awake" but has a tracheotomy — *what?!* This wasn't part of the plan. Another scary dip in the ride, then a slow climb: extremities moving, move from ICU to Neuroscience Acute Care Unit (NACU), able to sit, then a slight dip: shunt surgery, and an upward climb again: nose feeder removed, out of NACU into Neuroscience Inpatient Care, trach removed, able to speak, fitted for helmet, wheelchair tours outside. We were all pumped! 36 days post-op, and Bob communicates that "alertness and mobility took a swan dive." Allison had an infection and required antibiotics. *What?! Come on!! Enough already...* but apparently not. She "crashed" and ended up back in NACU, having seizures and an infected shunt. This roller coaster dip lurched in my stomach, and I wanted to scream or to cry. There was a delay in the shunt reinstallation. Allison became "quite inactive and uncommunicative" in Bob's words. I witnessed this for myself and, also for my first time, Bob's despondency. I worried for Bob as well as for Allison. After the new shunt and four weeks in NACU, Allison was returned to Neuroscience Inpatients and regained previous recuperative powers. The climb resumed and Allison's feistiness returned! The occasional AWOL experiences earned her an alarm bracelet.

Allison's Brain • 357

Many humorous episodes kept us all on our toes and encouraged. In the fall, she graduated to ABI, showing her potential for aggressive therapies and the climb continued up a steeper grade. Finally, on October 22, four months and twenty-four days; one hundred and forty-seven days; twenty-one weeks; 3,528 hours; 211,680 minutes after the initial operation, Allison was discharged. Home to live her life and, through self-determination and discipline, to gain more competencies in every avenue of her life.

But the roller coaster ride was not over. Another dip in December: titanium skull is not sterile, needing replacement with skin grafting. In April, Allison had a liver resection due to a cancerous tumour.

What more can one endure?! In Allison's case, if the body and mind are willing, she can endure and surmount what others may perceive as insurmountable.

Marya and Bob were amazing throughout. Allison appeared to be in dire straits at many intervals, yet they were optimistic. Didn't they get it? It turns out they did! Others had their doubts but would not let on to these two cheerleaders. They never outwardly wavered in their belief that Allison would come out of each challenge and that she would endure. It turns out that she did, with honours!

During this ride, I often questioned the wisdom of going through with this high risk surgery. What if they had left well enough alone, would Allison have been better off? She has proven that although this was one hell of a ride, she has come through with flying colours! This was the right decision.

... more stuff...

Loosely based on Howard Gardner's theory of multiple intelligences

Anecdotes of different facets of Allison's brain!

Allison's Linguistic Brain: Not always was Allison coherent, but she used her pet phrases in a natural manner. These rote fillers would always give me comfort that Allison was still in the building!

Allison often would ask if she is making sense or if I understood what she was saying — mostly I wouldn't. I would get her train of thought at times. I would relay to her what I thought she was saying, and she'd respond that it was close.

When I mentioned going to Ireland — she thought we'd gone already, then started saying something about Blarney. So I asked her: "Did you see the Blarney Stone when you and Bob were there?" She answered yes.

One time Allison was spooning the hot water from her mug. I suggested that I put the tea bag in instead and she said, "Oh red wine!" I responded, "you wish!" The nurse noticed that it was Red Rose Tea and probably that prompted her thinking that it was red wine.

Allison seemed to make linguistic connections that were relevant although at times it was a stretch.

Allison's Interpersonal Brain: Early on in her initial recovery when she was still quite weak and communicated very little, she grabbed me with both arms and pulled me to her and kissed me. We held hands a lot. It was a nice feeling.

When Allison was trying to remove the feeding tube from her nose, we had a hand battle! I won! I told her that I think this was the first time that I was more stubborn than her. I want this on record!

A month later Allison was attempting to remove her helmet. I explained that she needed it on to protect her. She gave a sigh of disgust and told me that I was so stubborn! Looked in a mirror lately, Allison?!!

She hospitably divided her hospital lunch to share with me — she was quite determined that I eat! She offered me her meal on many an occasion.

Allison politely told the nurse that I would be packing her up as she would be moving. "This hotel isn't suitable. We'll find something else."

Allison was always polite to staff, visitors and other patients. Her tone and comments would be pleasant. Not a negative word did I hear throughout her ordeals. She had a lot of patience.

Allison's Intrapersonal Brain: Allison was always inquisitive and engaged. She was honest about her capabilities and her deficits.

Allison's Brain • 359

She was focused on what was required to improve and methodical in attaining her goals. She would not waiver in her determination. I don't believe that thought would have crossed her mind.

Allison's Kinesthetic Brain: I brought in a laptop to show Allison some photos. She wanted to push the arrow button to advance the pics with her right hand, but her left hand kept taking over. It was a lot of effort for her, so I took over. Allison and I laughed when we observed that she was using her left hand to guide her right hand to her face so that it could scratch her itch.

Allison used her left foot to propel herself in the wheelchair. She was lifting her right foot as if she wanted it on the foot rest but would put it down on floor again. She did this repeatedly, so I asked her if that's what she wanted to do, and she said she was still deciding and laughed.

Allison's Logical Brain: Allison was pulling on her trach tube to pull herself closer to the machine, but I talked her out of that with a firm voice: "Allison, STOP THAT!" She laughed! She was curious as to how everything worked. She persisted and pushed her wheelchair closer to the medical machinery. She wanted to touch the buttons but I dissuaded her. Then she tried to open her seatbelt and, at one point, to remove the chair table. I asked her if she was trying to escape. She said: "Aren't you going to help me?!" I said that I thought I better not.

Someone had given Allison a bracelet which she was manoeuvring around her wrist intently when I came to visit one time. I asked her what she was doing, and she explained that she was trying to figure out how to put the power on.

While visiting and chatting, I noted that Allison was busily dismantling the table tray and armrest. She was attempting a Houdini move so she could escape the wheelchair! I managed, with some difficulty, to put it back together again.

Allison's Musical Brain: From very early on in her post-op, Allison was listening to music. Initially she was touching each fingertip to her thumb on each hand as if it was an exercise, but it was rhythmical in relation to the background music. Later on, she would use her full hands to conduct. She was definite in her choices of music when asked. When Allison became more vocal, she demonstrated that she knew most of the lyrics.

Allison's Spatial Brain: Allison persisted with me about something she was seeing on a calendar photo. I couldn't see what she was describing and was truthful in telling her so. She resolved that it must be in her head.

At ABI, we went outside for a walk. The nursing staff told me to allow Allison to guide me, by pushing the appropriate elevator buttons and deciding which direction to go. Upon leaving the building she purposefully turned around. I asked her at what she was looking. She responded that she was looking at the building sign so she would know where to go when she returned from the walk. Brilliant! I would never have thought that far in advance!

Janet Buske-Wischer

The one time I was afraid that Allison would not recover even to the point of being able to speak was when she took her sudden downward spiral a month or so after her surgery. I went into the intensive care unit at the hospital where I met Marya in the waiting area.

When we were finally allowed to go to her, Marya told Allison that there was someone who had come to visit. Allison did not respond at first, but she finally opened her eyes and looked at Marya and sort of looked around. Her eyes where glazed as though she saw nothing or registered nothing except that she seemed to know that Marya was there.

She did not speak, she barely moved... The difference in her manner at this time as opposed to the incredible recovery she seemed to be making two weeks before was profound. I did not know what to say or do, so I just sat with her for a little while (I believe Marya had gone by this time). I sang her a few songs, and she did not seem to hear or know that anyone was there. Allison closed her eyes, and I stayed a little while longer and then left thinking that she was not going to recover.

Sharon Chartier

My friend Allison has a "giant aneurysm" and likely needs brain surgery. Devastating news yet delivered by Allison in a matter-of-fact email to a group of friends and family in late 2011. She wanted all of us to know about her situation in an open, transparent way.

"So this is not a taboo subject. I am happy to email with you. Feel free to let our other friends and family know. Please don't feel doomy and gloomy. I don't feel that way."

So began a long journey that brought our friendship with Bob and Allison to a new level. Dan and Bob met almost twenty years ago through their legal work and enjoyed each other's company right from the outset. Not long after their initial meeting, Bob and his son Phil visited our cottage joining us for skiing and dinner. Meeting Allison came a little later, and our friendship continued over the years as our son Alexander was born and we watched Bob and Allison's children grow up into the wonderful adults they are today.

Allison is an impressive woman! She has many of the characteristics I admire in other women — calmness in the face of emergency, a great sense of humour, discipline, persistence. I am sure she was born with many of these traits but there is no doubt that thirty years of teaching honed them to a fine point. Managing groups of grade 7 and 8 students in several concurrent bands and on annual band trips would demand these traits and much more. Allison was always up to the task, and has been widely recognized for her teaching accomplishments.

No surprise then, when faced with news of her serious medical situation, Allison handled it with her usual aplomb. She was concerned about how her friends and family would take the news and didn't want anyone to worry.

"I feel fine — almost normal and not terribly worried, and I don't want you to worry either."

These traits, developed over her lifetime, stood Allison in very good stead throughout the journey of her brain surgery diagnosis, surgery, and recovery. It is my firm belief that these characteristics are what allowed Allison to survive and recover from this very serious condition.

Right from the start there were jokes and videos about rocket science vs. brain surgery, in particular a BBC Two video of a rocket scientist and a brain surgeon at a cocktail party each convinced that their field was the more difficult. Hilarious, except for Allison's circumstance.

Allison had great faith in the team of doctors and surgeons who were responsible for her care. If anyone had any doubt about Dr. Lesiuk (her main neurosurgeon) that disappeared when Bob learned that Dr. Lesiuk had been an astrophysicist before becoming a brain surgeon. What has this man not accomplished!? Tax lawyer perhaps?

I suspect the jokes about brain surgery vs. rocket science (vs. tax law!) will carry on for many years just as the famous "glass by the wine" expression has managed to do. We discovered that I was pregnant with our son, Alexander, on June 30, 1998, and celebrated Canada Day with Bob and Allison the next day. Since I now knew that I was pregnant, wine was off the menu for me but not the others. As dinner progressed the initial bottle of wine was consumed and Allison called the waiter over to ask whether this "glass came by the wine"… She has not lived that one down yet.

In March 2012, as attempts were made to schedule the large team (anaesthesiology, cardiology, neurosurgery, etc.) that was required to perform Allison's surgery, Allison joked that she would try to get a group photo on the big day. Throughout the lead up to May 28th, Allison's sense of humour was evident and kept her group of supporters, friends, and family positive about the eventual outcome.

Given the magnitude of the surgery, we were very interested to see what changes there might be to Allison's personality post recovery. Happily her good humour and ability to take things in stride are still intact. Eighteen months out from the surgery, Allison, on occasion, has some difficulty coming up with the word she is looking for. So, a sentence that she intends to say, such as "What a great day for a bike ride!" might be expressed as "What a great day for a bike

Allison's Brain • 363

route!" With a few seconds of thinking, the listener can figure out what she means to say, but then there is the dilemma of whether or not to correct Allison.

I wondered whether it was helpful to Allison to have these small slips pointed out, so I asked her how she wanted me to react. Her good humoured response was that she *did* want to know so she could make the correction. That situation could have gone either way, and I was very relieved to receive such a positive reaction. Not everyone is happy to have their mistakes pointed out! It demonstrates Allison's approach to her recovery, which is that this is a journey requiring continuous improvement and effort.

The delay between diagnosis and surgery (five and a half months) was very difficult for Allison and her family. Now that the aneurysm had been identified and the possibility of rupture had been estimated (40% over 5 years), there was a sense of urgency to complete the surgery as quickly as possible. Bob and Allison's lives were on hold given the uncertainty of the situation.

Despite being ignored by the administrative staff responsible for communicating with her, Allison kept following up over and over again. The surgeons were better at getting back to Allison than the admin staff! Her persistence definitely paid off when the surgery was finally scheduled.

Allison is a disciplined individual who could be extremely rigorous about what she ate and how much she exercised. In preparation for her surgery, Allison stepped up her exercise regimen to ensure that her body was a strong as possible before undertaking the massive task ahead of her. There were long walks, bicycle rides, yoga classes, and gym workouts all aimed at enabling a speedy recovery. At this early stage of the journey, there was great uncertainty about how quickly Allison would be up and about, so being in tip top shape going into this was important.

Following Allison's surgery as her appetite and ability to eat returned, it was interesting to see her new interest in food generally and dessert in particular. For someone who had always been so careful about what she ate, this was a new phenomenon and very interesting to watch. Was this new attitude to food a direct result of the surgery, a side effect of the medications, or simply a more relaxed attitude toward food? Having lost quite a bit of weight over the initial post-surgery weeks, it was encouraging to watch Allison eat and very interesting to see the new focus on sweets!

Allison's disciplined nature was also evident in the detailed diary she maintained (pre-surgery), logging all the phone calls and emails that generally went unanswered by hospital administration. Following the theory that the squeaky wheel gets the grease, Allison doggedly pursued information from the offices of the various medical personnel involved in an attempt to get her surgery scheduled. Sitting back and waiting for the hospital to organize itself was not going to work for Allison and likely made a difference in the outcome.

Allison's acceptance of her situation and the calmness of her approach to her impending surgery were much admired by friends and family. Her email updates about her upcoming surgery were factual, often humorous, and had not a hint of self-pity, which would not have been unexpected in someone suddenly afflicted with such a serious medical situation.

With surgery looming on Monday, Allison and Bob joined us for dinner at our home on Saturday evening. We were not sure what to expect, but Allison was calm, funny, and completely her usual self. It was Ottawa Race Weekend, and Marya was running the 10K that evening, so we casually strolled down to Queen Elizabeth Driveway and waved her on in a sea of runners. They drove away at the end of the evening, the roof of Bob's MG down, and Allison's hair blowing in the breeze. I had tears in my eyes as I thought about what my next experience with Allison might be.

Bob kept friends and family updated on Allison's status post-surgery with daily emails describing the medically induced coma and eventual surfacing as various medications were gradually reduced. For four of Allison's friends, our first opportunity to see her and provide some respite for Bob and Marya was during the period June 13th to 17th when Bob travelled to Toronto to receive his PhD

Allison's Brain • **365**

degree in Tax Law. Carol Anderson, Joan Duguid, Pauline Lynch-Stewart and I visited Allison during the periods when Bob would have been there. Bob referred to us as Marya's backup group. Given my musical abilities, this is likely as close as I will ever come to being part of a backup group. And it was for a trained opera singer!!

The four of us shared our experiences visiting Allison and her progress with each other so that we would be prepared for whatever might greet us when we arrived in the hospital. Some days were positive when Allison was alert and seemed to follow our one way conversations (monologues?). On other days, she was unresponsive and progress seemed to have reversed. This up and down cycle continued for many weeks with family and friends bouncing from hope to concern to fear to happiness — sometimes all in the space of a day! I can only imagine what Bob and Marya felt seeing her every day and trying to keep everyone's spirits up.

One afternoon, Allison was dozing, and I was reading by her side. I noticed a man dressed in a short sleeved summer shirt and casual pants carrying a heavy briefcase as he slowly approach her bed. I stood up feeling very protective and wary of this stranger. As he got to the foot of the bed, I introduced myself and asked who he was. This quiet, unassuming man was none other than Dr. Lesiuk, the brain surgeon/rocket scientist that I had heard so much about. He was very pleasant and following a question from me proceeded to explain the function of the various boxes, wires, and machines connected to Allison. I imagined that there were many other people requiring his attention at that moment and didn't ask anything else!

We were out of the country from the end of June to the end of July, and I was thrilled to see Allison's progress when I returned to the hospital to see her upon our return. We listened to Eric Clapton for a while, snapping our fingers to the music. I told her about our trip, the places we had been and some of our experiences. She smiled broadly when I told her how much Alexander enjoyed our visits to EuroDisney and Parc Asterix.

Allison progressed from the Intensive Care Unit to the Neurology Acute Care Unit to the Neuroscience InPatient Unit at the Civic Campus of the Ottawa Hospital over the course of the summer and was eventually ready to move to the Acquired Brain Injury Rehabilitation Centre at the General Campus on September 11, 2012. Bob and Marya had been told that the move to the rehab centre could happen in the next couple of weeks, but no specific date had been provided.

On September 11th, only a few days after hearing that Allison could move in the next few weeks, I arrived at the hospital to find out that she was moving right then. Neither Bob nor Marya had been advised, and I am quite certain that had I not been there she would have been moved without them knowing. Bob was sick with a cold and couldn't come to visit Allison for a couple of days, so I called to see whether he knew about the move. He didn't and neither did Marya!

Allison had been in the hospital for more than three months by now and had accumulated quite a collection of books, CDs, clothing and personal items. I found some boxes and packed up her belongings taking them over to the rehab centre in my car while Allison was transported by ambulance.

I was concerned about how Allison might react to this new situation, and as I explained what was happening to her, she said that, no, she was fine here (at the Civic) and didn't need to move. The Civic had been clear that a bed had come available unexpectedly at the ABI Rehab Unit and that if Allison did not move right away, someone else would take the spot. After some conversation, Allison agreed to go, but I wonder what would have happened had there not been a friend or family member there to help with the move. The nurses didn't seem to be interested in packing up her belongings and offered no explanation of what was happening to Allison. Information was only provided to me when I went to the nursing station and asked who could tell me what was happening.

Which brings me to the lesson I learned from all of this — the communication skills of hospital staff and administration need work! Right from the start of Allison's experience in late 2011, it was a struggle to have phone calls or emails responded to at all.

Allison's Brain • 367

Lots of great work was going on in the background in preparation for Allison's surgery, but none of that is visible to the patient who is left to worry that nothing is progressing. Think of the comfort for a family to know that although communication is sparse, her case is progressing through the system and is being addressed. There is lots of simple technology and automated tools that could help with this.

The decision to move Allison to the ABI Rehab Unit at the General Hospital was a major and very welcome step in Allison's recovery. It was made, though, by a nameless, faceless person somewhere in the hospital system with no attempt to let the family know what was taking place. Again, some attempt at communication could have made this process much smoother.

After a few weeks at the ABI Rehab Unit, Allison and Bob were able to drive up to our cottage for the weekend. It was wonderful to see Allison out of the hospital setting! Our son, Alexander, helped her with the iPad speech therapy program and she was, as always, very comfortable with him. We look forward to continuing to spend time with Allison and Bob marvelling at the recovery she has made.

Bravo to all!

Joan Duguid

I would like to preface this all by disclosing that I have a terrible memory and spend most of my time looking forward to what I am doing tomorrow. What is behind me is not always remembered in an orderly fashion, so I thank you for sending me the brief notes I wrote while visiting Allison.

My thoughts on Allison and her brain surgery start well before visiting her post-op. I distinctly recall discussing helmets with her as she did all her own research prior to her surgery. I, as well as several others, received an email one morning while I was on the road working. It revolved around a very descriptive detailing of how they would remove some of her skull leaving her with a skin flap which would need protecting in case of injury. The email was about types of helmets and where she might research them. I am a nurse, not squeamish at all, but it occurred to me that others receiving this might be. Reading this note while having their morning coffee seemed a bit much! Allison however, was beyond being squeamish and was deep into working towards the final goal of getting back to good health even before a scalpel had been lifted.

I mention this as I believe Allison's positive attitude and drive have been so important in her recovery. Faced with the same surgery, length of time and possible outcomes, I would not have gone forward... just saying. I admire Allison for her determination.

My first visit to Allison was in the neuro obs unit with Carol Anderson. The music was playing gently in the background. Not much of a response from Allison on this occasion but to be expected. Tubes and monitors all around. I went into nurse mode, cleaning around her trach, and I might even have suctioned her. I miss the buzz of a unit like that, but Carol told me it was overwhelming for her. Understandable and even more understandable when it is your friend all hooked up to these machines. Being able to be comfortable with the equipment made it more bearable for me as it gave me something to do.

My next visits were on the neuro floor in August. Allison was definitely more alert when awake but verbally not coherent. For the most part, when I was there, she was asleep as was I in the corner. I tried to show her slides of trips we had taken together, but she was far too tired and drifted off. I assumed she was tired as otherwise I would have to think she was bored and that could not be possible. At other times the helmet occupied our time together: she undoing it, and I trying to distract her from it. I had to chuckle at the time she had invested in researching the protective headgear and now the time she was investing in trying to rid herself of the damn thing.

When Allison moved to the rehab centre, I visited her there. The change was dramatic. She was up and about, knew the rhythm of the place and was, in her own mind, ready to leave. We were conversing! I noticed a dramatic difference in the staff contact as they worked with her and her visitors to get a whole picture of their patient. She had another visitor present and even though the conversation was

Allison's Brain • **369**

not always coherent, you had a sense that Allison knew what she wanted to say and do even though it did not always come across in a clear manner.

Much time has passed since the rehab centre and again the changes are dramatic. I notice when Allison is getting tired and her answers are not spot on, but for the most part she is back!! I love the last conversation we had at Burch's where she told me, and I paraphrase here, that "I could refrain from putting myself out there and stay quiet, or I can choose to participate and do my best and improve all the while because of trying." A life lesson indeed. To Allison!

The continuing love and support from Marya and Bob is evident. Truly a team effort in one person's recovery. Congratulations to you all.

Peggy Elliott

When Bob first told me about Allison's aneurysm, I was of course very worried and fearful for her as well. A trip to their house to visit Allison one afternoon, a few weeks after the diagnosis, for a cup of tea, led to her showing me the pictures she had, of course, on her computer, of the images taken by the MRI showing this huge honking ball of trouble. It made it more real, and my worry increased. Listening to her explain, in great detail, to me what it all meant, I was somewhat reassured, impressed at her own knowledge and telling myself that this aneurysm had picked the wrong bad-ass to mess around with! I swear that, during the time between her diagnosis and her surgery, Allison kicked some serious butt... advocating for herself and literally bullying the neurology department into getting things organized. The surgical team seemed to need her and lucky for her, for Bob, and for all the people who care about her, she got the ball rolling.

Before the surgery, on a run one day, Bob asked me if I would be interested in helping out during Allison's hospital stay, which was probably going to last for a significant period of time, and I of course said yes. He and Allison's daughter Marya arranged a calendar online where we could sign up to cover certain times for a visit and that part was easy. All the same, I was aware that, being Bob's friend more than Allison's, meant that my role was not a primary one, so I signed up for a couple of spots the first month and after that, I guess I went a total of three or four times.

The visits were not easy for Allison, from what I sensed, and I think maybe too much for her. She may have needed less people, less often — hard to say with hindsight because things seem different than when you are planning ahead. When I saw that she was struggling, I just cut the visit short.

Visits 1 and 2 were more of a recon. She was limited in her ability to interact, but able still to drink a mostly delicious mocha-chocolate Starbucks drink laden with sugar and whipped cream! I was surprised that she recognized me, seemed happy to see us. I have to admit that I struggled from time to time not to laugh at some of the rather outrageous things that she was saying... she did seem to understand pretty much what we said, and would try to answer in context, but the words that came out made no sense at all... her language was all over the place at that point, and she did not really seem aware of it, seemed to think she was making sense. Interestingly, she would use expansive and complicated words, so it seemed that her intelligence was intact, just the pathways for language twisted up and some dead ends.

Visit 3: I arrived to find her agitated and mobile. So my husband Andreas and I took her out on the floor for a stroll. Big mistake. But a lot of fun. She decided to seek exits. We had to go get an orderly, who she proceeded to flirt with — he was very handsome, young, fit... you get the picture.

Visit 4: One thing I did realize right away was that Allison did not, true to her character, want to be coddled or treated differently than usual. When we arrived, Bob and Marya were there waiting for us, and left shortly after. There were guests staying at Bob and Allison's. She knew that and persisted in asking us to bring her home and to call Bob to come get her. Trying to change her mind,

Allison's Brain • 371

and following Bob's pre-departure advice, I attempted to play a word game with her on her iPad. She was getting frustrated with me though I did not pick up on those feelings right away. Finally she asked me, "Is this what you want to do with your time today? Play little games?" Then she turned away, grabbed her newspaper, and proceeded to ignore me till I left. That was the moment I knew Allison was all there, and would be fine. Months later, when we were having a glass of wine in her living room, she apologized for that, but she did not need to. It was, and still is, for me a wonderful moment we shared.

Allison was amazing in keeping all her friends up to date with emails pre-surgery, and Bob continued after till it was no longer pertinent. I for one really appreciated that, and I think it was also a very useful way for them to manage the concern we shared without becoming overwhelmed themselves in the bombardment of questions. I just waited to hear from them, and knew they would let me know when it was possible or when there was news.

This book project is a great plan. I am looking forward to seeing and reading the end result.

Deirdre Garcia

I first met Allison in 1986 when she took the Savoy Society of Ottawa by storm with her role as Casilda in Gilbert & Sullivan's operetta *The Gondoliers*. I was in awe of her excellent singing and continued to admire this talent through all the subsequent operettas that she and I performed in. Not only was she wonderful on stage, but she immersed herself in Savoy's social scene, and we all enjoyed what I like to think were Savoy's best years during that period — Allison's sense of humour and fun were legendary.

After Allison had sung lead soprano roles for a few years, the directors decided to split the role of Phyllis in *Iolanthe* between Allison and another soprano, and they each played the role on alternate nights. Allison never let Jim Wegg the Music Director forget this, and she always gave him a hard time about her "half-role" assignment.

A few years later, Allison was appointed Music Director of Savoy, and her strengths as leader and teacher came into their own. We could now respect Allison in an entirely different role, as efficient and capable as always. I performed in most of the shows she directed until both she and I "retired" (for a while anyway) at pretty much the same time, about a year or two ago.

A few of us "retired" women were having lunch at Gloria Young's beautiful riverside home in the summer of 2011, and Allison told us that she was experiencing strange odours. Gloria went searching around her kitchen to find out what it could be, but found nothing. I gather it was shortly after that time that she received her diagnosis and her amazing and difficult journey started.

When she told me that she had to undergo brain surgery, I was totally amazed at her positive attitude and acceptance of what she had to face. She came to a 70th birthday party for my husband Tony on 25th February — shortly before her surgery. She was her usual fun self and was one of the people who wrote and sang a song to roast him.

After Allison's surgery, I was stunned to see what had become of such a fit, vibrant person. It was hard to believe that she could ever have recovered to the point where she is now. But every time I went to see her, there was improvement, and I am sure that her mighty spirit played a huge part in her recovery. But the devotion of Bob and Marya (along with a wide network of friends) was the real catalyst.

Shortly after Allison had been home from the hospital, I went to spend the afternoon with her because Bob had to go to work. I wasn't really sure what to expect. All was going well — but for a moment I was pre-occupied with fixing something for dinner and Allison disappeared. I was frantic. I went all over the house calling her name and getting no answer. Finally, I opened a door on the second floor, and there she was on the balcony, hanging out the

Allison's Brain • 373

laundry. The door was closed so she hadn't heard me calling. I was so relieved!

Lynn Graham

Allison and I have been friends since the early 1980s when she and her family moved onto Aylmer Avenue and she began her teaching career at Hopewell Avenue School. With our adjoining backyards and the friendships among our children — especially Anna and Marya — we have shared many of life's experiences. This friendship has continued in spite of both families relocating to other Ottawa neighbourhoods.

In looking back over my 2012 hospital visits with Allison, there were three distinct phases. In late June, I found Allison in bed in her hospital room, dozing frequently and with very limited cognitive capacity. However, I had brought a special edition of *Maclean's* and, as we looked at the pictures, Allison observed the two front covers, commenting that one must be French and the other English — not the case but a good try! I left that visit with a heavy heart, concerned for Allison's future and wondering if she would ever regain a normal life.

The next month, my visit with Allison took us out of her hospital room. She was in a wheelchair when I arrived, and we spent time in the lounge reading (me), looking at photos in a magazine and simply chatting. I felt Allison knew my voice and enjoyed the time with me but was not yet capable of recognizing me as her friend and former neighbour. One of the nurses seemed particularly interested in Allison, and I took the opportunity to explain that she was an amazing teacher and musician. This took me back to the years when my mother was suffering from Alzheimer's and the staff in her retirement home knew only the patient, not the accomplished woman she once was.

In August, my visit confirmed once again the progress being made by Allison. I laugh as I recall that evening although it really wasn't funny at the time. The first hour went well. I had brought several programs — such as *Jack and the Giant* and *Emperor Eddy* — from her Hopewell School musical productions and she recalled enthusiastically many of the details of the songs and the cast of characters. How delighted I was to see this improvement in her cognitive ability! However, the second half of my visit was frustrating for Allison as she tried repeatedly to get out of bed and convince me that I should take her home. She was very annoyed with my opposition, and eventually I had to ring for the nurse who came to the room and restrained her. This experience was upsetting for both Allison and me, but I knew upon leaving that she had made tremendous strides in a couple of months. She had even spoken in general terms of our former homes and neighbourhood, and I felt she knew exactly who I was.

Since Allison left hospital, I have seen her at her home and mine and in the community. Each time, she has shown remarkable progress to the point where, as far as I can tell, she is the Allison I knew pre-surgery. What Allison has accomplished is astonishing. What the medical system has done for her is truly commendable. Finally, I will always have the deepest admiration and respect for Allison's daughter, Marya, and Allison's husband, Bob. Their determination and love for Allison have been instrumental in making this transformation possible.

Louise Hall and Susan Smith

As colleagues and friends of Allison's, we have always been struck by her energy, sense of humour and determination. Over the years we have shared many laughs, and this is what characterized our get-togethers — the laughter, the silliness and the love of wine. As teaching colleagues, we have admired Allison's stubbornness *a.k.a.* determination in her professional life, demonstrated by her ability to be in control whether in the classroom, during her legendary musicals or on the well-loved band trips. We know Allison as an educator who challenged her students while teaching them independence, ensuring everything was well-managed and in control.

Allison's Brain • 375

Despite chaotic sounds coming from the music room, her classes were always well organized and productive.

Allison is not easily swayed. She has very definite ideas about how things should be done, and this purpose and resolve made us feel safe with her. Susan once asked Allison, "How do you always get approval for these things (expenditures, last minute field trip forms, school musicals)?" — She replied, "Susan, you don't ask for permission — you do it and then ask for forgiveness later." Allison is very sociable and refined in her special way, and this came through in the hospital where we noticed that her tone was always kind and gracious even though she could not find the right words.

From Louise: The Friday before her surgery, I brought Allison a special wedge-shaped pillow that we thought might be useful post-op. She was sitting on her porch, reading (I think it was Taylor's *My Stroke of Insight*). As we chatted, I was impressed by Allison's knowledge about how the brain heals itself, but it was mostly her composure that struck me. My next visit on July 8th was equally impressive with Allison sitting up and chatting away with Bob as I entered the hospital room. I quickly realized that what she was saying did not make too much sense. Soon after my arrival, Bob took his leave, telling Allison that he would return the next day. She asked him if he was going to meet the "people about the certificates." Bob wasn't sure what Allison meant and since she seemed confused, we dismissed it. During my visit, Allison's determination shone through as she insisted that we go for a walk. I tried coaxing her into a wheelchair and after a few moments of stubborn refusal, she suddenly complied in an almost child-like way — this astounded me as it was a side of Allison I had never seen. I kept my emotions in check. It wasn't until later that evening when I realized that when Allison had asked Bob about the certificates, it must have come from association when she saw me walk into her hospital room: one of my duties at Hopewell was to prepare all of the graduation certificates for our grade 8 students.

From Susan: I was teaching in a small African village when Allison was going through the worst of her struggles in June. It was very worrisome to be out of touch, having no news about Allison and her recovery. When I finally travelled to the nearest city and had access to the internet, I was relieved to see that Donna had been sending me regular updates on Allison's condition.

I didn't know what to expect when I first visited Allison in July. She was sleeping when I arrived, so I put on the CD of *Mama Mia*, thinking it might remind her of the performances we attended on the Toronto band trips. Allison awoke briefly when Nurse Delphin came in to take her blood pressure. As we were listening to *Mama Mia*, Delphin began to sing along. Lying there with her eyes closed, Allison raised her hand and began to direct Delphin as he was singing. This was the Allison I knew! Toward the end of my visit, Allison was grooving to the tunes of Roy Orbison. I still wasn't sure at this point if Allison knew who I was, so I showed her a couple of photos taken in recent years — one of Donna, Allison, and me wearing silly hats at Casa Loma, and another at our 'To Hell with the Bell' breakfast celebration on Louise's first day of retirement. Allison was interested in the photos but not yet making the connections.

I walked away from that visit with mixed feelings. I could see traces of Allison coming through, but I wondered whether the healing in the coming months would enable her to reconnect with the people and events in her life.

July 23rd — from Susan and Louise: Up to this point we had visited Allison independently, but in conversation we decided that it might be a good idea to visit together to renew a sense of our group dynamic. Seeing us together, she might connect with the "Hopewell friends" — begin to place us in a "historical" context of our past get-togethers — the fun and shenanigans of our particular sisterhood. It was a great visit with Allison.

On our next visit later in July, Nurse Jennifer was trying to give Allison her meds from a small cup. In an effort to console her, we compared the liquid meds to taking "shooters." Allison saw through our ruse and would have none of it! In some way, this was the true

Allison coming through: stubborn and determined to do it her way… The nurse left and said she would try later.

While we chatted, Allison was humming to background music and tapping her hands to the rhythm. She was holding down her part of the conversation in her own way — without the correct choice of words, but with expression and humour. She was so positive and light-hearted. She would make light of things, laughing at her own jokes even though they didn't make sense. She sang a few lines from "Only Love Can Break Your Heart", and the talk turned to holding a mic and organizing a girl band. Allison suggested we call the band Chicklets. We all laughed. After our visit with Allison, we realized that the name may have been triggered by the offering of chewing gum during the afternoon. It needs to be said that, after each visit, we would stop awhile to talk about our time with Allison — our impressions, hopes and fears, and our difficulty dealing with the unknown.

One moment we shared has become a treasured memory. Toward the end of August, when we arrived at her hospital room, Allison, in her red plaid pyjamas, greeted us in a perky way. We noted immediately the progress in her physical strength. She was sitting up and seemed to be feeling well. We shared laughs that reminded us of our 'get stupid nights' (inside joke), and even though Allison still did not always make sense, she was up-beat and engaged. Louise pulled out her cell phone with the intention of taking a picture, but decided to show photos of her Wheaten Terrier, Quincy. At this point, we posed for a few group pictures and then tried to decide which ones were keepers… Allison commented on our expressions which made us all laugh. In an effort to help her remember our names, we began to identify ourselves in the photo: Allison, Susan and… 'Dog-Face!' Allison blurted out. She was quite pleased with herself for remembering Louise's 'name'! The connection was there, but a little off target! Since then, we've had many opportunities to relive that moment and laugh — just like old times.

Pauline Lynch-Stewart

It is Thanksgiving Day 2013 and Allison's 62nd birthday. Her small dining room bursts with good cheer as friends and family gather to celebrate Allison and the season. I look to my left at her beaming face as she banters easily with her guests, laughing often, and I am inspired to raise my glass and toast our Allison: She is back! Thanks in large measure to her tenacious spirit and the love and good care of many people, Allison is well and truly back.

~~~

Allison's reputation had preceded her to the house across the road, where she and her husband Bob moved eight years ago. By the time she arrived, I had been informed by neighbours and friends that she was the formidable music teacher at the local public school, who directed and often wrote two full musical productions every year at the school, conducted several award-winning bands and choirs, provided musical direction to the Savoy Society's Gilbert & Sullivan productions, as well as organizing or participating in other community events. Clearly a woman in charge, and a force with which to be reckoned.

Since then, we have developed an easy, daily sort of friendship based on shouted greetings, chats on the road, borrowed eggs, and shared dinners. I came to know her as a kind and generous friend with a no-nonsense attitude to life and a cut-to-the-chase approach to conversation. "I noticed that your whole family was here for the weekend. What were you doing down in the park?"

I had a front-row seat to watch as Allison launched into her "retirement" with the same energy and determination displayed during her teaching days. Bob often joked that Allison made a to-do list every day and then just set about getting it done. On any given day it might have read: Bike ride to the store, work with Bob, tennis and lunch with Marya, seed the backyard, practice with Savoy for upcoming musical, teach piano lesson, dinner and a movie with Bob.

Allison's Brain • **379**

Allison and Bob spent a lot of time together, clearly enjoying one another's company. Every evening in the summer, we would see them on their front porch, chatting over dinner. Sometimes they would drive up to the Gatineau in Bob's MGB or attend an opera or some other musical performance. They went on frequent trips together to see friends, escape the Ottawa winter, or visit family in the prairies. Allison often accompanied Bob to one of his running or triathlon events to cheer him on from the sidelines.

~~~

The diagnosis of this "giant aneurysm" in the fall of 2011 put this wonderful, full life on hold to a great extent. The doctors had advised that Allison not stray too far from home, and once the winter had set in, she was particularly concerned about falling on the ice. From my perspective, the months before her surgery in May 2012 were coloured by her relentless pursuit of a date for the operation and her unshakable conviction that she was going to experience the best possible outcome. I recall Bob talking about how she waved off the neurosurgeon as he described the potential implications of the procedure: "But this is worst-case scenario you're talking about, right? I am going to have the best-case scenario," she confidently informed him, in what I imagined to be her best "This is the way it's going to be" teacher's voice.

In our conversations during this time, Allison was gracious in her acceptance of best wishes and support, but made it clear that she looked forward to the surgery as something that had to be done so she could get back to the life she loved. She expected to be home recuperating by Bob's 60th birthday on June 12th — although "not looking good" and being tired — and warned us that she could be back driving around "terrorizing the neighbourhood" within a month of the surgery.

~~~

In reality, Allison's early recovery looked nothing like this scenario. Instead of the milestones we predicted for Allison the first while — coming home, getting back on her feet, driving her car — we

380 • *Robert McMechan with Allison Woyiwada*

anxiously awaited news of her awakening after days of sedation, breathing on her own, the movement of a finger or toe or the squeeze of a hand. Two or three weeks after the surgery, we were struggling to come to terms with what seemed a very long road ahead, and learning to ride the bumps, setbacks and uncertainty of Allison's recovery.

I saw Allison for the first time sixteen days after surgery on June 13. I entered the room on her right hand side; Allison was awake, unmoving, staring dully ahead. She was being monitored and fed by a number of machines. Tubes drained the surgical site. She had a tracheotomy tube extending from her throat. Her face under her bandaged head was swollen and her left eye bulged from the socket. My initial reaction was pure shock. I remember thinking: *Dear God, this is not what Allison bargained for. This is not what any of us expected. We are not prepared for this.*

~~~

For Allison's entire recovery, but particularly during these initial weeks, Allison's daughter, Marya, and her husband, Bob, were simply heroic. They both spent hours and hours at the hospital every day, holding Allison's hand, talking to her, playing music for her, encouraging her to raise a finger, move an arm, speak. They regularly updated other family members and friends about her progress. They talked to dozens of health care professionals who appeared at her bedside, discussing issues, therapies, next steps. They coordinated a few close friends to be with Allison on the rare occasions they took time away. From the beginning, Bob and Marya have been formidable advocates for Allison's recovery.

For three or four weeks after Allison's surgery, Bob frequently joined us for dinner or a chat after returning from the hospital each evening. My heart just broke for him in these early weeks. He often arrived tired and worried; a few evenings he appeared almost shell-shocked, his voice strained. But he would share with us the news of the day and unfailingly recount a funny story — the neurosurgeon's comment that tax law was boring was a source of jokes for days. It was clear to us during this time that Bob's sense of humour, as well

Allison's Brain • 381

as his commitment to running and cycling, and his many wonderful friends and family members would help him to get through these difficult early days.

~~~

I visited Allison a couple of times during the month following the surgery. I would read to her from a book or newspaper, show her photographs, talk to her about the news in the neighbourhood. She seemed engaged, but it was difficult to discern her level of comprehension. As I was prattling on during my first visit, I became quite concerned that once she got her voice back she'd ask to have me taken off the visiting list. I could imagine her saying: "Bored? I thought I'd die!"

Allison's condition seemed to vary daily and even hourly during these early weeks. She was struggling with a number of medical issues — fevers, coughing and infections — on top of re-learning everything from swallowing to moving the right side of her body. I found it a great comfort to share thoughts and concerns with a small group of Allison's other friends who were spelling off Marya and Bob during these early weeks. A couple of them were incredibly upbeat and positive, detailing small victories in facial expression, movement of her right side or even speech, during their visits. Another friend, a nurse, reassured us that Allison's body was healing as it should, and that symptoms that were sometimes disturbing to us were normal and even healthy at this point in her recovery.

Many family members and friends reached out to Bob and Allison during this time, each bringing their own gifts. Don and I felt we could be of most value supporting Bob. Besides providing him with dinner and company, Don got him out cycling when he could. I set up a web-based application — Lotsahelpinghands.com — to help him to coordinate visits to Allison and other support. We dug out a bunch of very simple puzzles and games that he might be able to play with Allison. And I pursued information on the plasticity of the brain and sent him links of YouTube videos showing U.S. Congresswoman Gabrielle Giffords, who had been shot in the head in January 2011 and was responding very well to music therapy.

~~~

After our summer holidays, I went to see Allison again at the end of August 2012, about two and a half months after the surgery. I saw an enormous difference in her. She had moved to the Neuroscience InPatient Unit in the hospital. She looked much more like herself. I found her lounging comfortably in her own, new pyjamas. She was walking, talking, eating and laughing again.

We talked about some of the sights Don and I had seen on our trip, although it was strange conversation indeed. Allison seemed to understand what I was saying to her, and sometimes responded appropriately like, "Oh Bob wants to go there." Other times she looked me straight in the eye and delivered in her most authoritative Allison tone a sentence that made no sense at all like: "but they're going back and they want to but I said about the shoes and won't know." I pretended she made complete sense and simply continued the conversation without skipping a beat.

Bob, on the other hand, never let her get away with that. He would say to her: "I can't understand what you're saying, honey." He always responded truthfully to Allison and continually challenged her to articulate her thoughts. And slowly but surely, Allison has made great progress in fighting back the aphasia that played havoc with her speech. Recently, Allison told me that her speech therapist once taped one of her responses and played it back to her, and she couldn't believe what she sounded like: her words bore no resemblance to what she thought she had said.

~~~

Not surprisingly, when I think back on the last eighteen months, one of the great lasting impressions relates to the power of music in so many aspects of Allison's recovery. From early days after the surgery, music filled her hospital room and beckoned her back to consciousness. In the ICU, her family was so encouraged to see Allison mouthing words to *The Big Chill* soundtrack and conducting an orchestra with her finger. Weeks later, during one of the most poignant moments of her recovery, she shocked everyone by playing Beethoven's *Pathétique* from sheet music left on a hospital piano.

Allison's Brain • 383

Former students, colleagues, friends and family packed a benefit concert staged by Allison's musical daughter to celebrate her mother and raise funds for costly therapies. Months after the operation, music therapy allowed Allison to clearly sing her thoughts, long before she was able to reliably speak them.

~~~

Allison came home for the first time in mid-September — albeit just briefly on a day-pass from the rehabilitation centre — about three and a half long months after the surgery. Don and I didn't want to overwhelm her on her first day home, but Allison marched right over to our place after dinner — in one of the amazing flowing capes that she loves to wear — and chatted and laughed with us for a few minutes before returning to the centre. Since then, she has learned to slowly put the right words to the thoughts tumbling through her brain. And her daily commitment to that work is paying off now in lots of perfect sentences and even flawless conversations.

I think Allison is blessed to have access to such advanced medical care. She is blessed to have people around her who care for her so much and are committed to seeing her well. She is blessed with a wonderful fighting spirit, courage to surround herself with friends and family even as she struggles to communicate her thoughts, and the drive and determination to be "normal" as she puts it.

But I guess what has seemed so miraculous to me in all of this has been to witness the loss of so much of Allison's cognitive function and memory, to be searching her eyes for signs of Allison in there, and to watch her gradually re-emerge in all of her essential Allison-ness — the energy, confidence, flare, passion, humour. The brass-tacks nature of her conversation. Sometimes she still uses the wrong word or gets a story mixed up, especially if she's tired, and I know she will continue to strive to recover completely. But for now, I am just thankful that Allison is back. Cheers, my friend.

Pat MacDonald

I find it difficult to talk about someone's 'brain' without thinking of their 'personality', a more vague term that obviously has something to do with 'brains' but is also somewhat separate. Already being part of a journey involving brain trauma with my beloved brother-in-law gave me some insight into what happens when doctors go poking around in our head, so I knew a few things before they went in to explore Allison: I knew that she would face hurdles yet unknown; I knew she was a fighter; I knew the support she had from family and friends; I knew that, whatever happened, her personality would come out the other side. You can't come through something like this unchanged. It's not that it is worse, it's just that life will be different, and there may always be challenges. My brother-in-law has learned to adapt to his 'new brain', make allowances for it, to ask for help when he needs it, and to demand that people give him a chance to format ideas or 'get things out' when needed.

Now when I see Allison, I can look back to those days in the hospital and see how far she has come. I remember the first time I visited early in July. I was greeted with courtesy but looking back on it now, I am not sure that Allison actually remembered who I was. Knowing this, I had brought pictures of us from an old Savoy show and explained that we had been on stage together and that we had directed shows together. Although not asking specific questions, she was interested. All of a sudden she pointed to my hair, which is now grey, and then to the photos. I realized that her short term memory of me in the last few years had vanished. Good thing I re-introduced myself!

Music being so powerful in each of our lives, I asked if she wanted to go down to the piano. She did, so down we went, and even though speech was a problem, Allison was able to read the music and to play the piano although the right hand was having more difficulty. We tried some duets which 'kind of' worked. The exciting part for me, and I believe for her, was that she was actually at the piano making music! On future visits, Doug and I would bring music, and once when she still wasn't saying much, we started

Allison's Brain • 385

singing at the end of the bed and conductor Allison conducted —
along with the proper cutoffs!

What I remember most about those early visits was that, even
though she wasn't able to communicate through much speech,
she was still the Allison I've known these many years. We were
always greeted with courtesy and Doug with a hug, but when she
was tired or didn't want something the nurses were giving her, the
stubborn, and yes, opinionated Allison, jumped in and wanted her
demands met.

Like my brother-in-law, probably the main cause of recovery
and gaining back of language and other skills doesn't come from
any of us but from Allison's determination to continue to improve.
Now when we talk, a year and a half after the operation, it is like a
miracle that someone can have their brain taken apart and come out
of it in such grand style. Of course, there are words or expressions
that don't quite make total sense or that we will have to interpret
here and there. There may always be. This is a new Allison — yes,
but like the other Allison, a great one.

You go girl!

Marylen Milenkovic

The first time I saw Allison after her surgery, I was shocked and
scared. What I saw was this once vibrant woman curled up in her
bed unable to communicate on any level. This was around the time
I was considering breast reconstruction surgery after my two bouts
with breast cancer. After seeing Allison, I decided to put off my
decision or maybe never go through with the surgery. It brought all
memories of my previous treatments and surgeries back to mind. I
kept telling myself that at least I had the capability to think during
my treatments. My dear friend Allison couldn't at this time, and I
wondered if she ever would come back to us.

I had offered suggestions and reading for Allison to use in preparation for her surgery. She diligently did the exercises and prepared
in many ways. Different therapists have said that musicians have the

discipline to sail through brain therapies because of their years of practicing to achieve excellence. After witnessing Allison's recovery, I believe that to be true.

My numerous hospital visits with Allison consisted of observing her, trying to communicate with her, feeding her, taking her for walks and pushing her in her wheelchair through the hallways. On my first visit I thought I'd buy some picture magazines like *People*, *US* etc. Foolishly I thought she could look at the pictures of stars or famous people and it might jog her memory. At this point in her recovery she didn't know what to make of it and deftly flipped through the pages in about 5 secs and then put the magazines down. So I tried to talk with her, and she replied, but it was all gobbledygook. This way of communicating lasted for a long while. It slowly improved in that she actually spoke some words that I could actually understand even though they didn't make sense linked together.

What amazed me is that it all seemed to make sense to her in her mind. I knew she was improving when she directed me in which direction she wanted to go down the hallways. One of her earlier pleasures was looking out the few windows in the halls. I made sure to always take her to the windows so she could see outside because lying in her bed did not afford her a good view. Another time, when I was wheeling her through the hallways and downstairs, I started singing songs and she started singing with me. Some of the words came to her, but it was mostly melody. Later she actually could sing the words to an entire song and also harmonize. I knew she was connecting the dots then.

When I brought her to the room to put her to bed there was a nice slow jazz tune playing on her cd, and she waltzed with me with a smile on her face contented for the interlude. Whenever music was playing, which was constant, her hand was continually conducting the music with every beat. Music definitely comforted her.

A couple of times I found her on the floor all bloodied because she tried to get up out of her bed. That scared the shit out of me, for I thought the nurses weren't watching her as much as they should. I even reported one nurse to the supervisor. After those incidents

Allison's Brain • 387

they lowered the bed and surrounded her bed with mats so as to protect her from injury when she tried to escape again.

Feeding her was also a challenge in the early days of recovery because she either lost interest or didn't understand what the food was for. It was like trying to coax a baby to eat. She lost so much weight because she rarely ate anything. Gradually she started eating more, but I don't blame her for not trying as hospital food is notoriously awful.

You would have been so proud of Marya as she was with her every day in the beginning taking care of her. She anticipated every need and desire. Bob was also a guardian angel every step of the way along with Allison's army of friends. A highlight was the benefit concert that Marya organized and performed along side several of Allison's musician friends. The church was overcrowded with friends and colleagues, and I wish Allison could have been there but she were recovering from another surgery. I hope they taped the vent.

When Allison started to walk, with the help of two people, she was adamant like a toddler in wanting to walk and not be wheeled in her chair. One day when I took her walking with her friend Betty, she almost ran. She was so intent on walking, but she tired so easily. She also hated her helmet. She was always taking it off, and the nurses had a difficult time in keeping it on her head.

Allison had a number of setbacks with infections, surgeries etc. but each time she survived and came back working even harder. Her goal was to get out of the hospital. Let's face it, my seven years of cancer treatments don't compare to seven months of being in a hospital bed.

Welcome back, dear friend. I'm so proud of what you've accomplished and never doubted that you would do the work to recover. Love Marylen

Sharon Neill

Allison is a wonderfully gifted musician. She has spent her life involved with music, and as you will find out, music has played a huge part in her recovery.

My husband Al and I met Allison and Bob through the Savoy Society of Ottawa. Initially we watched Allison perform on stage as the leading lady in Gilbert and Sullivan musicals. She was a wonderful performer, and we fell in love with her. After a time, we performed on stage with Allison, and eventually she became the music director of the group. We shared many fun times together socially as well as on stage.

Bob informed friends about Allison's upcoming surgery in May 2012 and then provided updated accounts of her progress. I was apprehensive. I was scared for Allison because she was to undergo serious brain surgery. I felt unsure and was a little uncomfortable about going in to visit with her in the hospital. Would I be of any assistance to the family, not having medical knowledge of her condition and no experience with people who were seriously ill? I was asked for help, and that's all I knew. Being a mom myself with all that it encompasses, I felt it gave me some credibility.

Bob used the services of an organization called "Helping Hands." To know when it was a good time to visit with Allison, all I had to do was sign in on my computer to view a calendar. I could then choose a date when coverage was needed and a time that worked in with my schedule. I booked it right on line. It was a very good system and a way to give Bob and her daughter Marya a much needed break. I signed up for a weekly visit which sometimes turned into twice a week depending upon the need for coverage. I understood that the idea was to be company for Allison and to try to stimulate her in whatever way that I could.

If I remember correctly, on my initial visit I relieved Marya. As I entered the room, I heard music softly playing and a voice quietly speaking. Marya was sitting on her mother's bed chatting away. I thought — this is good. However, the conversation was one sided. Allison looked at me with dull, blank eyes and showed no signs of

Allison's Brain • **389**

welcome or recognition. She had a hollow, glazed appearance. Her replies to Marya were few and far between, and made absolutely no sense. I'm not certain that Allison was even aware that it was her daughter who was with her. It was unnerving to see her like that. I took the chair at the foot of the bed, wondering how I would reply to the disjointed comments when I would be left on my own with her. I immediately decided to be straightforward — if I knew what she was asking, I would tell her — if I didn't, I would also tell her. Thus began my visits.

Allison wore a blue helmet to protect her skull. It looked like a bicycle helmet.

Before I go any further, I must say that from day one to my last hospital visit with Allison, I really don't believe that she knew who I was. Even though I would say my name, not once did she call me by name. Allison was always pleasant and courteous — ever the gracious lady. There were times when she showed a stubborn streak, which I believe is part of the reason she is so well today. Her determination was something to see. Often I would check the record book to see who had been in, and then I would ask Allison if she had seen that particular person lately. In time she did acknowledge other visitors but not initially. She was very confused, and it appeared as though she was making things up. Initially there was not much response — just disjointed words and sentences.

Most of the time, I relieved Bob, and he was great to spend a few minutes to tell me how Allison was progressing. It was a good opportunity to see how he was doing. Despite the stressful circumstances, Bob held up extremely well throughout the whole challenging ordeal. It was wonderful to see how extremely caring and gentle he was with Allison. He was very concerned and determined that she would be herself again. Time spent with Bob was most encouraging, and I always felt better going in to see Allison after I took over from him.

Early on in my visits, I brought in some foot massage cream. I love a foot massage myself, so I thought perhaps she might enjoy one. By the expression on Allison's face, I could tell how much she enjoyed the foot massages. Perhaps it was just the fact that someone was touching her that made her feel good. The smiles and the moaning was a good sign :) I made that part of my visiting routine.

I understand that, after the initial surgery, some visitors took Allison outside of the hospital to enjoy the days of nice weather. Personally, I did not feel comfortable doing that. I took Allison around and around the corridors of her hospital floor. Initially she just sat in the wheelchair. There was no reaction to anything that I pointed out. I did a running commentary of where we were and what we were passing. I generally touched things so that she would know what I was talking about. She didn't appear to notice people we passed or nurses at their station. She didn't speak much as I pushed her in the wheelchair. Over time, Allison would slowly repeat and respond to whatever appeared to be new. I brought mundane items into the conversation and reinforced words for things that caught her attention. We went over numbers and letters on the elevator doors — whether selecting that number would take the elevator up or down. We looked at shapes pasted or painted on the hospital corridors. We went over words to songs. We vocalized about hospital supplies, nurses, charts, elevator doors. I talked about the view from each window — what you could see — what was in the distance — whether or not she knew where she was in location to things in the city. Allison tired very easily, so some of these trips were really short. I would take her back to her room and get her in to her bed. Later on, she appeared to be pleased to be out of the room. It was repetitive, but that appeared to be what was required, and it was something that I was comfortable doing.

Allison's short responses to small questions made sense. She knew who she was, and she knew that she had had surgery. I would ask whether she'd like to leave the room, and then I would go along with her response.

Still after several visits, Allison wasn't able to carry on a conversation — at times she would repeat what I would say. Then out of the blue, she would put a bunch of words together that had nothing to do with what I was talking about. She would be trying to tell

Allison's Brain • **391**

me something. She was very articulate, but her comments made no sense to the question asked. It was as though her wires were crossed. She was totally confused, but she herself felt as though she was responding correctly, and she did it with such conviction. Again, a bit unnerving because I didn't know the subject or the people she was talking about. I owned up to the fact that she was discussing people I didn't know or discussing a subject with which I was unfamiliar. She appeared to be comfortable with that. I felt that she was listening carefully to what you were saying.

Gradually after a few weeks, Allison would respond. She appeared as though she was actually carrying on a conversation and probably felt very much like she was, but nothing she said made sense in the beginning. I did my best not to question her but to correct or reinforce what she did know. Allison has an unbelievable vocabulary. Her ability to put words — and then sensible sentences — together took a few months. She showed great determination.

If I remember correctly, after the 1st of July, we were looking out a hospital window facing northeast, and Allison told me that she watched the fireworks on Canada Day. I was impressed that she was aware Canada Day just passed and that fireworks were a part of the celebration.

I was especially encouraged one day when Allison hummed and mouthed the words of a song that was playing. She actually knew the words.

On one visit, Allison seemed to not have control of the shaking on one side of her body. I watched her for a short time and she continued to shake at intervals. Nurses seldom came in to the room when I was there, so I asked one to check Allison to see if everything was ok. I had to leave the room while they came in and did some tests, and then I saw Allison again before I went home. That was pretty unnerving. I must say though that the medical response to my concern was immediate. I always informed the nursing station when I left Allison unless I was replaced by another visitor. I wanted them to be aware that she was on her own.

Never was I sure where I would find Allison upon arrival at the hospital. She was often moved from one side of the hall to the other. On one particular visit, I could not find her at all. Upon asking I learned that Allison was down on the intensive care floor. I was a little nervous to go down, not knowing what I would find, but since I had signed up to be there at that particular time of day I went. At first the receptionist on the floor wasn't going to allow me to visit since I wasn't a family member. I made them aware that I was asked by the family to sit with Allison. It was quite a shock to find Allison there all plugged in to devices. That was a huge step backward, and I was very concerned.

Allison was plugged into machinery that blipped and beeped. She lay totally still and did not open her eyes at all during my visit. I believe at this point she was in a coma. I touched her and spoke softly in the hope that she would know someone was with her. During my stay, the machinery made noises, and at one point the monitor line went absolutely flat. The bell beeped and I thought she was gone. I had a nurse come to check and he informed me that Allison's machinery was constantly monitored — not to worry. It scared the heck out of me. Again, the response by the nursing staff was immediate.

It was during my visits to this floor that I found another friend of mine was a patient across the hall from Allison. They shared the same nurse and the same surgeon. Dr. Lesiuk is obviously a very good surgeon, for both Allison and Marit have recovered wonderfully.

Music was a constant in Allison's recovery. Generally classical music was playing in the background, but I did change the CD occasionally. I recall myself waking at home in the middle of the night worried that I might have turned the music off. At times, when I arrived for a visit, I would think Allison was sleeping. However, as the music played, she would raise her left hand and keep time. Ever the conductor. How I loved to see that. It was hopeful, and I felt something was truly reaching her.

Friends and relations enjoyed a beautiful musical performance held as a fundraiser to help with Allison's medical expenses. It

Allison's Brain • 393

was well attended, and you felt the love and warmth for Allison throughout the gathering. We are so glad to be witness to Allison's amazing recovery.

My last visit was to Allison and Bob's home to bring a quilt that was made by a member of my quilting group. It was made with love and concern for someone in need, and Allison definitely qualified. I hope it made her feel comfortable and well thought of.

Since that time, I have lunched with Allison and friends in a restaurant several blocks from her home. Allison was her usual funny self, and it was heart-warming to see her looking and feeling so well. She held her own during all the conversations, but some of her responses were limited.

Well Bob, my memory is not as good as it used to be, and the sequence of how things happened may not be correct, but this is the best that I can recall.

I'm glad that I was able to help with Allison's recovery. I must say that people should not be overly concerned about their own abilities when it comes to helping others in need. There is always something one can do. I believe that a friendly face, some warmth, patience and a bit of chatter goes a long way when someone has to spend so much time on their own. An unwell person needs all the support and encouragement you can give.

JoAnne Sulzenko
Lessons from the 'Wings'

I am honoured to participate in this recollection, though I see myself as a 'bit player' in the drama of the past two years in Allison's life and the life of her family.

My association with Allison started at Hopewell Avenue Public School and developed through artistic collaborations into a friendship. I was and still am a big fan of 'Mrs. Woyiwada!' (Milestones in our relationship appear as a postscript to this submission for those interested.)

To my surprise, I had difficulty writing about my visits with Allison at the Civic Campus of the Ottawa Hospital. Perhaps because I grew up with neurological illness in my family, going into any hospital does not come easy. That I was afraid, particularly of the neurology floor at the Civic, I now admit with some shame. Which may explain, in part, why, even though I meant my comments to be all about Allison, I could not avoid the 'me' in the equation.

My narrative comes from the 'wings' and begins in the autumn of 2011, before I heard of the aneurysm.

NOVEMBER 2011

After a fourth very well received presentation of *A Child's Christmas in Wales*, the Dylan Thomas story, at Glebe St. James, which Allison and I had co-produced and she directed, Rob Clipperton and I approached her about returning for one final and fifth year. Never one to sit on the fence about anything, Allison said uncharacteristically that she wouldn't commit herself just yet. I shrugged off how she responded, though I can't say I was happy to hear it. She had played such a key part in the success of the annual productions. I encouraged her to think about our proposition, and we left it at that. I had no clue anything was the matter.

DECEMBER 2011

Allison 'announced' the decision she faced: to undergo major brain surgery to repair the huge aneurysm or accept the possibility of a rupture within years. Her news left me in shock. Who would have thought that something as innocuous as smelling garbage would equate to life-threatening pressure on the brain? I was not surprised when Allison rejected the do-nothing approach and chose to risk everything in order to take back her future.

What did astound me was how she embraced the challenge and involved her circle of friends in the process from the start. She told all of us, without sugarcoating but with optimism, as much as she could about what she learned she would need to go through. I admired her analytical and honest approach to the dangers and her bravery in the face of such a significant health challenge though I

Allison's Brain • **395**

could not help myself from fearing for her and from having disturbing thoughts about my own vulnerability.

That is when I wrote the following, three-verse tanka and posted it on my line-day poetry blog.

> Her sharp reflection
> in a mirror framed with vines.
> She stares at her face,
> the mask that hides what she knows:
> Under lips, that smile — her skull.
>
> What am I? she asks.
> Bones, flesh, gray matter, veins, blood?
> A prison of cells?
> Her body confines, defines
> her essence: When she lives, dies.
>
> Shackled and bound, she
> rejects her physical self;
> Seeks freedom elsewhere.
> Spirit, soul at liberty
> where cell walls wait to be breached.

JANUARY–MAY 2012

In her email updates, Allison shared both frustration and patience with the slowness of the 'medical system' to create the right conditions for the operation to proceed. As I read her blow-by-blow accounts, my admiration for her spirit, spunk and strength grew. To those of us on the receiving end of her notes, her commitment to undergoing the surgery in Ottawa never appeared to waver. The first of the many lessons that came to me through her experience was how it takes courage to choose to live and that the will to live is everything.

Finally, Allison wrote that the date was set; she expressed confidence in the team of surgeons, neurologists and cardiologists assembled to repair the aneurysm. Again, she embraced the opportunity, while admitting that there was no certainty about what the post-surgery weeks/months would bring. I couldn't help but worry. Then she passed the 'pen' to Bob.

Recognizing that I wanted to do what I could to cheer her, Bob and Marya on during what I knew would be long, post-operative days, I signed up for slots on Bob's outreach schedule when I knew I would be in Ottawa. Who else but Bob would have had the wisdom to involve the community of Allison's friends in ensuring she would spend as little time as possible alone on her ward? Who else would find a user-friendly interface that allowed for relatively simple, on-line enlistment, even for luddites like me?

AFTER THE SURGERY

After May 28, Bob kept communication lines open with Allison's community. If there was a longer-than-usual gap between his notes, anxiety weighed on me. As soon as a report arrived, I read it but not without with trepidation.

An amazing correspondent, Bob pulled no punches, though I felt he may have been selective in what information he shared so as to give us, his readers, no cause to lose faith in Allison's ability to recover. At the time, his approach made me remember a tender moment in Disney's film of *Peter Pan*. When Tinker Bell has been hurt, Pan urges everyone to chant their belief in her, because such affirmations would restore her to health. I know I kept my own inner 'mantra' of positive thoughts beamed toward Allison. Perhaps other friends did the same.

During those early days of high-risk healing, though they may have feared for her, Bob and Marya never lost sight of who Allison could and would be again. Their conviction fortified me as I became an irregular visitor to the Civic. Giving in to fear, not before the surgery, not during it and not during the long period of recovery that followed, was not an option for them. That brought another big lesson home to me.

THE SUMMER OF 2012
THE FIRST VISIT

I wanted desperately to believe in Allison's ability to recover even as I began to appreciate just how far she needed to journey to redefine herself.

The first time I came to her four-person room, Allison lay in a bed next to the window that overlooked open fields of the Experimental Farm. A CD player next to the head of her bed stayed on at a low volume all the time. Her head still in bandages, she was attached to various IV lines and monitors. I tried not to feel overwhelmed or scared by how foreign she appeared to me.

I had no idea if Allison would know me or what I could do or say during my timeslot. I remember I brought a book of poems or short stories to read aloud. I have forgotten which ones. I said, "Allison, it's JoAnne." No response. In some distress about what to do next, I looked around first at the orchid on the windowsill. So beautiful and strong. Then at Marya's picture, taped to the foot of the bed, to where Allison's eyes, somewhat unfocussed, strayed. "What a fine picture of beautiful Marya," I blurted. Then I think a read a bit as I crouched next to the head of her cot.

I'm not sure now how long I read before I noticed a favourite Beatles song playing in the background. I looked up and almost missed seeing Allison, who had not said a word or responded to my presence at all, with one finger 'direct' the music in perfect time. Whenever the chorus came on, she said "yellow submarine" at the right moment and with utter clarity. That music was a key to the 'room' where Allison was waiting as she built up her strength gave me hope and my next lesson.

THE SECOND VISIT

Allison had been moved to a bed across the same room. When I arrived, she was sitting up, and fewer bandages were evident. The IV was gone, too. While I am still not sure she recognized me, she responded to what I said in words or parts of phrases that often fit with the context. I watched her eat lunch without assistance, though not necessarily with the utensils provided and with a definite preference for anything sweet. Though I offered to read to her, she said, "No." She tired quickly of my presence. I left soon after, worried that I had not been able to offer much yet happy to perceive how much she had progressed since we last sat together.

THE THIRD VISIT

When I arrived the next time, Allison was asleep. She looked much more herself. I waited to see if she would waken so that we could 'chat' but did not stay when I saw how deeply and peacefully she snoozed in spite of the hustle of the ward.

THE FOURTH VISIT

I had been on the schedule for a few other slots, but circumstances at the hospital or in my commute intervened to make this fourth visit the last one. In seeking a last-minute substitute, Bob's email explained the titanium 'plate' in Allison's skull had been replaced earlier that day because of an infection.

I arrived at her new room on the neuro floor soon after she had returned from surgery. Allison 'wore' a headband of staples covered with transparent tape at her hairline and showed no discomfort. In fact, she looked well.

I had brought a sandwich and offered to have lunch together, if Allison wished. That's when I heard her roommate cry for help from the other side of a door not a metre from where Allison lay to recover from the morning procedure. The woman apparently had suffered a stroke and was on the toilet but didn't know it. She was begging to sit down.

Her desperation upset me and made me concerned that Allison would not be able to rest in such circumstances. At some point a nurse came in to reassure the woman but to no effect. When I asked if there was anywhere more appropriate for Allison to move, the nurse explained all beds on the floor were full.

Allison handled the situation far better than I did. She told me several times "Very difficult. Very difficult." When I offered again to stay and eat together, she repeated "very difficult," and added a definitive "no." I am ashamed to admit I was happy to leave that scene. I took with me, though, yet another lesson, along with my

Allison's Brain • **399**

uneaten sandwich: Allison had been able to focus on her own situation and recovery, rather than let herself be thrown by what was going on around her over which she had no control.

OTHER LEARNINGS
AUGUST 2012

When members of my book club gathered to set the reading list for the next year, our conversation turned to Allison, whom a number of women knew from Hopewell. Her surgery and recovery process inspired us to focus all of the readings, both fiction and non-fiction, on parts of the body, with specific emphasis on the brain.

During the year, we learned about how the brain works or does not from: Lisa Genova's *Left Neglected* and *Still Alice*, Oliver Sacks' *The Man Who Mistook his Wife for a Hat*, Norman Doige's *The Brain that Changes Itself*, plus Catherine Bush's *Claire's Head*. In the summer of 2013 we revelled in Betty Edward's *Drawing on the Right Side of the Brain*.

AUTUMN 2012

Given my travels, I didn't see Allison again until she came home from rehab when Andrei and I brought gourmet pizzas, one custom-ordered for each of us, to Glengarry Road. We enjoyed a fine dinner and a good conversation, if not like 'old times,' then definitely closer to them. Allison ate every morsel.

NOVEMBER 2012

Allison and Bob attended the fifth and final performance our group produced in Ottawa of *A Child's Christmas in Wales*. This was the first time I had staged the event without her directing hand, and I strove to maintain the high standards she had set.

The performance went ahead without a hitch. After we introduced Allison and Bob from the floor and gave her a bouquet of carnations, many friends and performers greeted her with real pleasure as she did them in return. Her presence that day, after all she had endured, enriched the experience. The event raised funds for the acquired brain injury program in recognition of the care Allison had received.

2013

My husband and I see Allison and Bob from time to time and delight with each encounter and each email update in her ongoing journey. We all roared at a comedy night in April. In May, Allison arrived at my annual garden party for mothers, sisters, daughters and nieces on her bicycle and in a spiffy helmet. Everyone there who knew her story was thrilled to see her.

OCTOBER 2013

Allison and Bob joined our table at a fundraising auction for Reach Canada. I scrambled to make sure that what they were served was vegetarian, a small change in the way they live their lives when compared to what they have survived and overcome together.

A surprise reunion brought many hugs and more laughter: Allison had taught music to Dr. Eileen McBride who squealed with pleasure at meeting her again.

Allison and Bob walked about and talked with everyone and enjoyed and partook in everything on offer. Unless you had known Allison before her surgery, you would have been hard-pressed to find evidence in her speech or demeanour of the drama that characterized the past two years for her and her family. The triumph of her path to recovery is almost the stuff of legends. May her progress continue.

POST SCRIPT — OUR 'HISTORY'
THE LATE 1990S

What I knew of Allison began in the mid to late 90s at Hopewell Public School in the Grade 7 and 8 music room. Our children, Alexa and Ben, each played instruments in different Hopewell bands over the years to the rhythm of Allison's baton. Without her ebullience, her love of young people, her fierce energy and drive to turn each child into a musician, I believe these most awkward, intermediate years would have been bleak for our kids. Her pièce de résistance: the famous, annual band trip to Wonderland that kept the kids dedicated year-long and provided a rite of passage into high school, as well. Allison's influence lasted long after Hopewell: Alexa took her euphonium into the Ottawa Youth Orchestra, while

Allison's Brain · 401

Ben played trumpet and flugelhorn throughout the music program at Arts Canterbury.

THE WRITER IN ME

I credit Allison in no small measure for how I came to write storybooks and poetry for children and families, my vocation since 1998. At the time Ben attended Hopewell, funding for music programs was under threat. I wrote then a short story about a little girl's quest to save her school bands. *Annabella and the TyCoon* raised more than $2,000 for music at the school. I remember how Allison completely bowled me over by asking Alexa to return to an assembly at Hopewell and play a brand new euphonium, financed from the book's proceeds and carrying the name 'Annabella' on a plaque.

DYLAN THOMAS

Our paths crossed from time to time after that until the summer of Allison's retirement from teaching. When we met over a glass of wine, I told her I wished to stage a public reading of *A Child's Christmas in Wales* by Dylan Thomas, a story which is a holiday favourite at our house. Much to my delight she signed on, and, for four seasons, we worked together with Rob Clipperton, Robert Palmai and James Caswell to herald the holidays with this fine event. Allison, always the impresario, directed the show and imported the musical talent. With Bob's help, we together raised thousands for a number of charities over the years and gained a loyal following.

OCTOBER 2011

The surprise party for Allison's 60th took place about fifteen minutes from our country home in Prince Edward County at a restaurant I recommended. All sworn to secrecy, we guests kept our backs to the front door. As Allison and Bob arrived, we turned around on cue. The expression of amazement and the joy with which she embraced friends, new and of old, made for an evening that celebrated her with panache. Nothing about that night presaged what was to follow.

JC Sulzenko is an Ottawa-based poet, playwright and author and the grateful mother of two of Allison's former music students at Hopewell Avenue Public School. www.jcsulzenko.com

Joan Veselovsky and Bette-Lou Paragg

Christmas Eve 2011, Bob's sisters, spouses and families were devastated to hear the diagnosis that Allison had a serious brain aneurysm. This is our Allison who had made our brother, Bob, very happy; she was the talented sister-in-law who had an entire wing of a school named after her and who had written and directed musicals.

Our immediate reaction was to send flowers to Ottawa to indicate that we were thinking of her. What else could we do to help? Throughout that Christmas season and the following year, we regularly prayed for Allison's recovery through our prayer circles. At long last, Allison had her extensive surgery. In June 2012, sister Bette-Lou, mother Sylvia, sister Joan and Bob's son Philip flew to Toronto to attend Bob's PH.D. ceremony at Osgoode Hall. Where was Allison? Only then did we fill in our mother about Allison's surgery; Mother had been recently ill herself, and we had not wished to cause her concern.

Then in September 2012, Ben and Joan made the long trek by car to Ottawa, driving along the shore of Lake Superior which took us two and a half days. While we were in Ottawa, Allison was allowed out of the hospital for her first supper with family since her May surgery. That week, we were overwhelmed at the gigantic response to the benefit concert organized by her friends and her daughter, Marya.

Since Allison's surgery and the shedding of our many tears, she is recovering while displaying her own determination for very hard work. Also assisting her recovery are her immediate family; the prayers and positive thinking of friends near and far; and the love and constant vigilance of our brother Bob.

At this time, we are elated to observe the progress Allison has made toward her recovery and extremely pleased that she and Bob can winter in Antigua.

Allison's Brain • **403**

Donna Walsh (aka D-unit, Dungeon Queen, etc.)

Allison has been a best friend of mine for over thirty years! Together we promoted school spirit, did fundraisers, added new programs and supported each other with our various educational projects.

I retired up at Christie Lake in 2008 and made it a point to keep in touch with my Ottawa friends. In the fall of 2011, the "girls" went out for dinner to catch up on our various news events. It was getting towards the end of the evening when Allison mentioned, in passing, that she was going to see a doctor because she occasionally smelt some pretty strange things that she shouldn't have been smelling. At home, she could smell garbage and would search the house for the source, often tossing out what she thought the offender may be but noticing that the odour would persist. While she was telling us this, I felt myself become quite anxious. Past experience with a former student taught me that smelling things that were not there was NOT a good thing.

Allison went to her doctor's appointments and kept us updated on what was happening. Around December, she let us know that there would be surgery scheduled "soon" as her aneurysm warranted an expedient solution. February arrived — no surgery. March and April passed by — no surgery. Finally in May, Ali's surgical team was all together to perform the all day, ground-breaking procedure! So many anxious moments were experienced as we waited until she was revived from the induced coma and we were allowed to see her! Thank goodness for Bob's updates! They certainly helped those of us who don't live in or near Ottawa!

My first few visits to Al reassured me that she was being well cared for! I would stand and watch "Sleeping Beauty", tell her what was going on outside the hospital, put in a CD and leave picture boards of people and events she knew and praying that some of the "old" Ali was listening!

On June 23rd, I was thrilled to see Ali sitting in her chair, giving the odd smile and saying a word here and there. I wasn't sure if "she was in there" until she looked at me, smiled and said, "Dungeon Queen." I almost whopped out loud with that! Years ago the

Science lab and Music Room were in the school's basement. We said we were in the dungeon. We were then christened by a friend of ours — "The Dungeon Queens" — a name that stuck for many years! I was THRILLED to hear Allison say our former title! YES! She WAS there!

July visits were reassuring! There were times when I'd come in for an afternoon visit and Al would be sleeping — sometimes after having done much therapy in the morning. Some of those times I would sit and chat with Ali, telling her how my week had gone and what was new in the family and on others, we'd listen to music together.

Allison was becoming more responsive during the August visits. She would usually be up in her chair and much more attentive. At times I'd have liked to come in but couldn't. Marya suggested I telephone while she was there and we'd try something. When I did, Marya put me on speaker phone so we could "chat"! It tended to be a "one-way" conversation but was still rewarding!

Al has now been home for some time. We've been able to get together for dinner, coffee and some laughs! With that Allison tenacity and stubbornness, much perseverance, dedication to rehab and that "never give up" attitude, Al is not quite her old self, she's even better! As I write this, she is currently involved with learning to play a new-to-her instrument and producing a musical at a school in Antigua!

You are an inspiration and amazing woman, Ali!

Eileen Wilson

I visited Allison at the Civic Hospital in early July 2012 just after Geoff and I returned from Jamaica. I wasn't certain what to expect when I entered Allison's hospital room. The calm and welcoming smile on Allison's face reassured me that I was welcome — but what to say, what to do?

Conversation was difficult, as I had expected, and I was saddened that the once articulate and gifted lady that we had met on many occasions was unable to clearly express her thoughts and seemed more comfortable looking at the photos in a magazine on her bedside table than speaking with me. Having just been in Jamaica, I had brought along two CDs, tunes that were still rattling around in my head from our travels there: one by Bob Marley and one by Harry Belafonte. I started the CD player and I was amazed as Allison began singing along softly with Harry, "Mama look at boo-boo dey..." and pumping her forearm authoritatively in time. As Allison shared her gift of directing, singing and musical memory with me during that brief visit, I experienced the power of music to communicate as words could not. Much has since been said about Allison's recovery and the ability of music training to uplift, to bring pleasure and to heal the injured brain. Her story is a musical miracle.

I did not see Allison for many months after the July visit; not until Allison, Bob, Geoff and I headed to the Scotties curling in Kingston in February 2013. What a surprise to travel with an articulate woman and converse about any number of subjects as we drove through the night to watch a fantastic curling game featuring the Rachel Homan team. Being from Manitoba, Allison is no stranger to curling and took an interest in the game although perhaps she was not quite as enthusiastic as we, her three companions who play the game ourselves. Again, I was amazed at the capability of Allison: from July when she could not enter into conversation, to a coherent and expressive travel companion. We laughed, we ate and we analyzed the curling shots. Allison and Bob have given much credit to her medical team, her family, her therapists and her many musical friends for helping her through the maze of her recovery. No one impresses me as much as the inner resilience Allison herself. The woman is a miracle.

Woyiwada, Marya

When I first began thinking about how my contribution to this text would be the most inspiring, I started looking back through old emails, dating right back to the moment I first became aware of my mother's potential brain issues. I could not, however, complete this process. I barely began it. Reliving, what I'm hoping is the most difficult thing I ever have to go through, was far too painful. The consistent unknown is terrifying, and the anticipation chilling. And the worst part, by far, is going to visit someone who is not my mother as I once knew her, day after day, never being sure if my efforts to influence her progress in a constructive way are at all beneficial. Had I been able to speak to someone who had been through what I was going through, I don't believe I would have struggled so much in finding motivation to spend so much time with a woman I did not know. For this reason, I have decided against repeating what you have already read through a different perspective. I have chosen instead to share a few words of wisdom, in hopes that someone who may be in a position similar to mine in the future might feel a little bit less isolated. If you're reading this because someone you love is going through something similar to what my mom went through, I hope these few pieces of advice will help guide you through it.

STAY POSITIVE

This is possibly more exhausting than any physical strain I can imagine, but you have no choice. Positivity is one of the most powerful remedies, both for you, and your loved ones. No one benefits from sharing negative thoughts, suffering from fear, or focusing on the negative. I'm not telling you not to be scared. You can't help but be, and there's no shame in it. Just don't ever let your fear get the best of you. Your optimism will take you, and everyone around you, a long, long way.

I recall a number of times, shortly after the surgery, that I had to shut out my grief and my concerns and replace them with happiness and strength. When my mother was in a coma and recovering from her coma shortly thereafter, for example, there were many times when Bob and I would spend an entire car-ride to or from the hospital in complete silence. We were, of course, both extremely concerned about my mother's condition. We had questions unanswered, we had worries unexpressed, we had thoughts of the worst possible outcome. Would we have benefited from dwelling on these? Not at

Allison's Brain • 407

this time. The last thing one needs to hear in a situation like this is that someone else has similar concerns. Concentrate on the affirmative, along with every single small step in the right direction.

Having difficulty seeing the positive? Keep records! We had a journal in the hospital that my mother's guests wrote in after each visit. This way, even if my mother was not displaying much progress at the times when I was visiting her, I was still able to see when she *was* earlier in the day, and measure her progress accordingly. If I had to do this all over again, I think I would keep a chart, or some form of graphic organizer that would include dates, and achievements. I found it extremely encouraging to read what other guests who did not visit quite as frequently had written, as my mother's improvements were much more evident to them. As a result, I was continually motivated to keep working hard. It's not easy no matter how you keep track of progress, but I think that having a table to refer back to would have been helpful, not only for myself, but also the other guests, the doctors, the nursing staff, etc.

FOCUS ON THE NOW

Coming out of a coma, as it turns out, is not depicted accurately in film! It is a lengthy process, and the longer and deeper the sleep, the longer the recovery. It's scary, too, after brain surgery. Infinite queries float around in your head. *Will she wake up? What if her abnormal brain activity never ceases? What if she can't walk? Or talk? What if she's a completely different person? Or what if she doesn't know who I am?* These questions will drift through your thoughts obsessively, but the fact is that you won't know the answer to these questions for quite some time. So instead of wondering where or who your loved one will be in the future, focus on where they're at in the moment. Rejoice in the first time they open their eyes. Don't concentrate on the fact that they can't move their right arm. Celebrate the small movements they makes with her left, and the yawns, and the sneezes, and the possibility that you think you may have just seen them try to wink at you. These things will be much more rewarding if you appreciate them when they arrive, instead of fearing that they may not come. I was never sure if my mother knew who I was until weeks after the surgery when she mouthed the words *I love you* and blew me a kiss. I never dreamed I'd be this excited to become aware that my mother knows who I am…

When you go and visit someone recovering from an extensive surgery such as my mother's, you really never know what to expect. One day it might seem as though there's been a huge step in the right direction. The next day, you may experience an even larger step backward. Don't let the bad days bring you down. And there *will* be bad days. They can be petrifying. But as they say: two steps forward, one step back.

DON'T LET SMALL COMMENTS BRING YOU DOWN

I have a newfound respect for our medical system, along with doctors, nurses, therapists, volunteers, and essentially everyone who works in the hospital. No matter what you may be feeling, these people are aware of their patients' conditions and are doing everything they can to support their well-being. Remember that time you had to wait eight months for an MRI? Well as it turns out, someone who has just suffered a fall post-brain surgery has to wait about eight minutes. And the nurses are incredibly knowledgeable, helpful, and considerate. That all having been said, what we have to understand is that these people see this kind of thing every day, and just like any other human being, may accidentally say things that can either be misinterpreted, or taken too seriously. Try not to dwell too much on every random comment that comes out of the mouths of the hospital staff. If they say something that can be interpreted in more than one way, assume their intention was for you to hear the one that doesn't upset you, and try to focus on that. I had many sleepless nights that were a result of misunderstanding, or dwelling on something that may have just been a comment in passing.

What might be even more important than how you react to your surroundings, is not communicating this to the patient. Do your best not to let your current emotional state have an influence on your visit. This may be easier said than done, but it's really important that you be encouraging and happy. So even if you've been crying in the car on your way to the hospital, stop outside the room, take a

Allison's Brain • **409**

deep breath, slap on a smile, and enjoy the fact that this person is still a part of your life.

ACCEPT THAT THEY DON'T KNOW, AND UNDERSTAND THAT THEY SPEAK GUARDEDLY

The brain is a complex organ that even the most knowledgeable people on the subject have only scraped the surface of. Leading up to the surgery, during surgery, and as your loved one is in recovery, if you're anything like I am, you're going to be full of questions. The problem is that the majority of these questions do not have answers. *How long will it take her to come out of a coma? Will she ever move the right side of her body? Will her speech improve?* There's really no way of knowing for sure, and the doctors are never going to give you false hope. Quite the opposite, in fact. They will likely give you the worst-case scenario, and even if they believe something to be true, that does not mean that they are correct. Every case in brain surgery is different, and your loved one is not a statistic. They say to prepare for the worst and hope for the best! These are very valuable words to remember.

HELP OUT IN ANY WAY YOU CAN

I never really knew for sure what to do to help the healing process. No one did. It was an awkward situation, especially because every day was a little bit different. In time, I found a routine that I felt worked for my mother and I. My mom would have three visits per day. One was with her husband, one was with a friend, and one with me. I would always arrive right before a meal so that I could help her with it. Those hospital meals have so many components, it can be complicated for someone in their right mind! When my mother was no longer on IVs, I even took her outside to eat. She really enjoyed this. I would bring myself something to eat also. I think it's important for the patient to feel as though there is some normality in her life, and having someone watch her eat certainly wouldn't help with that. So we would chat and catch up, just like we would have had she not been in the hospital. After what was usually lunch, I would try to bombard her with fun, educational activities, if she had the energy for it. As a teacher, I attempted to be well-rounded with her training, and focus on as many subject areas as possible. We practiced writing, mostly through short dictation tests. For reading, sometimes I would read to her, and other times I would have her read to me. I would ask her if she understood and encourage understanding through a variety of activities; this made it easy to measure her progress. We did puzzles, and played cards… We played war; I never thought I'd have to explain to my mother why a 10 is higher than a 9! At first she found the double-digit numbers confusing, so I removed these cards from the deck. But I was able to add them back in eventually. And then one day she was able to shuffle cards two different ways! That was exciting, even for her therapists! So in spite of the fact that I never felt confident that I was doing the right thing for my mother, I adjusted and eventually found something that worked. Just remember that you can't restrict yourself to using things like this to measure progress. The majority of progress is measured through general observations of the patient's day-to-day activities. I made up my own assessment tools.

For example, every day I asked my mother what she had for breakfast that morning. At first, the response was a blank stare. After a while, it was, "I didn't have breakfast this morning." It then developed into, "I don't remember." Eventually she started making things up. I knew full well what she had for breakfast, as I was the one who chose her menu! But the day finally arrived when she was able to tell me what she had eaten for breakfast that morning. Again, is it exhilarating to hear that your mom knows what she ate today? Maybe not. But seeing the progress was rewarding. Stay positive, and focus on the now.

IT'S OK TO RELY ON YOUR FRIENDS AND LOVED ONES
Your friends have no idea how to support you, nor do they know what you require, so cut them some slack and simply tell them. On the day of my mom's surgery, my wonderful friends organized a day of fun to keep my mind off of what was happening, or what *could* be happening to my mother at any given moment. It started with breakfast, followed by a nice walk through the market. Next came bowling in knee socks! After that, over a dozen of us met for lunch,

Allison's Brain • 411

and went to see a funny movie. Several hours at a pool hall was the next activity, and it all came to a close with dinner. Of course, it wasn't that much fun when I went to visit my mom post-surgery to find that she was being kept sedated, but being in such a good mood sure made it a lot easier. And who knew my friends would be able to turn what could have been the most difficult day of my life into what wound up being one of the most memorable ones.

As it turned out, however, during the days that followed, I was not in the mood to be in contact with my friends. I would send a group message here and there to keep them updated on my mother's status, but only out of courtesy. They would respond, but did not nag me with questions and understood if I did not reply. Some of them offered to help out in some way, or meet for a social activity. Sometimes I took them up on their offers, other times I did not. I think it's really important to do what you feel you need to do for your own sense of well-being, in spite of the fact that it might make your friends feel unneeded. I needed to be isolated a lot of the time, and other times the idea of being alone with my thoughts was dreadful. But when I canceled plans at the last minute, my friends always understood. And if I needed company, they would make me a priority and do their best to drop whatever they were doing to come and keep me company. This must have been pretty exhausting for them, as they may have had to do a lot more of the talking than usual, but they didn't seem to mind. I may have been blessed with the world's most amazing friends, but I always told my friends that, although I am forever indebted to them for being so supportive, understanding and uplifting, they will hopefully never be in such a position that would require me to return the favour.

STAY ACTIVE, AND KEEP BUSY

It's really important to have all or most of your usual activities on the go and to not put your life on hold because you never know how long a situation like this may last. Originally the doctors had suggested that my mother might be in the hospital for a week or two. After realizing during surgery that the aneurysm was much larger than anticipated, this changed. Of course, as I mentioned earlier, they never really knew how much it would change. In fact, when my mother arrived in rehab, there was mention of the possibility that she might never be able to return home. So it's really crucial that you keep doing everything you would normally do to keep yourself happy and healthy. My routine involved running in the morning before going to the hospital. After I got over the initial shock and accepted the fact that my mom was going to be in the hospital for a while, I kept playing volleyball on a regular basis. And later on, the organization of the benefit concert kept me distracted and busy. In fact, I believe throwing that concert to raise funds for my mom's recovery was one of my biggest achievements. I was on cloud nine for weeks following that, and considering the circumstances, I did not believe at the time that being in such a state of ecstasy was even possible. It is possible, however, if you avoid the need to deal with other stressors. So try not to indulge too much in things that only give you temporary satisfaction but bring you down in the long run. Things like being a couch potato, ordering a pizza, and having a few drinks may make you feel good in the short term, but I ultimately felt much better knowing that I was active, staying in shape, and eating right. Although, having an entire television series on DVD did help me a lot when I did need some down time.

I realize that everyone is different and that what helped me through this may differ from what you might need. If anything I have written here helps you in any way during a miserable time, then that makes it all worthwhile. I would have given anything not to have to figure this all out for myself. But if you only take one thing out of what you've just read, let it be this: Never give up hope! Your efforts and strength are not in vain.

List of Images and Photographs

#1.   Allison accepting award at Hopewell School, Ottawa, Ontario - 2008

#2.   Allison playing flute in Valkyr Mountains, British Columbia — August 2011

#3.   Allison and sister Linda at Clear Lake, Manitoba — July 2011

#4.   Allison and Laurie in France before Alpe d'Huez Triathlon - 2009

#5.   Aneurysm sketch

#6(1)   Aneurysm image — Jan. 16, 2012

#6(2)   Aneurysm image — Jan. 16, 2012

#7.   Allison and Marya, Gatineau Park, Quebec, Mother's Day 2012

#8.   Consent to Treatment, May 25, 2012.

#9.   Allison in Tulips, Ottawa, Ontario — May 2012.

#10.   Allison in Intensive Care Unit, Ottawa, Ontario — June 2012.

#11(1)	Bob at Convocation, York University, Toronto, Ontario — June 2012.
#11(2)	Bob's son Phil, sister Joan, sister Bette-Lou and mother Sylvia, Toronto, Ontario — June 2012.
#12(1)	Bob in Perth Kilt Run, Perth, Ontario — June 23, 2012
#12(2)	Allison's signature and Carol's illustration re Allison becoming a grandmother.
#13.	Allison being fitted for helmet, Ottawa, Ontario — June 2012
#14.	Allison outside in wheelchair, Ottawa, Ontario — June 29, 2012
#15.	Allison walking with Christine Moore, Ottawa, Ontario — June 2012
#16.	Picnic dinner with Allison in Hospital, Ottawa, Ontario — July 7, 2012.
#17.	Allison's Thank You note for pyjamas — July 2012.
#18.	Allison in Acute Care Unit, Ottawa, Ontario — July 20, 2012.
#19.	Lorraine England's boat — AWYN4ALLISON II, Ottawa, Ontario — July 21, 2012.
#20.	Allison and Bob on bus in Athens, Greece – 2500th anniversary of the marathon – 2010.
#21.	Allison's sympathy card message to Ruth McEwen, Ottawa, Ontario — August 2012.

Allison's Brain • **415**

#22.	Allison with blanket over her head, Ottawa, Ontario — Aug. 13, 2012
#23.	Allison with Stefanie, Micheal and Marianna Burch, Ottawa, Ontario — Aug. 13, 2012
#24.	Example of dictée Allison did with Marya — Aug. 2012
#25.	Allison in New York pyjamas, Ottawa, Ontario — Aug. 28, 2012
#26.	Allison eating Maryna's dessert, Ottawa, Ontario — Aug. 29, 2012
#27.	Susan Smith, Allison and Louise Hall, Ottawa, Ontario — Aug. 29, 2012
#28.	Allison at piano, Ottawa, Ontario — Aug. 31, 2012
#29.	Allison sitting on grass, Ottawa, Ontario — Sept. 1, 2012
#30.	Allison and Marya, Ottawa, Ontario — Sept. 2012
#31.	Allison's diary entries — Sept. 2012
#32(1)	Allison's Rehab Centre Weekly Agenda — Sept. 2012
#32(2)	Allison's Rehab Centre Weekly Agenda — Sept. 2012
#33.	Allison's first trip home, Ottawa, Ontario — Sept. 16, 2012
#34.	Allison's first trip home, Ottawa, Ontario — Sept. 16, 2012
#35.	Allison's first trip home, Ottawa, Ontario — Sept. 16, 2012

#36.	Allison lying on bed at Rehab Centre, Ottawa, Ontario — Sept. 16, 2012
#37.	Joan and Ben Veselovsky, Ottawa, Ontario — Sept 20, 2012
#38.	Allison at Red Dot Café, Osgoode, Ontario — Sept. 2012
#39.	Music Therapy Exercise — Sept. 2012.
#40.	Doug and Pat MacDonald as the Duke and Duchess, Ottawa, Ontario — Sept. 23, 2012
#41(1)	Host Rob Clipperton, Ottawa, Ontario — Sept. 23, 2012
#41(2)	Soprano Isabelle Lacroix, Ottawa, Ontario — Sept. 23, 2012
#41(3)	Tenor and Heart Surgeon Dr. Fraser Rubens, Ottawa, Ontario — Sept. 23, 2012
#41(4)	Michael McSheffrey and Nick Miller, Ottawa, Ontario — Sept. 23, 2012
#41(5)	Soprano Marya Woyiwada, Ottawa, Ontario, — Sept. 23, 2012
#41(6)	Jean Desmarais and Matthew Larkin, Ottawa, Ontario, Sept. 23, 2012
#42.	Sharon Chartier and Allison at Mont Tremblant, Quebec — Sept. 30, 2012
#43.	Allison and Bob at Mont Tremblant, Quebec — Sept. 30, 2012
#44.	Allison's birthday, Ottawa, Ontario — Oct. 14, 2012

#45.   Allison's birthday, Ottawa, Ontario — Oct. 14, 2012.

#46.   Allison's discharge from Rehab Centre, Ottawa, Ontario — Oct. 25, 2012

#47.   Allison's discharge from Rehab Centre, Ottawa, Ontario — Oct. 25, 2012

#48.   Allison, Bob and grandson Blake, Calgary, Alberta — Nov. 2012

#49.   Allison and Marya celebrating birthday, Ottawa, Ontario — Dec. 2012

#50.   Allison in Antigua — Jan. 2013

#51.   Allison and Bob in Antigua — Jan. 2013

#52.   Allison and Tyler at Mariposa Farm, Plantagenet, Ontario — Easter 2013

#53.   Allison at one year anniversary, Ottawa, Ontario — June 2013

#54.   Allison and Carol Alette playing duet, Ottawa, Ontario — June 2013

#55.   Allison on Canada Day along Le Petit Train du Nord, Quebec — July 1, 2013

#56.   Allison cleaning out back yard shed, Ottawa, Ontario — Sept. 15, 2013

#57.   Allison on Cascades Trail, Lake Tahoe, California — Sept. 2013

#58.   Allison with Blake at Lake Tahoe, California — Sept. 2013

#59.	Allison with Brahms Choir at Christmas Concert, Ottawa, Ontario — Dec. 2013
#60.	Allison atop Mount Obama, Antigua — April 2014
#61.	Allison with John Tobias — Jolly Harbour North Finger Beach, Antigua - 2014
#62.	Allison with Marion Byron, Music Education Officer, Antigua — Feb. 24, 2014
#63.	Invitation to *The Magic Book*, Antigua — April 15, 2014
#64(1)	*The Magic Book* — April 15, 2014
#64(2)	Allison conducting *The Magic Book*, Antigua — April 15, 2014
#64(3)	Allison with *The Magic Book* lead performers, Antigua — April 15, 2014

About the Authors

Allison Woyiwada had a 28 year career as a music teacher in Ottawa, Ontario, Canada. She has also performed in and directed musical productions for over 30 years, and has written 14 children's musicals. Allison has been a proud recipient of the Whitton Award (1993), Arts Advisory Award for Innovative Programming in the Arts (1997), Community Builder Award (2000), Hopewell School Music and Drama Award (2006), Capital Critics Circle Award as Best Director (community) (2006-2007) and a Lifetime Achievement Award from Hopewell School students (2008). A wing of the Hopewell Avenue Public School was dedicated to Allison upon her retirement from teaching, and the "Allison Woyiwada Music Award" is presented annually to Hopewell Public School students.

Robert McMechan is a tax lawyer in Ottawa, Ontario, Canada. He is a proud product of Deloraine, Manitoba, where he was raised by his parents Bill and Sylvia McMechan. After practising tax law (which he almost never found boring) for many years, he obtained a Ph.D. in tax law from Osgoode Hall Law School, York University in 2012. Robert is a co-author and author of nationally and internationally acclaimed tax publications, and he has been a tax law course instructor for 20 years for the Canadian Bar Association. Robert is an avid long distance runner, having completed 25 marathons, and he organizes and participates in a Canada-U.S. team that competes in 200 mile relays in Canada and the U.S. He is also a cyclist, swimmer and triathlete, and he has completed an Ironman in Penticton, B.C., finishing well-behind his daughter Laurie.

CPSIA information can be obtained at www.ICGtesting.com
Printed in the USA
LVOW11s0554090115

421911LV00001B/57/P